Billy
Southworth

BILLY SOUTHWORTH
A Biography of the Hall of Fame Manager and Ballplayer

John C. Skipper

McFarland & Company, Inc., Publishers
Jefferson, North Carolina, and London

LIBRARY OF CONGRESS CATALOGUING-IN-PUBLICATION DATA

Skipper, John C., 1945–
    Billy Southworth : a biography of the hall of fame manager and ballplayer / John C. Skipper.
        p.   cm.
    Includes bibliographical references and index.

    ISBN 978-0-7864-6847-8
    softcover : acid free paper ∞

    1. Southworth, Billy, 1893–1969. 2. Baseball managers — United States — Biography. 3. Baseball players — United States — Biography. I. Title.
GV865.S5919S5 2013
796.357092 — dc23
[B]   2013008266

BRITISH LIBRARY CATALOGUING DATA ARE AVAILABLE

© 2013 John C. Skipper. All rights reserved

No part of this book may be reproduced or transmitted in any form or by any means, electronic or mechanical, including photocopying or recording, or by any information storage and retrieval system, without permission in writing from the publisher.

On the cover: Illustration of Billy Southworth from the 1945 edition of *The Baseball Register*

Manufactured in the United States of America

McFarland & Company, Inc., Publishers
  Box 611, Jefferson, North Carolina 28640
    www.mcfarlandpub.com

For Carole Southworth Watson

Table of Contents

Preface   1
Introduction   5

1. "The closest man friend I had"   9
2. "Each burning deed and thought"   16
3. "What would McGraw do?"   25
4. McGraw   35
5. The Cardinals Rule   46
6. A Strikeout for the Ages   59
7. Transitions   69
8. "Every species of discouragement"   78
9. Down and Out   87
10. The Redbird Renaissance   97
11. A Special Year   105
12. Two More Just Like It   125
13. William Brooks Southworth   136
14. Brave New World   145
15. Spahn and Sain and...   156
16. From Better to Bitter   164
17. The Transition Years   173
18. A Final Tribute   180

Appendices
  A: Career Statistics   187
  B: War Years Managers   189
  C: The 1942 St. Louis Cardinals   190

D: The 1943 St. Louis Cardinals	191
E: The 1944 St. Louis Cardinals	191
F: The 1948 Boston Braves	192
G: Winning Managers	193
Chapter Notes	195
Bibliography	203
Index	207

Preface

One of my earliest recollections of connecting with baseball is my oldest brother, 11 years older than me, showing me how he could pick up St. Louis Cardinals baseball games on the radio. This was no easy trick for we lived in Oak Park, Illinois, solid Cubs and White Sox country, and this was in the 1950s.

I was about nine years old and just beginning to get in the habit of hearing Jack Brickhouse broadcast Cubs and White Sox games on WGN-TV in Chicago. In those days, WGN didn't televise road games but aired every home game of both teams.

My brother, who was in college, was an avid Cardinals fan. He owned a black 1941 Ford. At night, in the summertime, we would go out to the garage at the back our house, he would turn on the ignition of the '41 Ford and then turn on the radio. Very carefully, like he was panning for gold, my brother would move the round dial that allowed him to go from one radio station to another. There wasn't much space on the dial between the big Chicago stations of WCFL, WLS, WBBM, WGN, WIND and so many others.

But on many nights, if the air was clear and the stars were aligned just right, my brother could find KMOX in St. Louis where Harry Caray was doing the play-by-play of the Cardinals games.

My brother told me Harry Caray was the only announcer in the world who could get you excited over ball two. He also could cause your anticipation to skyrocket by simply telling you who was on deck, as in "Holy cow — Musial will be next!"

On July 3, 1954, my family went to the Cubs–Cardinals game at Wrigley Field and on that day, my brother dived into a crowd of spectators and came up with a treasure that remains in my home today, nearly 60 years later. It is a foul ball hit by Cardinals third baseman Ray Jablonski. I thought it was a pretty big deal that he got it and an even bigger deal when he gave it to me to keep. I don't have to go to retrosheet.com to find out who won the game.

The Cubs won, 4–1. My brother had neatly printed Ray Jablonski's name and the score of the game on the ball.

I grew up appreciating the nuances of baseball, the facts and figures of the game, and the names in front of those statistics. To this day, I might have trouble reciting the names of the members of the president's cabinet but I can attest without fear of contradiction that Hank Sauer hit 41 home runs for the Cubs in 1954.

As an adult, I became a professional writer, not a sportswriter per se, but someone who enjoyed baseball, enjoyed research and enjoyed the challenge of turning both of them into a really good story. In researching my book *The Cubs Win the Pennant*, I was reminded that Billy Southworth won three straight National League championships with the St. Louis Cardinals from 1942 through 1944 and that his Cardinals team finished second in 1945 — the last year the Cubs won the National League championship.

One of the facts that stuck in mind is that Southworth's son, Billy Southworth, Jr., was killed in a plane crash in Flushing Bay, New York, just before the 1945 season started and that his body was not recovered until August. His father, managing a team while grieving the loss of a son, had to leave his team and go to New York to identify his remains.

I have always been struck by the fact that all of us, no matter what our profession is, have lives "outside the office" and many times events outside the public eye have a profound effect on what the public sees, whether the public is aware of it or not. It is for that reason, more than anything else, that I wanted to dig deeper than statistics and learn more about the life of Billy Southworth. The first full year of his terrific reign as manager of the Cardinals was 1941, the same year the old black Ford was manufactured that provided those radio accounts of the Cardinals in our garage in Oak Park.

Three of Ray Jablonski's teammates on that 1954 Cardinals team were Musial, Red Schoendienst and Al Brazle, three men who played for Southworth more than a decade earlier. By 1954, Southworth's managing days were over. The Cardinals manager was Eddie Stanky, who was an infielder on one of Billy's Boston Braves teams late in the waning days of his managerial career.

I set out to try to connect the dots in the life of Billy Southworth and discovered, as is so often the case, that the dots do not connect on their own. Rather, it is only when one can look back at the events of an entire life that it becomes apparent how one dot connects with another.

What is conveyed in the following pages is the remarkable life of Billy the Kid, his triumphs, his tragedies, his rise, his fall, the motivations that drove him, the demons that followed him.

I am indebted to the National Baseball Hall of Fame in Cooperstown, New York, and the Boston Braves Historical Association for the resources that provided the data so necessary in a book such as this.

Any researcher has to have the raw materials to work with, and in this case, I reveled in the splendid writings of some of the great sportswriters of the 20th century—Grantland Rice, Red Smith, Bill Corum, Joe Williams, Tommy Holmes, Dan Daniel, Bob Considine and so many others whose words brought meaning and understanding and perspective to Billy Southworth.

Great thanks also to the late Bill Voiselle, the Boston Braves pitcher who won 13 games in the year of "Spahn and Sain" and was an integral part of the Braves' championship season. The author interviewed Voiselle 20 years ago in connection with another book project (*Inside Pitch: A Closer Look at Classic Baseball Moments*). Neither he nor I could have envisioned at the time how valuable his insights would be to this book.

Similarly, several years ago, I interviewed Elayne Savage, a California psychologist and therapist, for an article for *The Globe Gazette*, the daily newspaper in Mason City, Iowa, my hometown. The subject matter had nothing to do with baseball. Rather, its focus was on how people react to tragedies in their lives. The insights she had about her own personal experience turned out to be remarkably similar to Southworth's encounters with tragedy.

A special thanks to Ray Mileur, curator of "The Birdhouse" website and super fan of the St. Louis Cardinals, who, was especially helpful in connecting some dots regarding Southworth's election to the Hall of Fame and details about the induction ceremonies.

Bob Brady of the Boston Braves Historical Association provided specific help and guidance which is much appreciated.

My friend and colleague Arian Schuessler provided his usual technical and personal support to help make this project succeed.

And lastly, a profound thank you to Carole Southworth Watson, daughter of Billy Southworth, for the time she spent in five interviews with me, providing what box scores and batting averages and won-loss records cannot provide—the human side of the man. Her loyalty to her father was refreshing but so was her candor in reflecting on his life. This book would have been incomplete without her insights.

Introduction

Billy Southworth was the most successful baseball manager of the 1940s and one of the most successful of all time. His St. Louis Cardinals teams won three consecutive National League championships, winning more than 100 games in each of those seasons. In 13 years of managing, his teams went to the World Series four times, won it twice and he is one of a handful of managers to guide two different teams to the fall classic. His teams never finished lower than fourth in an eight-team league and his .597 winning percentage is the fifth highest in baseball history.

But as sportswriter Bill Corum pointed out, Southworth's life was full of instances where he was taking bows or hearing bow-wows. One cannot fully appreciate the complexity of Southworth's life without recognizing the ups and downs he had, on and off the field, fueled by the relationships he cherished, the tragedies he experienced and the demons he tried to fight off.

If you came in contact with Billy the Kid, as he was called all of his life, you hit the highest pinnacle of a relationship with him if he considered you a pal. Lida Brooks was a pal who sang in a church choir with him and he married her. That relationship wore thin over the years and they divorced. His marriage to Mabel Stemen was rock solid for 34 years and they shared a love and devotion for each other until the day he died. But part of the initial attraction was the pal he saw in her, the pal in his life that he craved. His children, Billy Jr. from his first marriage and Carole from his second, both thrilled in being his pal.

Billy was a good hitter and an outstanding outfielder who played for the Cleveland Indians, Pittsburgh Pirates, Boston Braves, New York Giants and St. Louis Cardinals. In 1928, Cardinals owner Sam Breadon chose him to manage the Cardinals farm team in Rochester and he led them to a first-place finish. In 1929, when the Cardinals got off to a slow start, Breadon demoted manager Bill McKechnie to take Southworth's place in Rochester and brought Billy to St. Louis to manage the big league club.

Having no experience as a major league manager, Southworth tried to emulate the demeanor of John McGraw, his manager in New York, whose tyrant-like tactics had produced many championships with the Giants. But Southworth was no McGraw; he was, in fact, the guy who had been a teammate, a drinking buddy, with many of the players just two years before; he was now their manager and his tough guy approach made him a "heel," as one player called him, before the team ever got out of spring training. By mid-season, Billy was back in Rochester and McKechnie was back in St. Louis.

Billy began having problems off the field. In 1928, Lida delivered twins who died at birth. Not necessarily related to that tragedy but nonetheless not long after that, Billy began finding solace in another pal, John Barleycorn, a popular way in those days of referring to alcohol. Though he continued to win championships at Rochester, within the Cardinals organization his reputation with drinking began to overshadow his accomplishments on the ball field, particularly with general manager Branch Rickey, whose moral views were priestly.

Within just a few years, Billy found himself out of baseball altogether and selling cotton seed oil in Columbus, Ohio, to make a living. By this time, his marriage was on the rocks and his career was in shambles. But he had kept in contact with Rickey over the years, hoping to have another shot at managing. He got it when he vowed he had stopped drinking. He had remarried and was trying to put his life back together.

But the road back to the major leagues was not easy. It was filled with long rides on dusty roads in Asheville, North Carolina, in Memphis and eventually back in Rochester where he had experienced his biggest success. In 1940, when the Cardinals stumbled once again coming out of the gate, Breadon once again called on Southworth, now 11 years older than in his first stint, to try to right the ship.

In his many years of managing in the minor leagues, Billy worked with dozens of young ballplayers, trying to develop them into major league–caliber players. He knew from his own experience playing under McGraw, and in his previous brief major league managing role, youngsters needed structure, discipline and encouragement rather than a dictator hovering over them. Older players didn't need an overbearing boss either. They needed someone to show them there was a role for them, not necessarily a starring role, but an important thread in the fabric of a winning team.

By teaching kids how to develop their skills and encouraging older players to make the best use of what they had left, to instill the will to win in all of them, to hustle and to always think "team," that was the Southworth formula.

On December 7, 1941, the Japanese bombed Pearl Harbor and from that day forward, baseball, like most every other aspect of American life, changed greatly over the next few years. Seasoned ballplayers went off to war, leaving teams with whoever was left. Some were young men who were a lower military priority because they were married with families or had some physical ailment that made them unfit to serve, 4-F in military parlance. Others were older men, who, because of their age, were low priority for the military or because they too had a deformity or illness that made them 4-F.

It was a set of circumstances that fit well with the new Billy Southworth because one thing about his personality that hadn't changed over the years was his yearning to be a pal. The St. Louis Cardinals of 1942, filled with wannabes and wannabes-once-agains, were ripe for someone to lead them, exhort them, encourage them and yes, when they needed it, to be their pal, their confidante, their counselor. A hallmark of those Cardinals teams that won 106, 105 and 105 games respectively in 1942, 1943 and 1944 is the confidence they had in their manager and the confidence he had in them.

One of the drawbacks of reaching the top is the inevitability of the eventual fall from it — and the higher the mountaintop, the greater the plunge. It sometimes happens through circumstances no one could have predicted. In February 1945, as Southworth contemplated the upcoming season and the quest for a fourth straight National League championship, his only son, Billy Jr., a highly-decorated World War II pilot, was killed when a plane he was piloting, far from any war zone, crashed into the waters of Flushing Bay in New York. His body was not found for several months. Southworth had not only lost a son, he had lost the best pal he ever had. He was a father who had now lost three of his four children, dating back to the day the twins died at birth. His grief was overwhelming.

He countered it in two different ways. He threw himself into his work and guided the Cardinals as best he could to a second-place finish, losing out to the Chicago Cubs in the last week of the season. The second way he staved off the emptiness of his soul was to reacquaint himself with an old pal from years past, alcohol, a companion that was never too far away.

At the end of the 1945 season, the Boston Braves approached Billy to manage their ball club, which hadn't won a pennant in 34 years and hadn't come close in recent years. They made him a financial offer he couldn't refuse and perhaps part of his motivation was to once again throw himself into his work in new surroundings. Within three years, the Braves were in the World Series and once again Billy the Kid was being heralded as a miracle man.

But the Braves were a different team than the Cardinals. Though just a few years apart, they were teams of two different eras — separated by a world war. Unlike the Cardinals, the Braves did not revere their manager. Many resented him and thought he was taking too much credit for their championship. While the St. Louis players understood and accepted Billy's penchant for platooning, playing the percentages and always thinking "team," several of the Boston players looked at it as lost playing time, fewer at-bats, fewer opportunities to improve their individual statistics.

Another factor was Billy's drinking which, in the opinion of many players, interfered with his decision-making on and off the field. In the spring of 1949, there were reports in Boston newspapers of a near mutiny of the players. Southworth and the Braves front office denied the reports, as did several of the players, but clearly the seeds of discontent had been planted, a situation totally foreign to Billy's experience as a major league manager. In August, he was asked to take a leave of absence. Some reports said he was suffering from exhaustion. Others said he was on the verge of a nervous breakdown. He went home to Sunbury, Ohio, to rest.

He returned to manage in 1950. The Braves had tried to help him by trading away some of the trouble-makers from 1949 but the team was mediocre and the Philadelphia "Whiz Kids" were hot. The Phillies won the pennant and Boston finished fourth. Fifty-nine games into the 1951 season, with the Braves struggling at 28–31, Southworth resigned as manager, saying simply he thought someone else could do a better job. For the next couple of years, he did some scouting and other work for the Braves, but for all practical purposes, his career was over.

In 2007, 59 years after his last championship season and 38 years after his death, Billy Southworth was elected to the Baseball Hall of Fame.

◆ 1 ◆

"The closest man friend I had"

Billy Southworth shivered as he stood on the barge and stared into the waters of Flushing Bay, New York. His thoughts rolled over and over again in his mind as to what happened and why. And, as was the case today, yesterday and the day before, there were no answers. His grief was overwhelming, as if someone was pressing an anvil down on his heart and wouldn't let go.

He was the most successful baseball manager of his time — the best since McGraw, some said — having won three consecutive National League championships in 1942, 1943, and 1944 with the St. Louis Cardinals, knocking the Dodgers and Leo Durocher off their pedestal, and aiming for a fourth title in 1945.

Billy had a way of getting the most out of "the boys," as he often called them — Stan Musial, Enos Slaughter, Whitey Kurowski, Johnny Beazley and so many others — providing strategy and guidance on the field, sometimes being "Father Confessor" to them in his apartment at Lindell Towers in St. Louis and somehow striking the balance between boss and pal.[1]

"Billy was a brisk, orderly man who had a young ball club and knew how to handle it," said Musial, who came up with the Cardinals as a rookie in 1941. "He could instill confidence in a kid. I know he gave it to me by telling me I could do the job."[2]

Billy thrived on being a pal. You were in good stead if you achieved that status with him. He came by it naturally, for when he was growing up, the youngest son of Orlando and Marriah Southworth, he liked to tag along with his brothers Ervin (who went by his middle name of George), Calvin, Pressley and Arley as they played baseball. He was too young to play with the big boys — and there was no room for him in the covered wagon they used to go to and from the games — but he enjoyed helping out where he could, including letting them use some of his old socks to fashion makeshift baseballs. In that way, he felt like they were pals.[3]

As Billy grew older, he became a pretty good ballplayer in his own right, so good in fact that he signed a professional contract with Portsmouth in his home state of Ohio at the age of 19. It was there that he met Lida Brooks, daughter of a local minister. They sang duets in the church choir and fell in love. They were married on June 29, 1914, but not by the bride's father. He thought they were too young to tie the knot so Billy and Lida eloped. For Billy, it was the beginning of a life's journey that was to include glorious triumphs and unspeakable tragedy.

By that time, Billy, having spent one year in Portsmouth, was called up to the Cleveland Indians where he got into one game as a defensive replacement and then was shipped to Toledo where he played in 1914 and part of 1915. After a few games with the Indians, they moved him across the country to Portland where he played in 1916.[4]

His son William Brooks Southworth was born in Portland in 1916. Almost from birth he was known as "Billy Jr." although he did not carry his father's middle name of Harold. For reasons unknown, Billy Sr. hated his middle name. In fact it created an uncharacteristic fighting mood in him if someone teased him about it. So when Billy Jr. was born, he was given the middle name of Brooks, his mother's maiden name. He was his father's pride and joy from the day he was born and as the youngster grew up, he developed the same interests as his father, including the love of baseball. "From the time he was born, it was as if he just latched on to Dad's ankle and never let go," said his step-sister, Carole Southworth Watson. "There was no doubt about it. They were pals."[5]

After the 1916 season, Cleveland sold Billy to Pittsburgh and the Pirates assigned him to Birmingham, Alabama, in the Southern League — more than halfway across the country again. But things were looking up. He had a couple of good years with Birmingham and, in 1918, when Pirates outfielder Casey Stengel joined the Navy, Billy got called up to the big club and remained a major league ballplayer from then on.[6]

He was traded to the Boston Braves in 1921 and to the New York Giants in 1924 where he played on John McGraw's pennant winner and experienced firsthand the manager's iron-fist approach of controlling his ballplayers. From there, it was on to the Cardinals in 1926 where he played on another pennant winner and helped the Cardinals win the World Series against the New York Yankees. It was in that Series that he watched as Grover Cleveland Alexander, old, weather-beaten and perhaps hung-over, made a relief appearance and struck out Tony Lazzeri with the bases loaded in the seventh game to help preserve a Cardinals victory.

By this time, Southworth's knowledge of the game and his ability to get along with his fellow ballplayers caught the attention of Cardinals owner Sam Breadon, who named Billy player-manager of the Cardinals' Triple A farm club at Rochester in the International League. It was a huge career move for Southworth but it was during this time that the first of many tragedies tarnished his success. In the offseason of 1927, Billy and Lida learned they were expecting twins and were as excited as any young couple could be. But Lida had a difficult pregnancy and in May 1928 she delivered a boy and a girl who died at birth.

A devastated Southworth came home to bury his babies and comfort his wife, Then he had to return to concentrate on the first managerial job of his career. His Rochester team finished in first place and played Indianapolis of the American Association in the Little World Series. For Southworth, it was quite an accomplishment for a man whose personal life was torn apart just months earlier.

Billy Southworth, Jr., now 12 years old, was an active kid who not only inherited his father's interest in baseball but also the ability to play the game with vigor. As he matured, he developed good looks that would one day catch the eye of Hollywood talent scouts and producers. Billy Jr. also had his father's love for hunting and fishing.

On a cool October afternoon in 1928, as his father prepared his Rochester club for its playoff game, young Billy was home in Columbus where a neighbor kid was shooting blackbirds. As Billy watched from a seemingly safe angle, the neighbor kid lurched, the gun went off and young Southworth was drilled with hot lead in his stomach and legs.

Billy was in the Rochester dugout when a messenger handed him a telegram which said, "Come home at once. Billy has been shot." The boy survived but years later, in recounting the incident, Billy Sr. offered a telling comment about his relationship with his son who now was his only child. "He was only 12 but then somehow I kind of looked at him as the closest man friend I had."[7]

Meanwhile, in St. Louis, Breadon had a habit of being quick on the trigger finger to fire his managers. Rogers Hornsby, the Cardinals' second baseman and great hitter, had managed the club in 1925 and 1926 but was traded to the Giants after winning the World Series because of a dispute with Breadon that was settled with the trade. Catcher Bob O'Farrell was the player-manager in 1927 but O'Farrell's batting average dipped as he tried to do both jobs and, more significantly, the Cardinals didn't win the pennant. So O'Farrell was demoted, replaced by veteran manager Bill McKechnie who had a record of success with other clubs he led.

Breadon's maneuvering seemed to work as the Cardinals won the pennant again in 1928 but were swept by the Yankees in the World Series. So Breadon made another change in managers, bringing Billy up to manage the Cardinals and moving McKechnie down to Rochester. The Cardinals got off to a good start, but after a mid-season slump, Breadon changed his mind again and moved Southworth back to Rochester and brought McKechnie back up to manage the Cardinals.

Billy was a tremendous success in Rochester, winning championships in 1930 and 1931. He started the 1932 season at Rochester but was moved to Columbus and was fired before the end of the season.

Those who knew him marveled at his resiliency. He had the reputation of "a man who was on the mat many times in his life and always picked himself up."[8]

It was at about this time that Billy started drinking more than he had in the past. His daughter, Carole Southworth Watson, says her dad was not an alcoholic but acknowledges his drinking did have an impact on his career and his life.[9]

In 1933, Bill Terry, his old teammate with the Giants and now the Giants manager, hired Billy as a coach but the relationship fizzled in a hurry. As the team headed north at the end of spring training, Terry and Southworth had words with one another after a stop at a restaurant. Carole Southworth Watson, reflecting 80 years later, said she had heard that Terry was heckling Billy about his middle name "and there might have been some hard liquor involved." The next day, Terry was seen with a black eye and Billy got his walking papers from the Giants.[10]

He dropped out of baseball for a while as not even his beloved Cardinals were willing to take a chance on this man with the brilliant baseball mind but with increasingly troublesome erratic behavior. His home life collapsed when Lida left him. Billy returned to Columbus where he got a job as a cottonseed oil salesman for Capital City Products, Inc. He began dating the company's bookkeeper, Mabel Stemen, and they were married on January 7, 1935. Carole was born later that year.[11]

Billy had kept in contact with Branch Rickey, the Cardinals general manager, who was a shrewd judge of baseball talent and created the first major league farm system in which the Cardinals signed players to minor league contracts, developed them and elevated them to the major league club when there was an opening due to injury or another player being demoted to the minors. While other clubs depended solely on scouts scouring the countryside for young talent, the Cardinals were developing their own through Rickey's farm system.

Rickey had given Billy his first shot at managing a major league team. But Rickey was also a man of high principles who didn't attend ballgames on Sundays and expected his managers, coaches and players to have lifestyles that were beyond reproach. Nobody talked about it publicly, but Rickey did not believe Southworth lived up to that standard because of his drinking. No one ever questioned his moral fiber and all who knew him admired the devotion he had toward his son.

After getting married for a second time and settling down, Southworth begged Rickey for another chance. He enticed him with three words, "I've quit drinking." Rickey gave him a job managing the Cardinals' Asheville, North Carolina, team, a Class B ball club. It was far from the major leagues but Billy was back in baseball. And by the end of the year, he was back in first place.[12]

The Cardinals moved him to Memphis where he managed the Chicks in 1936 and 1937. In 1938, Breadon made another managerial move in St. Louis. Since the days of the McKechnie–Southworth switch and the switch back in 1929, the team had been led by Gabby Street until 1933 when Frankie Frisch took over. Breadon replaced Frisch in 1938 with Ray Blades and moved Southworth from Memphis up to familiar territory at Rochester.

In 1940, when the Cardinals lost 29 of their first 44 games, Breadon saw the need for yet another change. Blades was fired and replaced by Southworth. Billy's elevation to the big leagues represented a remarkable transformation and fulfillment of promises by both Billy and his boss. Six years earlier, his career was in shambles and he was selling cottonseed oil in Columbus. He straightened himself out, promised Rickey he had stopped drinking, and, in turn, Rickey gave him a second chance and kept his promise of bringing Billy back.

The Cardinals jelled under their new manager, won 69 and lost only 40 the rest of the way and finished in third place. In 1941, the ball club built on the foundation Southworth had created the previous season and finished in second place, behind the Brooklyn Dodgers.

The next three seasons are a permanent part of baseball lore. St. Louis won the National League pennant in each of those years, won more than 100 games in each of those seasons and won the World Series twice. There was no better team in baseball and there was no reason not to believe the Cardinals would win a fourth championship in 1945. Billy Southworth, practically ostracized from baseball a little more than a decade before, was now the toast of St. Louis.

Back home, he had built a large home on an acreage in Sunbury, Ohio, where wife Mabel and 10-year-old daughter Carole lived in comfort and rooted for the Cardinals. Billy Jr., who had shown some promise as a minor league ballplayer, was the first professional ballplayer to enlist in the armed services when he saw America's entry into World War II drawing near. He flew many successful bombing missions over enemy territory, sometimes wearing a St. Louis Cardinals baseball cap, not only for good luck but to keep something of his father's close to him.[13]

He was back in the states on February 15, 1945, when he took off from Mitchel Field on Long Island, New York, on a routine flight when one of the plane's engines caught fire. Major Southworth tried to make an emergency landing at LaGuardia Airport but the plane toppled into Flushing Bay and burst into flames. Five people died, including Billy Southworth, Jr., whose body was not found in the wreckage. It was months later when the body washed to the surface and a heart-broken father identified his son by the scars left from bullet wounds he had sustained as a youth.

Once again, Billy Sr. had to pick himself up, as he had done so many other times in his life. But this time it was different. Having already suffered the loss of twin babies, now his only son, his pal, whom even when he was 12 his father had described as "the closest man friend I had," was gone.

Time passed but the broken heart simply wouldn't heal. After the crash, Billy and Mabel accompanied search teams on a barge that combed the waters of Flushing Bay for two weeks, searching for young Southworth's body.[14]

The demon of death awakened another demon as Southworth began to drink again. And frequently, years after the body was recovered, when he would come to New York, he would go to Flushing Bay, the memories would return, the questions would once again linger and he would wonder what might have been. And, as always, there were no answers.[15]

Billy got off the mat one more time and managed the Boston Braves for a while. But even as he experienced success in Boston, as he had everywhere else he managed, the demons followed him and were responsible, at least in part, for his departure into baseball oblivion.

His friend Bill Corum, legendary sportswriter and columnist, described Southworth as a man of high character. "Billy's done a lot of living, not all of it on the sunny side," said Corum. But through it all, Corum wrote, he learned to be fair and kind. "His defeats, in and out of baseball, have taught him a philosophy of living — not just the glib phrase 'you can't win 'em all' but an acceptance of the fact. So he is a fellow that stands up."[16]

Sportswriter Tommy Holmes put it this way: Southworth's story "is an intensely moving and human chronicle, punctuated by brilliant highlights, deep shadows, a personal reclamation and one great personal misfortune."[17]

For Billy Southworth, all the championships and the accolades that went with them were hollow. The longing for his son, his pal, his best friend, was real.

The Southworth story has two images embedded into it, each with profound significance. One is of a man in a baseball uniform, standing on the steps of a dugout, hand cupped over his mouth, shouting instructions and encouragement to his ballplayers.

The other is of a little man in an overcoat, with cigarette in the corner of his mouth, standing on a barge in Flushing Bay on the south side of the East River, eyes moist but intent, gazing into the waters as a search team tried in vain to find his son.

◆ 2 ◆

"Each burning deed and thought"

In the late nineteenth-century, Orlando Southworth put his family and all their belongings in covered wagons and moved from Ohio to Nebraska in search of a better life. He was a blacksmith, a man of little education who worked with his hands and lived by God-fearing principles that he and wife Marriah Marie strove to pass on to their youngsters.

They were from Pike County in southeastern Ohio, people whose lives were guided by Christian principles, a strong work ethic and family loyalty. Orlando was born on September 12, 1857, and was four years older than Marriah. He was 20 and she only 16 when they married. Together they worked hard and raised a large family.

George Irvin Southworth was the first-born son in 1879. Calvin Warwick Southworth came along two years later, Gracie was born two years after that and Pressley Clay Southworth two years after that. Arley Waine Southworth was born in 1890 and Opal was born in 1899.

In between Arley and Opal, William Harold Southworth was born in Harvard, Nebraska, on March 9, 1893, the youngest of the five boys with a 14-year spread between oldest and youngest son. When they were old enough, the seven Southworth children were all expected to contribute to the family income and to be in church on Sunday mornings.

"From my father, I learned determination, persistence and honesty of effort and purpose," Billy Southworth said, reflecting as an adult on what it was like growing up in the Southworth household. "From my mother, I learned that anything worth doing is worth doing well. From father and mother, I learned the merits and rewards of living up to the teachings of the Golden Rule."[1]

Orlando Southworth had a quality about him not usually associated with the tough, grimy work of a blacksmith. He had a love of poetry, particularly that of Henry Wadsworth Longfellow, and young Billy would listen as his father forged iron and, as the sparks flew, would recite from "The Psalm of Life":

Tell me not in mournful numbers, life is but an empty dream;
For the soul is dead that slumbers, and things were not what they seem.
Another Billy's father often recited was from "My Lost Youth":
Often I think of the beautiful town that is seated by the sea;
Often in thought go up and down the pleasant streets of that old town
And my youth comes back to me.

"Naturally," said Billy, "his particular favorite was 'The Village Blacksmith' and he knew every line of it. It was the first poem I memorized as a small boy. My father put particular emphasis on one verse, the last":

> Thanks, thanks to thee my worthy friend,
> For the lesson thou has taught;
> Thus at the flaming forge of life
> Our fortunes must be wrought;
> Thus on its sounding anvil shaped
> Each burning deed and thought.

Billy Southworth could recite the verse as an adult and said it gave him great comfort, perhaps, because with it, he carried a part of his father with him, and also for its message of every deed and thought being forged into a man's soul from his childhood just as a blacksmith molds metal into shape and form and substance.[2]

Billy carried the nickname "Billy the Kid" for much of his life, stemming from an acquaintanceship his father had with William F. Cody, the cowboy who was the original "Billy the Kid."[3]

Times were not always kind to the Southworth family. Orlando did some farming, in addition to his blacksmithing, and two successive droughts plus a fire at the family home convinced him to pack up his family and move back to Ohio. Billy was just a toddler. Family legend had it that he made the trip in a covered wagon but he remembered it differently. He said one of his earliest memories was boarding the train with his mother and sisters and making the long, cross-country trip. Orlando and the four older boys took two covered wagons, filled with the family's belongings and headed back to Wakefield, Ohio, the original Southworth homestead.[4]

When the older Southworth boys weren't going to school or doing chores, they liked to play baseball and they were good at it. George, Calvin, Pressley and Arley all joined the local Wakefield team. Billy often tagged along and chased after foul balls and wild throws but he was too young and too small to participate with his older siblings and their teammates. It was in Wakefield that he frequently sacrificed the yarn of his socks, wound tightly, so the boys would have a "baseball" to play with.

Orlando Southworth was continually struck with wanderlust, a desire to look for new places to ply his trade and make a better life for his large family. So after a couple of years in Wakefield, the family moved to Mount Sterling and eventually to Columbus, the place Billy was to call home for the rest of his life. All of the moving had been done by the time he was nine years old.

At the Avondale Elementary School on the west side of Columbus, Billy, at age 12, finally got the chance to play baseball on an organized team. He was a good hitting, fleet-footed catcher and the captain of a team that won three consecutive championships in the interscholastic league. At West Side High School in Columbus, he continued to develop his skills as a catcher and his all-around play was noticed throughout Columbus and the surrounding area.

Officials of the Chenoweth semi-pro team in the Capital Cities League needed a catcher and agreed to pay Southworth $5 a game if he would catch for them on Sundays. He agreed, providing an even bigger audience for his skills as a ballplayer. By this time, Billy was out of school and working as a bellhop at the Southern Hotel in Columbus.[5]

He had gotten his first job at the age of 12, setting pins at a bowling alley in Columbus, earning spending money and contributing to the family income. It was a part-time job he had for four years while going to school. He also worked as a messenger for the Toledo and Ohio Railroad but he had a habit of hopping freights to get him from one location to another. His brothers made him quit so that he wouldn't accidentally get maimed or killed. So he settled for a job in a safer environment, the Hocking Valley Railroad shops in Columbus, working on engine grates. Guided by his father's work ethic, Billy learned his trade well and was eventually earning $75 a month, big money for a kid in those days.[6]

An opportunity arose for him to be a bellhop at the Southern Hotel in Columbus and Billy jumped at the chance. It was cleaner, had better hours (to fit his baseball activities) and he made pretty good money in tips, and not only because of his courteous, helpful service to hotel patrons. He was becoming well known in the Columbus area for his baseball skills and hotel guests loved to have him accommodate them so they could talk a little baseball with the young star. His family expected he would probably eventually go back to the railroad someday where men earned a good living at respectable jobs.

Billy's career path was taking other turns, however. The ball club at Kenton, 65 miles from Columbus, offered him a baseball contract for $5 a game. So Billy played baseball during the day and bellhopped at night, taking the train back and forth from Columbus to Kenton. Before long, that became too grueling and, given the choice, the young man decided his future was better in Kenton than at the Southern Hotel in Columbus. He quit his bellhop job and moved to Kenton where he became the star catcher.

Kenton was a quaint community, the county seat of Hardin County, situated on the Sciota River. Town historians are quick to point out that this little hamlet was once home to Jacob Parrott, a Union soldier in the Civil War, who in 1873, became the nation's first recipient of the Congressional Medal of Honor. None of that mattered to Billy Southworth. For him, it was a city where he was being paid to play baseball.

He needed more than just his baseball income so he took a job as the night counterman at Mother Shields Restaurant for $12.50 a week plus some meals. He spent the summer of 1911 playing ball for the Kenton Reds. It was during this time he made the switch from catcher to outfield, a position he played for the rest of his career. There are many published reports as to why he made the transition. Bob Hooey, Billy's friend since boyhood who grew up to be sports editor of the *Ohio State Journal*, a daily paper in Columbus, reported that Southworth injured his throwing arm while making a belly-flop slide into third base during a game. He was relegated to right field to keep his bat in the game.[7]

But Billy, in an interview with *The Sporting News* in 1930, told a different story. He said the change happened a year later when he reported to a new team that already had two good catchers. "I was informed by the manager that if I wanted to play baseball, I would have to make good in the one position in the outfield that was open," said Billy. "I got a glove and went to right field, a position I had never played. There were six young men trying for the place and, after a bitter fight, I got the call."[8]

Billy the Kid had a good season with Kenton in 1911, hit the game-winning homer in the biggest game of the year and it was said that Connie Mack, owner and manager of the Philadelphia Athletics in the American League, had taken an interest in the boy.

The toughest part of it for Billy, still just an 18-year-old, was living away from home and being away from his family. He said his good-byes to Mrs. Shields at the restaurant and to other friends in Kenton and returned to Columbus. When he got there, he learned his old job at the Hocking Valley Railroad shops was open and he went back to work there as something useful to do at least until the next baseball season arrived.

One night, when he had put in a full day and was in a restroom washing the grime off his hands and arms, he chatted with an old co-worker, a fellow by the name of Jerry Ryan, who had spent his whole adult life in the railroad yards of Columbus. He walked with a severe limp, the result of his foot being crushed in an accident at work and he had other lingering ailments.

Young Billy felt sorry for his co-worker and got to thinking about what his life would be like when he reached Ryan's age if he spent all his working years in the yards. At one point in their conversation, Ryan shook his head wistfully, pointed to his crushed foot and said, "This is all I have to show for my life's work."[9]

At about this same time, the professional ball club in Portsmouth, Ohio, had made an offer for Billy to play for them at a salary of $90 a month. Contemplating that, and thinking about the conversation with Jerry Ryan, young Southworth made a decision. He wanted to be a major league ballplayer some day and the route to fulfill that dream went through Portsmouth and not the railroad yards of Columbus.

Sitting at the family dinner table in January 1912, Billy told Orlando Southworth, the blacksmith who respected the hard labor of the men who worked in the yards, that he had quit his job so he could become a ballplayer. It was a difficult decision for Orlando Southworth to understand, why someone would give up good, steady, honorable work with a future to it for the sake of playing a game and getting paid for it. But Orlando understood and appreciated passion and determination, two values that had guided him, and because of that he gave his son his blessing to pursue his dream.[10]

Portsmouth was a bustling city on the Ohio-Kentucky border, about 90 miles south of Columbus. It was the county seat of Scioto County and offered a sports-friendly environment for a teen-age kid coming to town to play ball. Within the next 20 years, it would have a professional football team, the Portsmouth Spartans, that would eventually move to the bigger market of Detroit, Michigan, where it remains today as the Detroit Lions. Portsmouth also claimed a rich baseball heritage. One of its most famous residents was Branch Rickey, who was born in nearby Stockdale, spent much of his youth in Portsmouth and grew up to be a baseball executive who would have great influence on the life of Billy Southworth.[11]

It was at Portsmouth where Billy made the transition from catcher to outfielder. He hit .278 and returned to Portsmouth in 1913 for his second year in professional baseball. He had played in 77 games and was hitting .306 when, on July 25, his contract was sold to Cleveland in the American League. The boy who at one time set pins in a bowling alley, worked in the railroad yards and as a cashier in a restaurant, was now in the major leagues. In terms of distance, Cleveland was only about 240 miles from Portsmouth and half that distance from his home town of Columbus, but professionally it was in another world.

Billy rode the bench for two weeks, soaking in this new world and the people who inhabited it. There was Napoleon "Nap" Lajoie, star second baseman, destined for the Hall of Fame. So popular was he in Cleveland that the ball club took on his name and was known as the Naps. There was "Shoeless Joe" Jackson in the outfield, one of the greatest hitters of all time, who had put together three straight years with Cleveland in which he hit .408, .395 and .373. His career was to come to a screeching halt seven years later when, as a member of the Chicago White Sox, he was implicated in a scheme to fix the 1919 World Series. Commissioner Kenesaw Mountain Landis banned him for life from major league baseball. His lifetime batting average was .356.[12]

The team's shortstop was Ray Chapman, a journeyman ballplayer who was literally a song-and-dance man off the field who was known as a great story teller, a fellow who could carry a tune and who had friendships with entertainers including Al Jolson, one of the most famous singers of his era. Chapman is remembered in baseball lore for a tragedy that occurred on August 16, 1920, when he was struck in the head by a pitch thrown by Carl Mays of the New York Yankees. Chapman was rushed to a hospital where he died the next day, the only major league player ever to die from an on-field injury.[13]

The Naps manager was Joe Birmingham, an outfielder who played nine years with Cleveland and was in his first full year as manager after taking over in mid-season 1912. Birmingham would manage the club for five years. His career as player and manager was undistinguished except that in 1906 he scored the only run in Addie Joss's perfect game and in 1913 he benched Lajoie for a while, drawing the scorn of Cleveland fans and writers.

Billy Southworth knew he was a small player on a big stage but he soaked in all the knowledge that he could, heeding the Longfellow admonition he had learned from his father, "our fortunes must be wrought (on) each burning deed and thought." He made his major league debut inconspicuously on August 4, 1913, when he was inserted into a game as a defensive replacement. Not long after that, he was shipped to Toledo to finish the season. His big league totals were an empty sheet:

G	AB	R	H	D	T	HR	RBI	AVE
1	0	0	0	0	0	0	0	.000

But Billy looked on it as something to build on, and indeed he would. He was not only learning what it took to stick in the major leagues but, at the age of 20, he was also learning the intricacies of the game, little things that years later he would remember and use as a manager.

"I had to hustle," Billy said, "because I was a small fellow. This is a big handicap in trying to impress a big league manager. I knew I had to put out that much more and do things to attract attention than a fellow with better physical equipment."[14]

Billy played in Toledo again in 1914 and was to rejoin the Naps when the American Association season ended in early September. But he broke his ankle sliding into second base on the last day of the minor league season and was sidelined the rest of the year, never making it back to Cleveland.

In 1915, Charlie Somers, owner of both the Cleveland Naps and Toledo Mud Hens, came up with a novel way of trying to stave off the upstart Federal League from putting a team in Cleveland to compete with his Naps. He moved his Toledo ball club to Cleveland. They became the Cleveland Bearcats and played in the Cleveland ball park when the Naps were on the road. Hence, there was no ballpark available for a Federal League team.

Somers' plan worked but it created some inconveniences for his transported Toledo team. They had to work around the Naps schedule for their home games and therefore did not play their home opener until May 14 and at one point had a month-long road trip. They finished the season at 67–82, good for only seventh place in the American Association. Billy got off to a good start with the Bearcats and was moved up to the Naps on June 1. He appeared in 60 games but hit only .220 and was dispatched to Portland in the Pacific Coast League. But he learned some important lessons with the Bearcats, who had several players who would one day make their mark in the major leagues or who had already been there, among them Sad Sam Jones, Greasy Neale, and Jimmy Sheckard.

Sheckard had been an outstanding outfielder with the Chicago Cubs with a strong throwing arm who set records for most assists in a season. His big league days were over when he played for the Bearcats and he took young Southworth under his wing and taught him lessons that separated the great ballplayers from the average ones.

"He explained the importance of playing the hitters. He taught me to keep repeating to myself the count on the hitter, and to keep figuring, with the changing count, what the batter would probably do and what I would do if the ball came my way," said Billy.[15]

Sheckard told him when the pitcher is ahead in the count, he will try to pitch to the hitter's weakness, which means he might throw high and away or low and inside or some other variation, depending on the hitter. But if he gets behind in the count, for instance if it goes to 3-and-2, the pitcher has to put it over the plate — and the batter knows that too.

"The outfielder, if he is wise, will shift a few feet on the 3-and-2 count because the hitter, who couldn't pull an outside pitch, is likely to pull on 3-and-2," said Billy, who at age 20 was developing a mental storehouse that he would use not only in his playing career but also as a manager teaching young ballplayers.[16]

Sheckard managed the Bearcats for a while and gave young Southworth a lesson in discipline he never forgot. One day in a game where the Bearcats were down by a run, Billy came up with runners on first and second. Sheckard, coaching at third base, gave him the bunt sign. The next pitch was right down the middle of the plate. Billy swung away and hit a triple, driving in what turned out to be the tying and winning runs.

He was proud of himself but Sheckard was upset with him for acting on his own and benched him for several games. "Sheck taught me something," said Southworth. "I never ignored another sign. I had learned to let the manager do the managing."[17]

He was only at Portland long enough to appear in 25 games in 1915 but he hit .320 and seemed primed for another shot at the major leagues, hopefully this time hitting higher than .220 as he had the previous year in 60 games with the Naps.

Everything seemed brighter for "Billy the Kid" in Portland. Lida gave birth to the couple's first child, William Brooks Southworth, who would always be known as Billy Jr. And Billy Sr. sparkled on the diamond. He became well known for his diving catches in the outfield and, playing the full season, he hit .300 and had 188 hits in 171 games.

A scouting report on Billy the Kid listed his speed as "medium fast" and that he was a good hitter. Written in longhand, the report sized him up this way: "He played in 171 games last year. Made 97 runs, 188 hits, 8 three-base hits, 12 home runs. Stole 32 bases. Bat Av. 300. Records show he is as strong a driver (hitter) as Bodie, Gusto or Wolters, same league."[18]

Billy knew he was a good ballplayer and now he was a new father. When the season ended, Billy asked for a $25 a month raise from the $300 a month he was making and he decided to hold out for it. He got his answer and it wasn't the one he was expecting. Cleveland sold him to the Pittsburgh Pirates in the National League and Pittsburgh assigned him to the minor league club in Birmingham.

Once again, Southworth traveled across the country to continue his chosen profession, In 1917, he was having another good year, but broke his shoulder diving for a ball in the outfield and missed 33 games. He finished with a batting average of .285 with 102 hits in 103 games. But his limited play proved to be another stumbling block in his quest to climb the ladder back to the big leagues.

In 1918, Southworth got off to a great start and was hitting .285 for Birmingham when Casey Stengel, the Pittsburgh right fielder, joined the Navy. The Pirates needed a right fielder and Southworth got the call. He appeared in 64 games and hit .341, higher than anyone else in the National League. Because he played in so few games, National League officials awarded the batting championship to Brooklyn's Zack Wheat, who hit .335 but played the full season.

So Southworth didn't win the batting title and, in fact, would never again hit for such a high average. But when he took his position in right field for the Pirates, he would never play another inning of minor league baseball.

In a winding road that took him from Columbus to Kenton to Portsmouth to Cleveland to Portland to Birmingham, Billy Southworth had finally made it. He was a big league ballplayer.

3

"What would McGraw do?"

The Pittsburgh Pirates were a power house in the National League at the start of the 20th century. Under player-manager Fred Clarke, the Pirates finished in first place four times, in second place five times and third place three times in 16 years.

One of the catalysts of those teams was Honus Wagner, their shortstop, who Branch Rickey said was the greatest ballplayer he ever saw. Wagner played his entire 21-year career with the Pirates. When he retired, he had 3,420 hits and a lifetime batting average of .328. He led the National League in doubles seven times, in triples three times, in runs batted in five times and in stolen bases five times. In 1917, his last year, Pirate owner Barney Dreyfuss named him as manager, replacing Jimmy Callahan, who had

Honus Wagner, one of the Pittsburgh Pirates' greatest players, served as manager for a short time (Library of Congress).

taken over for Clarke. Wagner managed five games and decided he didn't like it. He stayed with the organization but never managed again anywhere.

The Pirates' fortunes started to slip in 1914 as age started to catch up with Wagner and Clarke and some of the others. Pittsburgh finished seventh in 1914, the year the "Miracle Braves" came out of nowhere to win the National League pennant. Pittsburgh moved up two notches to fifth place in 1915. Those were the two lowest finishes for Clarke and the Pirates since he became manager in 1900.

So in 1916, Dreyfuss turned the reins over to Callahan, a good ballplayer in his day, but he was not able to turn things around for Pittsburgh. The Pirates finished sixth in 1916. When they lost 40 out of their first 60 games in 1917, Callahan was fired. Dreyfuss called on Wagner, his superstar, to manage the team. Wagner accepted the challenge reluctantly but loyally as a favor to his boss. But the Pirates lost four out of five under Wagner, who gladly returned to his job as fulltime shortstop.

Dreyfuss looked for another man to answer the call and found it in a most unusual place — the football field. He hired Hugo Bezdek, football coach at the University of Oregon who also did some scouting for the Pirates in the Pacific Northwest.

Fred Clarke was one of the great managers in the early 1900s, guiding the Pittsburgh Pirates to several championships (Library of Congress).

Bezdek was born in Czechoslovakia and came to the United States as a teenager. He attended the University of Chicago where he played both football and baseball and was an All-American fullback for coach Amos Alonzo Stagg. He coached football at the University of Oregon and the University of Arkansas before returning to Oregon where his team won the 1917 Rose Bowl. He had never coached baseball but he had a reputation as a good trainer of athletes who had a good rapport with players — and he was a winner, at least in football.[1]

Callahan had lost two-thirds of the games he managed (20–40 record) and Bezdek came within a game of duplicating Callahan's won-loss percentage (30–59 record). Squeezed in between was Wagner's effort, losing four out of five. It all added up to an eighth-place finish.

In 1918, Bezdek's first full season, the players were more comfortable with their new manager and were anxious to get a fresh start. Bezdek brought two attributes from his football coaching days that seemed to work well with the Pirates. One was his emphasis on training and physical fitness. He put the players through a rigorous training regimen in spring training that he hoped would pay off in the dog days of summer. The other was his ability to relate to the players, even to the point of admitting his lack of baseball knowledge at certain points during a game. He would talk strategy with his players and ask questions like, "What would McGraw do here?" Three of his young ballplayers, Bill McKechnie, Casey Stengel and Southworth, went on to have Hall of Fame careers as managers when their playing days were over. Southworth said he used a lot of what he learned from the old football coach in his managerial career.[2]

While in Pittsburgh, Billy the Kid found a new way to train and to stay in shape. He struck up a friendship with Harry Greb, a local boxer who one day would be the middleweight champion of the world. One thing led to another and Southworth began boxing against Greb in Pittsburgh gyms. "He handled himself so well that Mr. Greb wondered why Billy hung around in baseball when he could get paid real money for the innocent fun of fighting," as one newspaper put it. The answer was that boxing was fun for Southworth, and good training too, but baseball was his business.[3]

The Pirates broke camp in 1918 like all ball clubs do, full of high hopes for the coming season, but Southworth wasn't with them. Pittsburgh's outfield was pretty well set with Stengel in right, Max Carey in center and Carson Bigbee in left.

Carey was the star of the team and a future Hall of Famer. As a center fielder, he had great range. He still holds the National League record for assists in a career, 339, and double plays for an outfielder, 86. He was also a great base stealer. Carey broke in with the Pirates in 1910 and had six straight seasons with 38 or more stolen bases, leading the league in 1913, 1915, 1916 and 1917. His speed and quickness in center field allowed him to cover a lot of ground, not only accounting for the number of fly balls he caught but the ability to prevent runners from taking an extra base on balls hit in the gap.

Carson Bigbee, the left fielder, was fairly nondescript, particularly compared to his outfield counterparts, Carey in center and Stengel in right. Bigbee was an adequate fielder who was best known as being a good contact hitter.

Stengel was a happy-go-lucky journeyman ballplayer who had a flair for keeping things interesting on and off the field. He began his career with Brooklyn in 1912 and went 4-for-4 in his first big league game.

Stengel came over to the Pirates in a trade in January 1918 along with second baseman George Cutshaw. While Stengel was the more flamboyant of the two, Cutshaw was a key player the Pirates wanted to shore up their infield. He was one of the best fielding second basemen of his era, leading the National League in putouts five times, in assists four times and in double plays twice. In addition, he was a good base stealer and a tough man to strike out.

The rest of the infielder consisted of third baseman Bill McKechnie, a likeable fellow whose knowledge of the game outshone his physical skills and later led to a successful managerial career; Buster Caton at shortstop, also known as Howdy, who was the successor to Honus Wagner until Rabbit Maranville was acquired in a trade a few years later; and Fritz Mollwitz at first base, who was born in Germany. Walter Schmidt, another player whose skills were adequate but not noteworthy, did the catching.

The pitching staff was anchored by Wilbur Cooper, a strong lefthander whose 202 career wins with the Pirates is still the franchise record for southpaws. Cooper was coming off a 17-win season in 1917, accounting for one third of the Pirates victories. Cooper was an exceptional fielder who had a knack for picking runners off third base. He also had a .239 lifetime batting average, exceptional for a pitcher.

Erskine Mayer joined the Pirates in mid-season 1918 after several decent seasons with the Philadelphia Phillies where his achievements were dwarfed by the accomplishments of his teammate, Grover Cleveland Alexander. Mayer won 20 games in 1914 and 21 in 1915. Another hurler, Earl Hamilton, had a career full of ups and downs. As a member of the St. Louis Browns, he threw a no-hitter against the Tigers in 1912. After several good seasons, he was 0–9 with the Browns in 1917 and they dispatched him to the Pirates. In a remarkable turnaround with the Pirates, Hamilton was 6–0 with an 0.83 earned run average, six complete games, one shutout with Pittsburgh before his season was shortened when he went into military service.

Stengel also joined the military, creating a need for another outfielder. Southworth was enjoying another good year at Birmingham, hitting .314. In July, he got the call to join the Pirates. Three years earlier, when the Cleveland Naps had given him a serious look, he had faltered, hitting only .220 in 60 games. He was older now and had paid his dues in the minors. He was determined to prove he belonged in the big leagues.

Billy made his first appearance with the Pirates on Saturday, July 2, at

Forbes Field against the Cincinnati Reds. He went 4-for-5, scored two runs and drove in two more as the Pirates beat the Reds, 7–6, in 10 innings. The Pirates were putting together a little bit of a winning streak but were mired in fourth place, 16 games behind the league-leading Chicago Cubs.

The next day, the Pirates won again, besting Cincinnati, 8–5. Billy contributed three hits in five at-bats and drove in two runs. He now had seven hits in his first 10 at-bats and had four runs batted in for his first two games.

The Pirates hosted the Reds in a July 4 doubleheader at Forbes Field and won both games. In the first game, Billy had two hits in five at-bats and one of them, a single, drove in the only run of the game. In the nightcap, he walked three times and got a hit in his only other at-bat and stole his first base as Pittsburgh continued its winning ways with an 8–4 victory. On the following day, the Pirates took on McGraw's Giants and won, 10–4. Billy had another game with three walks but was hitless in his other two at-bats, the first time he had finished a game without a hit.

The next opponent was the Boston Braves in another doubleheader and another sweep for the Pirates, winning 17–1 and 5–4. Billy got five hits in eight at-bats in the two games and got his first extra-base hit, a triple in the second game. He also picked up his fifth stolen base.

The Braves bounced back to beat Pittsburgh, 5–0, on July 8, ending the Pirates' eight-game winning streak. Billy was hitless in four at-bats. But his totals for his first week in a Pirate uniform were impressive:

AB	R	H	D	T	HR	RBI	AVE	SB
30	9	15	0	1	0	8	.500	5

Southworth's early accomplishments were well recognized. The July 6 edition of *The Sporting News* carried a story with the headline "Hail Southworth as a Phenom." The story said, "The youngster has made a fine start in fast company and is pronounced by many competent judges of ball players to be one of the most promising men to break into the big show in some time."[4]

The Pirates moved up in the standings during Southworth's productive first week. On the day he arrived, Pittsburgh was in fourth place, six games below .500 at 28–34 and 16 games behind the Cubs. They also trailed the Giants, Braves and Phillies. A week later, the Pirates had hit the .500 level at 35–35 and had snuck past the Braves and Reds into third place. They still trailed the Cubs by 14½ games but at least they seemed headed in the right direction.

Billy continued to hit the ball well and the Pirates were getting solid pitching from Cooper, Mayer and Hamilton as well as the usual stellar play from Carey. But they didn't have enough to move up further in the standings and in fact finished fourth with a 65–60 record in an abbreviated season due to America's entry into World War I. The Cubs got great pitching from the trio of Hippo Vaughn, 22–10, Claude Hendrix, 20–7, and Lefty Tyler, 19–8. Their best all-around ballplayer was shortstop Charlie Hollocher, who hit .316, led the league in hits and was dazzling defensively for Chicago.[5]

The Cubs had picked up Grover Cleveland Alexander, the great Phillies pitcher, after the 1917 season. Alexander won 31, 33 and 30 games respectively in 1915, 1916 and 1917 so there was no reason to believe he wouldn't win 30 or come close to it again. But Phillies management feared he would be in the service in 1918 and decided to peddle him for players who would be around the whole season. They turned out to be right about Alexander leaving to go to war and he wasn't much use to the Cubs, having a 2–1 record when he departed. But the Cubs won the pennant without him and he had many good years when he returned to the big leagues.

Wilbur Cooper won nearly one-third of the Pirates' victories, finishing with a 19–14 record. Mayer won 9 and lost 3 and Frank Miller contributed 11 wins while losing 8. It was Hamilton, the St. Louis Brown castoff, who pulled off the huge turnaround by going 6–0 after being 0–9 with the Browns in 1917.

Cutshaw had a good year with the bat, hitting .285 and Carey's batting average was a little below par but respectable at .274. But the hitting sensation for the Pirates and in the whole National League was Billy Southworth, who hit higher than any other everyday player at .341. The problem was that his "everyday" status didn't start until July and he only played in 67 games. So the batting championship was awarded to Brooklyn's Zach Wheat who hit .335 in 105 games.

Bezdek remained with the Pirates through the end of the 1919 season and the ball club steadily improved. In 1920, he was offered the job of athletic director, football coach and baseball coach at Penn State University where he resumed his Hall of Fame career as a football coach. His legacy with the Pirates is that of a skilled tactician who took over a team in turmoil in 1917 and returned them to respectability.

The Pirates were 30–59 after Bezdek answered Barney Dreyfuss's call for help in 1917. They improved to 65–60 in 1918, thanks in great part to the pitching of veteran Wilbur Cooper and the hitting of newcomer Billy Southworth. In 1919, his last year, Pittsburgh was 71–65. He was replaced by George Gibson.

The Pirates had become a team in transition, mixing veterans with young players and making trades that would eventually build the ball club back up as a pennant contender. Stengel returned from the Navy in 1919 and appeared in 89 games before being traded to the Philadelphia Phillies.

Southworth had solid years in 1919 and 1920, hitting .280 and .284 as the Pirates regular right fielder. In 1919, he got off to a slow start, leaving some writers to wonder whether his first-year heroics were a fluke. As *The Sporting News* reported, "Record keepers and dope slingers were generally not willing to give outfielder Billy Southworth of the Pittsburgh Pirates credit for the honor of being the National League's best batter last year. He'll be on top again and no question about it if he keeps up his good work and he's been at it long enough to prove he is a consistent performer."[6]

Southworth established himself as a major league ballplayer as a member of the Pittsburgh Pirates where he was a teammate of Casey Stengel (courtesy Southworth family).

In 1920, he rapped out 155 hits, the most he had in any season to date. But the trade winds were blowing in Pittsburgh and on January 23, 1921, Billy was traded with Walter Barbare, an infielder, and Fred Nicholson, a well-traveled outfielder, to the Boston Braves for shortstop Rabbit Maranville. Southworth and Maranville were the keys in the trade for both clubs. Billy was expected to add some punch to the Boston lineup and be a good defensive outfielder. Maranville was considered one of the league's best shortstops and would fill a gap with the Pirates at that position that had existed since Honus Wagner retired.

Southworth became a team leader almost immediately and was named captain, an unusual distinction for someone who just joined the team but also an indication of a void that needed to be filled.

The club was managed by Fred Mitchell, who started his major league career as a pitcher and relieved Cy Young in 1901 in the first game played in the American League. But he wasn't good enough to make it as a pitcher so he went behind the plate and was a catcher for the remainder of his playing career. As a manager, he led the Chicago Cubs to the National League championship in the war-shortened 1918 season.

One of the catchers on the Braves was Hank Gowdy, a Columbus native who Billy knew from the days they both played in the Ohio State League. A pitcher just getting started in the big leagues was Johnny Cooney who would have a long and successful career as a coach after his playing days were over.[7]

As the 1921 season began, the trade looked like a good one for the Braves. Southworth was his usual steady presence in the outfield and he hit .308. Barbare had the difficult task of replacing Maranville at shortstop but had one of his best seasons, hitting .302. Nicholson, in a reserve role, got into 83 games and hit .327. Boston's top pitcher was Joe Oeschger who won 20 and lost 14.

But the Braves finished fourth, a familiar position, for Southworth. McGraw's Giants were the champions again but the surprise of the league was Pittsburgh, which finished second, just four games behind the Giants. And with good reason. Maranville did exactly what he was expected to do, playing great defense at shortstop and hitting .294. Charlie Grimm, playing his first full season in the majors, hit 17 triples to go along with his .274 batting average. The Pirates also had two other kids on the rise, third baseman Pie Traynor and outfielder KiKi Cuyler who would eventually team up with the Waner brother, Paul and Lloyd, to bring championships to Pittsburgh.

The Pirates' surge to second place was also due to great years by some of Southworth's former teammates. Cutshaw hit .340, Bigbee hit .323 and Carey hit .309. On the hill, Cooper was 22–14 and Babe Adams contributed with 14 wins and only five losses.

In 1922, the roof caved in on the Braves, who won only 53 and lost 100. Oeschger, who won 20 games the year before, had the worst year of his career by winning 6, losing 21. But the most crippling blow to Boston was when Southworth, the team captain and leading hitter, dislocated his knee and missed most of the season. He appeared in only 43 games and hit .323. The Braves had two losing streaks of nine games, one of eight games, one of seven games and three of six games. In one stretch in September, they lost 12 out of 13.

Billy the Kid was back at full strength in 1923 and had one of his best years. Appearing in 153 of the Braves' 154 games, he had 611 at-bats and used them to hit .319 with 29 doubles, 16 triples, 6 home runs and 78 runs batted in. But the Braves as a team still faltered, finishing seventh with a 54–100 record — only one more win than they had in 1922 when they finished eighth.

Billy's play did not go unnoticed on the otherwise bad performing team. Boston sportswriter Burt Whitman said, "Bill was one of the best. We always bracketed him with Harry Hooper as the greatest of all Boston right fielders. When you needed a whale of a catch, Southworth would make it for you."[8]

The *Sporting News* said, "Like a meteor, Billy flashed across the Boston horizon.... Running to and from his position, pepping up his mates, even when defeat seemed certain, Billy changed the aspect of many a game and often turned the tide by the inspiration he furnished his colleagues.[9]

But pep and inspiration from one man could

Casey Stengel's career intertwined with Southworth's. At Pittsburgh, when Stengel went into the military, Southworth was called up from the minors to take his place. A few years later, Southworth was traded for Stengel (Library of Congress).

not prevent the Braves from finishing eight and seventh in consecutive years.

Clearly, some changes had to be made and they turned out to be of the bombshell variety. Veteran manager Fred Mitchell, who four years earlier had guided the Cubs to a league championship, resigned. Then on November 12, Southworth, the heart of the Braves ball club, was traded to the New York Giants along with Oeschger, the pitcher with great and horrible years consecutively for Dave Bancroft, Bill Cunningham and Casey Stengel.

In 1918, Southworth got his big break when Stengel joined the Navy, creating a place in the Pittsburgh outfield for Billy to fill. Now, their careers were intertwined once more as they would take each other's place in the outfields of Boston and New York. It would not be the last time their careers intersected.

Boston fans and the Boston press were livid. One Boston paper headlined the story, "Ball Club Goes to Help McGraw and His Giants." Another commented, "Oeschger goes to the Giants.... With him goes the ball club — Billy Southworth."[10]

For Billy, it was yet another move but this one was from a second-division team to a champion, an opportunity any ballplayer would relish. But this one also carried a big challenge with it, as Southworth would soon find out. His name was McGraw.

◆ 4 ◆

McGraw

When John McGraw was an infielder for the Baltimore Orioles in the 1890s, he was a great hitter, an expert umpire baiter and a player who took every opportunity to bend the rules or just ignore them. His objective, to win the ballgame, superceded any other principle. It was in Baltimore that he developed "the belligerent, quarrelsome, unprincipled on-field personality that would become basic to his reputation as a player and manager — and to the McGraw legend."[1]

Playing shortstop in a game at Savannah in 1893, McGraw began swearing at the opposing manager to the point where the manager stormed onto the field and knocked down the young, feisty ballplayer. Orioles manager Ned Hanlon broke up the fight and prevented a potential riot involving players and fans. A week later at Chattanooga, McGraw held a runner by the belt to prevent him from advancing on a fly ball, while the lone umpire on the field was watching the flight of the ball. He also had a reputation for slapping runners with the ball, rather than tagging them, sometimes bloodying their faces but the players always remembered what they were up against when they came in contact with McGraw.[2]

Under Ned Hanlon, the Orioles won three straight championships with teams that featured McGraw, Wee Willie Keeler, Hughey Jennings and Wilbert Robinson, all future Hall of Famers. When Hanlon moved on, McGraw was player-manager for a couple of years.

The Baltimore ball club was successful because of the keen insights of its players — many of whom, like McGraw, became successful managers in later years — and also because of some new tactics they developed. The hit-and-run, the squeeze bunt, the art of hitting the cutoff man and the "Baltimore chop" — hitting down on the ball so that it would hit the ground and bounce high enough that there would be no play on the runner going to first — were all part of the Baltimore Orioles repertoire.[3]

After two years as player-manager with the Orioles, McGraw began the

1902 season with Baltimore but then got a chance to manage the New York Giants. The ball club finished eighth that year but within two years, McGraw had the first of his 10 championship ball clubs. In typical McGraw fashion, he refused to have his team play in the World Series because he didn't consider the American League's Boston Americans a worthy opponent.[4]

McGraw went on to manage the Giants for 31 years, 4,424 games, winning 2,583 of them. His teams won 10 National League championships, 3 World Series championships, finished in second place 11 times and third place five times.

When Billy Southworth reported to spring training in March 1924, he was once again entering a whole new baseball environment, one that would help shape the rest of his career as he came under the thumb of "Little Napoleon" in the Giants dugout.

Previously in his big league baseball life, with the Naps, Pirates and Braves, he played with athletes who went out on the field and tried to win every day. The Giants expected to win every day and had a swagger about them that started with their manager. The everyday lineup had five future Hall of Famers in George "High Pockets" Kelly at first, Frankie Frisch at second, Travis Jackson at short and Ross Youngs and Hack Wilson in the outfield. Three players who appeared in fewer than 100 games in 1924 also made it into the Hall of Fame — Southworth (who actually made it into the Hall as a manager), Bill Terry, an up and coming first baseman, and second baseman Freddie Lindstrom. Jennings, McGraw's good friend dating back to their playing days in Baltimore, was now one of his coaches and was also destined for the Hall of Fame.

Playing for the Giants turned out to be quite an adjustment for Billy. For one thing, Ross Youngs was McGraw's right fielder. Southworth was expected to play center field, a new position for him, Also, the off-the-field environment was different in New York than in Pittsburgh or Boston, It was while he was with the Giants that Billy started to have a couple of beers with the boys after work, either to try to fit in with the team or perhaps to relieve some of the pressure he was feeling on the field. But the biggest adjustment was playing for McGraw.[5]

Billy did not know McGraw except by reputation at the time he was traded to the Giants but he certainly knew of him. "Like every other ballplayer, I was a great admirer of his. He was quite a man. You had to play winning baseball for him," he said.

McGraw's temper was infamous, even with his own ballplayers but Southworth said he could change moods in a hurry, particularly when he was out of the clubhouse. "He'd bawl you out in the clubhouse and then he'd ride you downtown in his car. Or if you went, say, to Moore's (restaurant) for ham and cabbage and he saw you, he would call you over to his table and insist that you eat with him or, if he thought you'd rather stay at your own table, he would pick up your check," said Southworth. He said it was easy to see why so many of his players later became managers. "You'd have to be dumber than he sometimes thought you were if you didn't learn something about running a ball club from him."[6]

McGraw had his eye on Southworth since watching him play for the Braves in 1921. He recognized Billy was a good hitter, a fearless fielder and someone who had good instincts — in other words, a smart ballplayer. But Southworth had been injury plagued and the Giants manager wanted to make sure Billy was physically fit before he tabbed him as his center fielder.

When Southworth played for the New York Giants, shown here in 1924, he didn't always get along with his manager John McGraw but he learned many lessons from him (Library of Congress).

It was a tough go almost from the get-go for Billy the Kid who appeared in 94 games but hit only .256, his lowest average since 1915 when he was with the Indians. It also stopped a streak of three consecutive years of hitting over .300, all with the Braves.

For all of the Giants' success, winning National League championships three years in a row and not finishing lower than second for a decade, they seemed to be in constant turmoil on and off the field. McGraw was a human grenade and everyone around him was wary of who or what might pull the pin and cause the explosion. Yet McGraw was also sickly, suffering from chronic sinus problems (in the days before antibiotics) that left him bedridden for long periods of time. Hughey Jennings had several stints as interim manager over the years.

The front office ran a successful baseball operation despite some questionable business practices away from the ballpark that drew the scrutiny of federal authorities. Charles Stoneham, the multi-millionaire owner of the Giants, was indicted for stock fraud in 1923 for some shady dealings in divesting his financial interests in a couple of companies in which Stoneham's National Exhibition Company was a stockholder. The National Exhibition Company owned the Giants.

The federal probe was hampered because two of the other partners in the companies under investigation had burned all their financial records. The legal mess was further muddied when Stoneham's lawyer was indicted for his part in destroying the records and faced a second indictment for trying to bribe a federal juror. In January 1924, Stoneham faced a new indictment, this one for mail fraud in connection with another business deal.

Grand juries determined he was a liar and a crook but his baseball cronies, the National Exhibition Company stockholders, re-elected him president and McGraw vice president. "I am in baseball to stay permanently and that's all there is to it," said Stoneham.[7]

Southworth leaps to catch a ball while playing for the Giants in 1924. He and manager John McGraw had trouble connecting so Southworth was traded to the Cardinals in 1926 (courtesy Southworth family).

The turmoil was not limited to the front office. Early in the season, McGraw was sidelined, not by illness this time but by an unfortunate and painful fall. Crossing a street outside Wrigley Field in Chicago, he stumbled off a high curb, injuring his right knee. As the ball club took the train to Pittsburgh, McGraw was on crutches but doctors determined the injury required a cast on the knee and bed rest. The manager retreated to his home in Pelham, New York, and Jennings took the reins for the next five weeks.

During that time, the Giants put together a 10-game winning streak to forge ahead in the National League standings. But Southworth, the team's starting center fielder, broke his hand and was out for most of the rest of the season. He played in only 94 games and was replaced by Hack Wilson in the starting lineup. Billy's injury was painful to him in more than one respect. As a newcomer on an established good team, he was anxious to make a good impression on a manager not easily impressed. Beyond that, McGraw had been interested in Southworth for a long time but held off in acquiring him because he thought he was injury prone. So the broken hand was a symbol of frustration for both McGraw and Southworth.

Late in the season, another controversy developed concerning the Giants, this one on the field. On September 27, the National League pennant was still up for grabs. The Giants were in first place and would clinch the pennant by winning two out of three in a season-ending Series against Philadelphia or if the Dodgers lost any of their remaining games against the lowly Boston Braves.

Prior to the Giants-Phillies game, New York outfielder Jimmy O'Connell reportedly approached Phillies shortstop Heinie Sand and offered him $500 if the Phillies would take it easy on the Giants that day. Sand turned him down but reported the conversation to Philadelphia manager Art Fletcher. Three days later, Fletcher met with National League president John Heydler. By the end of the day, Commissioner Kenesaw Mountain Landis had been given a full report. According to newspaper accounts, the scenario began when Giants coach Cozy Dolan told O'Connell to make the offer and told him that his teammates would all chip in to come up with the $500. O'Connell said Frankie Frisch, George Kelly, Ross Youngs and others all knew about it and approved.

Landis had been hired as baseball's first commissioner to clean up the game after the infamous Black Sox scandal of 1919 when eight players of the Chicago White Sox were accused of throwing the World Series against the Cincinnati Reds. Though the players were exonerated in court, Landis banned all of them from baseball for life. Now he had another potential scandal to deal with and he did not waver. O'Connell and Dolan were each banned from major league baseball, the same fate as the eight Chicago players. Landis cleared all of the other Giants, saying there was no evidence linking any of them to the bribe.[8]

O'Connell was a marginal player on the Giants roster and was in only his second year in the major leagues. The outfielder got into 52 games in 1924 and put up a .317 batting average. With the abrupt end to his career, his lifetime average, a lifetime of two partial seasons, was .270.

Dolan's career as a player lasted parts of seven seasons as an infielder, mostly with the Phillies and Cardinals in which he compiled a lifetime batting average of .252. He hooked on with the Giants as a coach two years after retiring as a player.

Many skeptics wondered how an incident like this could have taken place without McGraw knowing about it. McGraw said, "The only explanation I can give is that they (O'Connell and Dolan) are a couple of saps. If you search the country over, you probably couldn't find two bigger ones."[9]

The Giants won the game in question and, by the end of the weekend, had won their fourth consecutive National League championship, a record unmatched in baseball history until Casey Stengel's New York Yankees won five straight between 1949 and 1953. For Southworth, whose hand was healed, it would be his first opportunity to play in a World Series.

Jennings wound up managing 44 games during the regular season and compiled a 32–12 record in McGraw's absence, statistically a better record than McGraw's won-loss total of 61–48. Six of their eight starting position players—Frank Snyder, High Pockets Kelly, Frankie Frisch, Travis Jackson, Ross Youngs and Irish Meusel all hit over .300, and the two that didn't, Heinie Groh and Hack Wilson, hit .281 and .295, respectively.

McGraw and Jennings were able to get the most out of a pitching staff with no starter winning more than 16 games. But they didn't lose many either. Jack Bentley was 16–5, Art Nehf was 14–4, Hugh McQuillan was 14–8, Virgil Barnes was 16–10 and Mule Watson was 7–4.

The Giants began the season winning 11 of their first 12, had another streak in which they won 12 out of 14 and won 15 of 17 in the stretch that included the 10-game winning streak with Jennings at the helm. They closed out the season by winning four of their last five. They had the easiest time with Southworth's old team, the Braves, winning 17 of 22 from them. They had the toughest time with another former Southworth team, the Pirates, who had the only winning record against New York, 13–9. Buoyed by their fast start, the Giants were 44–22 at the end of June and had only one subpar month the entire season, August, when they split 30 games.

Their World Series opponent was the Washington Senators, who managed to break through the New York Yankees' dominance to clinch their first American League pennant. By contrast, the Giants were making their tenth World Series appearance and their eighth in the last 14 years. While McGraw was in his 23rd year managing the Giants, the Senators' player-manager Bucky Harris was in his first year at the helm. On paper, all signs pointed to a Giants victory.

The first game, played on October 4 at Griffith Stadium in Washington, matched Walter Johnson, the Senators' aging but still immensely popular hurler, against Art Nehf, the Giants' 16-game winner. The two veterans scratched their way out of one jam after another in a game that wasn't settled until Southworth, a late-inning defensive replacement, scampered home with what proved to be the winning run in a 12-inning, 4–3, victory for the Giants. Both starting pitchers went the distance. Johnson struck out 12 but he allowed 14 hits and six walks. Nehf allowed 10 hits but benefited from home runs by Kelly and Terry.

Southworth entered the game in the 12th inning and scored what proved to be the winning run. Then, in the bottom of the 12th with the Senators mounting a rally, Billy the Kid came up with a key defensive play. With a runner on first, Sam Rice singled to center. As the base runner moved from first to third, Rice tried to take second but was thrown out by Southworth.

The second game, also at Washington, matched Jack Bentley of the Giants with Tom Zachary of Washington. The Senators jumped out to a 3–0 lead on a two-run homer by Goose Goslin in the first inning and a solo shot by Harris in the fifth. The Giants clawed their way back with a run in the seventh and two in the ninth to tie it, but the Senators pushed across a run in the bottom of the ninth to win it, 4–3. Southworth did not play in the game.

The Series moved to New York for Game Three where the Giants took a 2–1 Series edge with a 6–4 victory. Hugh McQuillan got the win, though he only pitched three innings, for in those days a starter did not have to work five innings to qualify for a victory. Firpo Marberry, who registered a save in Game One, was the starter and loser in the third game. Rosy Ryan, who relieved McQuillan in the fourth, helped his own cause by hitting a home run. Southworth came in as a defensive replacement in the ninth inning. No balls were hit to him and he did not come to bat.

Goose Goslin hit his second home run of the Series and the Senators pounded out 13 hits against Virgil Barnes and two relief pitchers as Washington evened the Series with a 7–4 victory in Game Four. Marberry, appearing in his third straight game, picked up his second save of the Series. Billy pinch-hit in the seventh inning — his only at-bat in the World Series — and reached on an error.

In Game Five, the last matchup at the Polo Grounds, once again featured the Game One starters, Johnson and Bentley. The Giants torched Johnson for 13 hits enroute to a 6–2 victory to take a 3–2 lead in the Series, which headed back to Washington for Game Six, and, Game Seven if necessary. Southworth did not play.

The Giants struck first in Game Six, with a run in the top of the first inning but Tom Zachary was practically untouchable after that. He scattered seven hits but the Giants didn't score beyond the first inning run and lost, 2–1. Art Nehf pitched into the eighth inning when Rosy Ryan relieved him, Together, they allowed just two runs on four hits, just enough for the Senators to stretch the Series into a seventh and final game. Once again, Southworth's role was as a pinch-runner in the ninth inning.

The very start of Game Seven proved to be an indicator of how strange this game would be from beginning to end. Harris sent Warren "Curly" Ogden to the mound, a seldom-used righthander. He faced one batter and then was replaced by lefthander George Mogridge. McGraw had stacked his lineup with lefthanded hitters and was forced to make many switches early in the contest to get the hitting matchups he wanted against Mogridge.

McGraw went with Virgil Barnes who gave up a homer to Harris in the fourth inning but had a 3–1 lead when he was relieved by Nehf in the seventh. The Senators pushed across two runs in the eighth inning to tie it. Harris then pulled another surprise and brought in Walter Johnson, hoping his venerable star could hold off the Giants until the Senators could push across a run. Johnson had pitched 12 innings in the Game One loss and was pounded for six runs and 13 hits on nine innings of work in Game Five.

Johnson managed to shut down the Giants in the 9th, 10th, 11th and 12th innings. In the bottom of the 12th, with one out and the Giants' ace Bentley working his second inning in relief, Muddy Ruel, the Senators' catcher, hit a routine pop up behind the plate. Hank Gowdy, the veteran Giant catcher, tossed his mask down and began circling under the ball, preparing to make the catch. But Gowdy tripped over his mask and was unable to make the play. Ruel, given new life, drilled a double to left center field. Harris let Johnson bat for himself and he hit a ground ball to short that Travis Jackson misplayed, putting runners on first and third. Senators outfielder Earl McNeely then hit what looked like a sure double-play ball to send the game to the 13th inning. But the ball hit a pebble and bounced high over the head of Freddie Lindstrom

Southworth slides as he is forced out at second base in the fourth game of the World Series on October 9, 1924, won by Washington, 7–4 (Library of Congress).

at third base. Ruel scampered home with the winning run. The Senators had won their first World Series. Johnson, the second-winningest starting pitcher in baseball history, got the win in relief.

Bentley, the hard-luck loser, said years later, "That was one of the strangest games I ever played in. With one out, Gowdy did a sun dance on Ruel's pop foul and stepped into his mask and dropped the ball. Ruel doubled and then there was an error at short. Then McNeely hit the grounder. That was a hell of a way to lose a World Series."[10]

Southworth's only role was as a pinch-runner in the 11th inning. Altogether, he got into five games as a pinch-runner or late-inning defensive replacement. He got up to bat only once and reached on an error. But he had one big moment as a pinch-runner when he scored the eventual winning run in the 12th inning of Game One.

Years later, reflecting back on his days with McGraw, Billy said, "While I was playing for him, as much as I admired him, I made up my mind I'd do some things differently if I ever had a ball club. Baseball is a team game. Everybody must do his part and everybody must know what to do. In my opinion, the McGraw system of pulling all the strings destroyed initiative."[11]

The biggest falling out between Southworth and McGraw occurred after a game in Pittsburgh in 1925. Billy had a great day at bat and in the field, getting four hits in five at-bats and making a couple of diving catches in center field. In the ninth inning, the Giants were up by a run but Max Carey, Billy's old teammate, led off the bottom of the ninth with a double. The next hitter, Clyde Barnhart, usually hit to right-center so Billy moved over and Irish Meusel, the left fielder also moved more toward left center. Barnhart hit a fly ball to left-center. Billy started to move in that direction but saw Meusel in position to make an easy catch. Carey tagged up and went to third, beating Meusel's throw. The next batter hit a ground ball to Heinie Groh at third but he juggled it. He recovered it in time to throw the hitter out at first base but Carey scored with the tying run. The Pirates eventually won the game in 11 innings.

"Naturally, I felt as bad as anybody about losing the ballgame but at least I consoled myself with the thought it had been no fault of mine. I figured if I hadn't made those four hits and those two diving catches, we would have lost in nine innings," said Billy.

As he went into the clubhouse, the players sat with their heads down as they usually did, waiting for McGraw to critique their work. McGraw usually had the same routine. He would come in, wash his hands and face, comb his hair and then put talcum powder on his hands and rub it on his face. Then he would turn around and address the team.

On this day, Southworth had grabbed a ladle of orangeade and was sipping it. McGraw said, "If you over there by the orangeade will put that dipper down, maybe I can talk to you, too." Billy apologized, to which McGraw said, "You're sorry? You should be. You cost us the ballgame."

Billy was flabbergasted. "Me?" he said. "What did I do?"

"It's not what you did," said McGraw. "It's what you didn't do. You could have caught that ball Barnhart hit and thrown Carey out at third base."

Southworth explained that Meusel made the catch easily and made a good throw to third. Carey just beat the throw.

McGraw started pacing as he responded. He told Billy he had a better arm than Meusel and should have made the play. "When I used to see you playing in Boston, I thought you were smart," he said, "I'm on to you now. You just looked like a good ballplayer on a lousy club."

Billy had had enough. "That may be," he said. "But you'll have to admit I was right on this play."

McGraw didn't back down either. "Even if you were right," he said, "you were wrong with me."[12]

Southworth played in 123 games in 1925 and had a pretty good year, hitting .292 as the Giants finished second behind the Pittsburgh Pirates. But it was clear by now that he and McGraw were just never going to click. Before the start of the 1926 season, McGraw informed Billy he was going to have to take a salary cut because he didn't do as well as expected. And that was an indication that he should be ready to pack his bags. "When I cut a player's salary it's an indication he better get a move on," McGraw once told a reporter.

On June 14, 1926, when Southworth hitting .328, he was traded to the St. Louis Cardinals.[13]

◆ 5 ◆

The Cardinals Rule

The year 1926 was a year of many cultural and political changes in the United States. In April, Walter Varney Airlines, later to be renamed United Airlines, made the first commercial air flight, from Pasco, Washington, to Elko, Nevada. The "Book-of-the-Month" Club started with an offering of *Lolly Willows*, by Sylvia Townsend Warner. U.S. Senator Smith W. Brookhart of Iowa was ousted from his Senate seat when a majority of the Senate sided with his opponent's election challenge.

In 1926, baseball was clearly the national pastime. St. Louis represented the western edge of major league baseball, a distinction it would hold for 31 more years before the Giants and Dodgers moved to California. Like New York, Chicago and Philadelphia, the city was home to two major league teams, the Cardinals in the National League and the Browns in the American League. Unlike New York, Chicago and Philadelphia, St. Louis had never had a championship team. Going into the 1926 season, there was no reason to believe that distinction would change, what with the Senators and Yankees being the strongholds of the American League and the Pirates, Southworth's former team, the defending World Series champions, looking like the team to beat in the National League.

Coming out of spring training, the Cardinals may have led the league in diverse personalities. Their player-manager, Rogers Hornsby, was a no-nonsense Texan who is still regarded as one of the greatest hitters in baseball history. His .424 batting average in 1924 is the highest in modern-day history. His .358 lifetime batting average is second only to Ty Cobb on the all-time list.

In 1925, he won his sixth consecutive batting title, hitting .403 with 39 home runs and 143 runs batted in, also winning his second Triple Crown. Midway in the season, he took over as manager for Branch Rickey, so 1926 was his first full season at the helm.

Hornsby was a perfectionist who was so consumed with baseball he skipped his mother's funeral so he could play and manage in a World Series. He did not drink or smoke and he did not attend movies or read newspapers for fear of hurting his eyesight. He did not play golf because he said when he hit a ball, he wanted someone else to chase it.[1]

Because of his overbearing personality, he had trouble getting along with owners and other players and therefore wasn't destined to last too long with any team that snatched on to him because of his great hitting.

Hornsby's starting pitching corps in 1926 consisted of 25-year-old Flint Rehm, southpaw Bill Sherdel, veteran Jesse Haines and Vic Keen, a steady righthander. Art Reinhart and Hi Bell were spot starters.

Rehm, a hard-throwing righthander from South Carolina, broke in with the Cardinals in 1924 and had two mediocre seasons before experiencing his breakout season in 1926 when he would win 20 games. His legacy in baseball is more as a drinker than a player, including a time in 1930 when he disappeared from the ball club for several days and claimed he had been kidnapped, held captive in a hotel room and forced to drink excessively.[2]

Haines was a veteran who played all but one game of his major league career with the Cardinals and was considered the ace of the staff. His money pitch was his fastball but he developed a knuckleball that extended his career. He threw the first no-hitter in Cardinal history and won 210 games, the most by a Redbird hurler until Bob Gibson came along 40 years later.

Sherdel kept his teammates loose and opposing hitters unnerved by often singing or whistling while he was on the mound. He was a little guy who wasn't overpowering but won 165 games in the big leagues with finesse and good control. Sherdel was an effective relief pitcher as well as a starter. He once came into a game with the bases loaded and nobody out and got the batter to hit into a triple play on the first pitch.

First baseman Jim Bottomley, nicknamed "Sunny Jim" because of his friendly disposition, was a line-drive hitter who consistently hit over .300 and set a National League record by driving in 12 runs in one game. He was no slouch defensively. Bottomley holds the National League record for most unassisted double plays in a season by a first baseman with eight.

The Redbirds had two players who had severe vision problems and yet had productive major league careers. Outfielder Chick Hafey, who along with Haines and Bottomley were eventually elected to the Hall of Fame, battled sinus problems similar to John McGraw's in the days before antibiotics. He also had poor vision and was one of the first ballplayers to wear eyeglasses. Despite these drawbacks, Hafey hit .329 or better in six straight seasons and, one year, got 10 straight hits in a span of three games.

George "Specs" Toporcer, a reserve infielder, is believed to be the first big league ballplayer to wear glasses. Branch Rickey, Hornsby's predecessor as Cardinals manager, said he once saw Toporcer come off the field, take off his glasses, and run his hands along a wall so that he could get to the clubhouse. Toporcer played a reserve role on the '26 Cardinals. He was primarily a second baseman, Hornsby's backup.

Third baseman Les Bell was an average ballplayer in 1924 and 1925 when he first came up. He was adequate both offensively and defensively but Hornsby had confidence in him and Bell had what every pennant contender needs — someone to come up with a "career year." Bell had it in 1926, leading the team in hits with 189 and in batting average with .325.

Shortstop Tommy Thevenow was a sparkplug who consistently came up with clutch hits but was not much of a power hitter. In September 1926, he hit two inside-the-park home runs within a week and also hit one in the World Series. He never hit a home run out of the park in his career. After his last inside-the-park shot in 1926, he never hit another home run of any kind for the last 12 years of his career, a span of 3,347 at-bats, a National League record.

The Cardinals began the season with Heinie Mueller, Ray Blades and Taylor Douthit, all .300 hitters, in the outfield and Bob O'Farrell, another .300 hitter, behind the plate. O'Farrell and Blades would each have a shot at managing the Cardinals in later years.

O'Farrell was a good defensive catcher, one of the best at gunning down base stealers with his strong, accurate arm. In 1925, while playing for the Cubs, a foul tip broke through his mask and fractured his skull. While he was recuperating, the Cubs inserted Gabby Hartnett in his place. Chicago was well satisfied with Hartnett and unsure of O'Farrell's future so they traded him to the Cardinals.

The Cardinals opened the 1926 season at home on April 13 by beating Pittsburgh, 7–6. Hornsby, who hit .424 two years earlier, banged out three hits in the home opener. Opening Day elsewhere had some thrillers. Brooklyn beat the Giants at the Polo Grounds as the Dodgers' Jess Petty just missed throwing the first no-hitter on opening day in baseball history. Frankie Frisch's double spoiled the near no-hitter. The Giants recovered from that loss to win seven in a row before Petty beat them again in Brooklyn.

In the American League Walter Johnson made his 14th opening day start for the Washington Senators and got locked into a classic pitchers' duel with Philadelphia's Ed Rommel. The game went 15 innings before the Senators pushed across a run to give Johnson the victory. While Washington and

5. The Cardinals Rule

Philadelphia had trouble scoring, the Yankees and Red Sox engaged in a slugfest. New York squandered an early 11–1 lead but hung on to beat Boston, 12–11.

After winning their opener, the Cardinals took two out of the next three from the defending champion Pittsburgh Pirates. They had a four-game winning streak going when they lost to the Cubs on April 18, 5–4, in 14 innings. They ended the month losing two of three to Chicago and went into May with an 8–8 record. Meanwhile, with the Giants, Billy Southworth got off to the hottest start in his career and was hitting over .400 for the first month of the season.

In May, the Cardinals floundered and were three games below .500 at 15–18 after losing to the Phillies on May 19. By the end of the month, after splitting a four-game Series with the Chicago, the Cardinals found themselves in fifth place, one game below .500 at 23–24. In a grueling, 31-game month, St. Louis was 15–16.

The standings were dismal for both the Cardinals and the Giants and their two feisty managers, Hornsby and McGraw.

	W-L	GB
Cincinnati	29–16	...
Chicago	23–17	3.5
Pittsburgh	23–18	4.0
Brooklyn	21–19	5.5
St. Louis	23–24	7.0
New York	20–22	7.5
Philadelphia	16–24	10.5
Boston	12–27	14.0

Hoping to shake things up a bit for their respective ball clubs, on June 14, the day before the trading deadline, McGraw sent Southworth to the Cardinals in exchange for Heinie Miller. In Miller, McGraw got a trueblood center fielder. In going to St. Louis, Southworth could return to the comfortable confines of right field, his most natural position. The acquisition of Southworth was a turning point in the Cardinals' season and in Southworth's career.

Looking back years later, Billy said McGraw treated players not as individuals but as cogs in his machine and every player knew it. "I was a veteran when I came to the Giants and by temperament and experience, I was unable to subordinate myself to McGraw's rigid system," said Southworth. "So when he decided, in 1926, that I was, from his viewpoint, hopeless, he traded me with no personal feeling one way or the other."[3]

If it is possible to have two turning points with in eight days, St. Louis accomplished it with the acquisition of Grover Cleveland Alexander from the Cubs.

Alexander, who still is tied with Christy Mathewson for the most wins by a National League pitcher, 373, was nearing the end of a spectacular career that included a 28-win season as a rookie with the Philadelphia Phillies in 1911 and three consecutive 30-plus win seasons with the Phillies — 31–10 in 1915, 33–12 in 1916, and 30–13 in 1917. Phillies management, apparently

Rogers Hornsby, the greatest hitter of his day in the National League, piloted the Cardinals and Southworth to their first World Series championship in 1926 and then was fired (National Baseball Hall of Fame Library, Cooperstown, New York).

thinking Alexander would be going off to war in 1918, sent him to the Chicago Cubs. Old "Pete," as he was called, did go in the army and served overseas for a year. The Cubs won the pennant without him.

When he returned, Alexander was a changed man. He had a hearing problem from being so close to all the shelling. He also had epilepsy and his penchant for drinking had magnified to the point of being a problem on and off the field. The Cubs put up with their eccentric righthander because he still managed to put in some good years for them, including two 20-plus win seasons.

In 1926, Joe McCarthy, destined to be one of the greatest big league managers, was hired to replace Bill Killefer as manager of the Cubs. It was McCarthy's first managerial job and he learned quickly that one of his problems was going to be handling Alexander, now 39 years old who didn't pay much attention to training or rules or the dictates of a cocky new manager. Though he was one of the greatest pitchers of all time, he had become a distraction.

Teammate Jimmy Cooney recalled how Alexander would hide liquor bottles in the lockers of rookies to try to avoid McCarthy's wrath. He also went in the clubhouse between innings of games and sniffed ammonia, thinking that would prevent epileptic seizures.[4]

On June 22, the Cubs placed the veteran old pitcher on waivers and the Cardinals picked him up. He was reunited with his old friend Killefer, who was now a Cardinal coach.

In an eight-day period, Hornsby's Cardinals had acquired Southworth, a veteran outfielder looking to redeem himself with a new team, and Alexander, who needed to redeem himself if he was to stay in baseball.

Southworth sized up his new team this way: "Hornsby had rounded up a good, solid team, a pretty hard-bitten bunch that was the foundation for the famous Gas House Gangs of later years." The starters were formidable with Bottomley, Hafey, Hornsby, Thevenow, Bell, Douthit, O'Farrell and now Billy; and Rhem, Sherdel, Haines, Bill Hallahan and now Alex. "We got good pitching and good hitting and Hornsby flogged us pretty good," said Southworth.[5]

The acquisitions began to pay off almost immediately. The Cardinals were in the midst of a winning streak when Southworth joined them and they won their sixth straight on June 20, beating the Braves, 9–0, with Bill Sherdel getting the shutout. Billy had three hits in five at-bats and scored three runs.

The winning streak was snapped the next day in a zany game with the defending champion Pirates. Pittsburgh won 13–11 as the teams combined for 28 hits without any of them leaving the ballpark. The Cardinals moved into second place on June 26, beating the Cubs, 8–7, with Hornsby's three-run homer being the big blow.

The next afternoon, 37,000 fans poured into Sportsman's Park in St. Louis as Alexander took the mound in his Cardinal debut, facing the team that had dumped him. Alex didn't disappoint. He mowed down the Cubs, allowing just two runs on four hits but the Cardinals could not muster more than two runs themselves. So Alexander took the mound again in the tenth inning, held the Cubs at bay and got the win when his teammates pushed across a run in the bottom of the 10th. Southworth had another big day, hitting his first home run as a Cardinal and scoring two runs.

The Cardinals ended the month with Jess Haines besting the Pirates, 6–2. They turned their season around in June, going 16–8 for the month and were 39–30 for the season, 3½ games behind first place Cincinnati but 2½ games ahead of third place Pittsburgh. Southworth, back in his comfortable right field position, was hitting the ball well and the Cardinals were 10–4 since acquiring him. The standings at the end of June were:

	W-L	GB
Cincinnati	43–27	...
St. Louis	39–30	3.5
Pittsburgh	34–30	6
Brooklyn	35–31	6
Chicago	34–34	8
New York	34–35	8.5
Philadelphia	26–41	15.5
Boston	25–42	16.5

The Cardinals' 3½ game second place cushion over third place Pittsburgh quickly evaporated when the Pirates swept St. Louis in a three-game set at Forbes Field to open July. They had a long train ride back to St. Louis where they were to open a Series with the first place Reds — and the Cardinals were noticeably sluggish. Cincinnati jumped on Sherdel for three runs in the first inning and Cincinnati went on to hand the Cardinals their fourth straight loss, 7–3, before a sell-out Fourth of July crowd at Sportsman's Park.

The next day, they split a doubleheader with the Reds, losing their fifth straight in the opener, 4–0. Les Bell, having the best season of his career, had three hits, matching what the entire rest of the team could do. In the nightcap, Southworth came out of a mild slump and hit a two-run, tie-breaking homer in the eighth inning as the Cardinals won, 7–5.

The next day, Alexander pitched well and had a 2–0 lead going into the ninth inning. But Ole Pete gave up two in the ninth and the Reds touched him for three in the 11th to beat the Cardinals, 5–2. The Redbirds were reeling now, having lost three straight to the Pirates and three out of four to the Reds. They salvaged the fifth game of the Series with Cincinnati and hoped to gain back some ground as the lowly Boston Braves headed into St. Louis for a five-game Series.

Southworth went 3-for-4 and scored three runs in the next game as St. Louis beat Boston in the first two games of their Series and now had a modest three-game winning streak. On July 11, they split a doubleheader with the Braves as Billy the Kid rapped out three more hits in a 7–2 win in the opener but Flint Rehm and two relievers were pounded in the second game, won by Boston, 19–5, the Cardinals' worst drubbing of the year. The Braves then took the fifth game of the Series, 8–6.

The Cardinals were 44–38, in third place behind the Reds who led the league with a 48–36 record and the Pirates, 1½ games back at 43–34. But the race was tightening up as Brooklyn was in fourth place, four games out, percentage points ahead of the Cubs who were also four games out, followed by the Giants, in sixth place, but only 5½ behind Cincinnati. By contrast, in the American League, the New York Yankees, behind the big bats of Babe Ruth and Lou Gehrig, were cruising. With a 52–29 record, they were seven games ahead of the second place Washington Senators.

Southworth continued to do his part, hitting a two-run homer in the bottom of the ninth to beat the Phillies, 9–7, on July 18, hitting another homer on July 22 in a 5–3 loss to the Giants, getting two hits and scoring two runs in a 6–1 victory over New York the next day, getting a double and scoring twice in a 5–3 loss to the Giants on July 24, then getting yet another home run in a 6–5 win over the Giants the following day. He had three hits in a 9–5 victory over the Phillies on July 27. The Cardinals ended the month losing a doubleheader to the Giants. The standings going into August:

	W-L	GB
Pittsburgh	55–40	...
Cincinnati	56–45	2
St. Louis	53–46	4
Chicago	50–48	6.5
Brooklyn	51–49	6.5
New York	48–49	8
Boston	40–57	16
Philadelphia	38–57	17

The Pirates had surged into first place by winning 22 of 30 games in July. Cincinnati relinquished the top spot by having a 13–18 month. The Cardinals were 14–16. The questions going into the last two months of the season included whether Pittsburgh had hit its stride, as it had the year before, and would now run away from the pack; could the Reds and St. Louis mount any kind of threat; and did McGraw's Giants have enough firepower to turn their season around.

St. Louis opened August ominously, losing two more games to the pesky Giants, but their fortunes soon changed. They reeled off six consecutive wins against Brooklyn at Ebbets Field. Their longest winning streak of the year ended when Boston's Larry Benton shut them out on five hits on August 9. But the Cardinals won the next two games of the Series behind Rhem and Haines to move 12 games above .500 at 61–49. After Alexander lost a tough 3–2 decision to the Cubs, the Cardinals mounted another surge and moved into a tie for first place with Pittsburgh on August 20, beating the Giants, 6–2, at Sportsman's Park. Southworth had the game's only extra-base hit, a double.

The Cardinals extended their winning streak to eight straight with wins over the Giants but dropped into second place on August 24 after splitting a doubleheader with the Braves. On August 26, they dropped a 3–2 decision to Philadelphia and, at the end of the day, found themselves in a virtual three-way tie for first place with Pittsburgh and Cincinnati. The Pirates were officially on top because they had three fewer losses than the Reds and the Cardinals. They also had three fewer wins. The Cardinals had 13 games yet to play against Pittsburgh and Cincinnati. How they fared in those contests would be a big factor in determining the National League champion.

The first of the showdown games occurred when the Pirates came to Sportsman's Park on August 29. Pete Alexander threw a masterpiece, allowing just two runs and striking out eight in a game that went 10 innings. But the Cardinals could only manage two runs on three hits. The game had two long rain delays and was finally halted after 10 innings and the 2–2 tie. Counting the rain delays, the game lasted five hours — and nothing had been decided.

With the makeup game scheduled for the next day, it meant the two teams were to play doubleheaders on consecutive days in the dog days of summer in St. Louis. They split a pair on August 30 and the next day, the Cardinals, behind the pitching of Sherdel and Alan Sothoron, swept the Bucs and moved into sole possession of first place. The standings heading into September:

	W–L	GB
St. Louis	75–54	...
Cincinnati	74–54	0.5
Pittsburgh	71–52	1
Chicago	69–58	5
New York	60–64	12.5
Brooklyn	60–70	15.5
Philadelphia	47–75	24.5
Boston	48–77	25

One game separated the top three teams with 26 days to go in what was shaping up to be one of the best pennant races in National League history.

The Cardinals were the hottest team in baseball in August, winning 22 and losing only 9. But Cincinnati had the same number of losses as the Cardinals but had played one less game. And third place Pittsburgh was two ahead of both the Cardinals and the Reds in the loss column.

The Redbirds started September with their fourth straight win over Pittsburgh and then took a doubleheader from the Cubs with Alexander throwing a 2–0 shutout against his old team in the opener and Southworth hammering out three hits in a 9–1 victory in the nightcap. St. Louis had now won six in a row.

Cincinnati remained on the Cardinals' heels and beat them, 4–2, in the first of a five-game stretch in which St. Louis would play the Reds and the Pirates, all on the road. An unusual happening in the loss was that Bob O'Farrell, the Cardinal catcher not known for his speed, hit two triples.

The next day, September 4, the Reds moved into first place with a 5–0 win, shelling Sherdel for four runs in the first innings and coasting from there. The Cardinals turned to Alexander, their grizzled veteran, to right the ship and he came through as St. Louis went back into first place by a half-game with a 7–3 victory. For Alexander, a few months short of his 40th birthday, it was his fifth consecutive victory and his 12th of the season, nine of them coming with the Cardinals.

Hornsby's crew then took the train to Pittsburgh where they split a doubleheader on September 6 after which Sherdel shut out the Bucs, 8–0, in the final game of the Series. The Cardinals left town with a two-game lead in the standings, heading for Boston and then Philadelphia, the two worst teams in the league. Things were looking up.

In the first game at Braves Field, Southworth banged out two hits and Alexander was holding his own once again as the teams traded scores and were tied 3–3 going into the eighth inning. But Alexander faltered as the Braves scored six runs and eventually won the game, 11–3. The next day, the two teams split a doubleheader with Billy the Kid contributing three hits. He continued his torrid hitting with three more hits the next day but they weren't enough as the Braves outlasted the Cardinals, 5–4, in 14 innings. Alexander took the loss in relief. The defeat dropped St. Louis into a first place tie with Cincinnati.

It was on to Philadelphia where the Cardinals pummeled the Phillies in four straight games by scores of 9–2, 23–3, 10–2 and 10–1. Southworth contributed another three-hit game in the 10–2 victory. St. Louis had a one-game lead over Cincinnati with eight games left in the season but that lead shrunk to a half game the next day when the Cardinals split a doubleheader with the Phillies. Rhem, who had become the ace of the staff, won his 20th game in the opener but the Cardinals lost the nightcap, 3–2, with Alexander giving up a run in the bottom of the ninth.

Losses to the Giants and Brooklyn the next two days saddled St. Louis with a three-game losing streak — but the Reds had lost five in a row so the Cardinals clung to a two-game lead with four games left to play. They made it 2½ games with three to play when they disposed of Brooklyn, 15–7, despite a shaky outing by Art Reinhart. Cincinnati was idle.

On September 26, the Cardinals headed for the Polo Grounds in New York, sending Rhem to the mound in a game in which they could clinch the National League championship. But the Giants, with nothing but pride to play for, jumped on the Cardinal ace for three runs in the first inning.

"Hornsby poured acid on us when we came back to the bench," said Southworth. "He told us we hadn't been taking our full cuts at the ball for several games and to get out there and swing."[6]

Sherdel relieved Rhem in the second inning and held the Giants scoreless until the bottom of the ninth. Meanwhile, the Cardinals started taking their full cuts. They rallied for five runs in the third inning, capped by Southworth's two-run homer. St. Louis held on to win, 6–4, bringing the Cardinals their first championship of the 20th century.

Southworth's homer against his old team, McGraw's Giants, proved to be the game winner. He did not hide the satisfaction he felt. "I couldn't have asked for a better setting, in the Polo Grounds against the Giants who had traded me," he said. "That was the timeliest home run I ever hit and to have hit it against the Giants, with McGraw snarling his defiance from the bench, made it doubly thrilling and satisfying."[7]

The Cardinals dropped the last two games of the season, which had become meaningless, as Hornsby began planning for the World Series against the New York Yankees, who easily won the American League championship. The final National League standings:

	W-L	GB
St. Louis	89–65	...
Cincinnati	87–67	2
Pittsburgh	84–69	4.5
Chicago	82–72	7
New York	74–77	13.5
Brooklyn	71–82	17.5
Boston	64–85	22.5
Philadelphia	57–91	29

Rhem finished the season at 20–7, the best he would ever do in the big leagues. Sherdel, the lefthander, was 16–12. Haines was 13–4, Vic Keen was

10–0, and Ole Pete Alexander was 9–7, including several clutch performances down the stretch.

Southworth hit .320 for the season, including .317 in 99 games with the Cardinals. The Cardinals were 29–26 and struggling to stay above the .500 level when they acquired Southworth from the Giants. They won 60 and lost just 39 the rest of the way. But most of the others in the starting lineup had good years too. Les Bell was the surprise with his .325 batting average to lead the team and chipping in 17 home runs and 100 runs batted in. Bottomley drove in 120 and led the club with his 19 home runs. Other .300 hitters were Hornsby at .317, Douthit at .308 and Blades at .305. Bottomley and O'Farrell weren't far behind at .299 and .293, respectively.

Their next task was daunting, taking on the Yankees in the World Series. Led by their feisty little manager Miller Huggins, who a decade earlier managed the Cardinals and mentored a young Rogers Hornsby, now was in charge of a powerhouse that was coming into its own. Winners of 91 games, the Yankees had baseball's greatest star, George Herman "Babe" Ruth, who hit .372, belted 47 home runs and drove in 146. First baseman Lou Gehrig, in just his second full season with the Yankees, hit .313 with 16 homers and 112 runs batted in. Rookie second baseman Tony Lazzeri didn't hit for quite as high an average (.275), but hit 18 home runs and drove in 114. He hit 60 home runs in the minors the previous year. Those three men, in the middle of the Yankee lineup, became known as "Murder's Row." They accounted for 372 runs batted, an average of better than two a game. Ruth's total of 47 home runs was more than half of the entire Cardinal team total of 90.

Herb Pennock, a tall lefthander, was the Yankees' ace pitcher in 1926, winning 23 and losing just 11. Urban Shocker was 19–11 and Waite Hoyt was 16–12. A fourth starter, Sam Jones, won 9 and lost 8. Pennock and Hoyt were future Hall of Famers.

The Yankees had won the American League championship four out of the last six years, including three in a row from 1921 to 1923. They were one year away from being considered one of the greatest teams of all time as youngsters Lazzeri and Gehrig developed into full-fledged stars and Ruth hit 60 home runs.

The Cardinals were gritty but had never played in a World Series. Their catcher had suffered a skull fracture the year before, two of their players had severe eye problems, another was frequently out of the lineup with sinus problems. Their shortstop had never hit a ball out of the park and two of their pitchers were well known for the highballs they had off the field.

Some odds makers had the Yankees as 15–1 favorites over the upstart

Cardinals, and, five days before the start of the World Series, St. Louis was dealt another blow. Hornsby received word his mother had died in Austin, Texas. Grief stricken and with a huge decision to make, he chose to stay with his team. His mother, he said, would not have wanted him to miss the World Series. The funeral was postponed until the Series was over.

◆ 6 ◆

A Strikeout for the Ages

Billy Southworth had now played for two of the most overbearing, dictatorial managers in all of baseball in John McGraw and Rogers Hornsby. Both were obsessed with winning and expected the same from all of their players. The difference between the two for Billy the Kid was that he never could quite measure up to what McGraw wanted but was exactly what Hornsby needed. The difference in how he was treated translated to the results Southworth produced on the field.

But as Southworth said many times over the years, McGraw was the type of person who could scold you unmercifully one moment and offer to buy you dinner the next. And so it was that the manager who dumped Southworth in mid-season contacted him before the start of the 1926 World Series with a little advice.

Part of McGraw's success over the years was that he paid attention to every detail of the game — the tendencies of pitchers and hitters on the opposing team, the habits and strategies of opposing managers, the way certain umpires called balls and strikes — anything that might make the difference between winning and losing. He was not a man who celebrated "moral victories." Success or failure was dictated by the final score.

And McGraw was a National League man through and through. He was the manager who refused to have the Giants play in the 1904 World Series because he didn't think the American League's Boston Americans were a worthy opponent. A few days before the 1926 World Series, McGraw talked to Southworth about one of those little details that could have an effect on the outcome of a game to bring victory to the National League.

He warned him about the ground in right field in Yankee Stadium, which he called "the hill." McGraw told him the field sloped slightly upward as it approached the right field wall and advised Billy to go out and "practice that hill" because, he said, "that's where the heaviest hitters hit." Southworth ran into McGraw several days later, after the Series had begun, and asked his old manager how he was doing. "Fine," said McGraw, "but keep on practicing that hill."[1]

When the Series opened on October 2, a rainy day in New York, Hornsby was embroiled in controversy — not a new thing for him. He and owner Sam Breadon had a business relationship which could best be described as they tolerated one another in order for each of them to succeed. But when Breadon scheduled the Cardinals for an exhibition game on an off-day in September, Hornsby blew up, accusing the owner of being more interested in making money than in winning the pennant. So, already saddled with grief over the death of his mother and chronic back pain for which he refused to take any pain pills, Hornsby was held in disfavor by the man who signed his paychecks.

A crowd of 61,658 poured into Yankee Stadium for the World Series opener. Two lefthanders, Pennock for the Yankees and Sherdel for the Cardinals, were the opposing pitchers and locked into a classic duel. Douthit led off the game with a double for St. Louis and, as happened so often during the regular season, was driven home by Bottomley on a two-out single. The Cardinals had sent a message in the very first inning — they were no pushover.

But trouble brewed right away in the bottom of the first when with one out, Sherdel, perhaps a little nervous, walked the bases loaded. He almost got out of the inning unscathed when Gehrig hit a double play ground ball to short. But he beat Hornsby's throw to first and the tying run scored.

Both pitchers then settled down and the score remained 1–1 until the bottom of the sixth when Ruth singled, was sacrificed to second by Bob Meusel and scored on Gehrig's single. Lazzeri followed with a single but the inning ended when Hafey threw out Gehrig trying to go to third. That run was enough for Pennock who retired 19 out of the 20 Cardinal hitters after Bottomley's RBI single in the first. He finished with a three-hitter and a 2–1 Yankee victory.

Southworth had a quiet day at the plate and in the field. He went 0-for-3 with a ground out, a pop to the catcher in foul territory and a fly out to left field. Patrolling right field with the hill McGraw warned him about, he handled one fly ball flawlessly.

Game Two matched Alexander, the Cardinals' mid-season acquisition from the Cubs with Urban Shocker, the Yankees' 19-game winner. Both teams were scoreless in the first, but the Yankees touched Alex for two runs on three hits in the second inning and it looked like it could be another tough day for the Cardinals. But after Earl Combs led off the third inning with a single, Alexander retired the next 21 Yankees. The Cardinals tied the game in the

6. A Strikeout for the Ages

Southworth got to play with and against some great ballplayers in his day. Here, as a member of the Giants, he poses with Joe Dugan of the New York Yankees in spring training 1926. Later that year, Southworth was traded to the Cardinals (courtesy Southworth family).

third inning on a two-run single by Bottomley and the game remained tied into the seventh inning. With two on and two out in the seventh, Southworth lined a long home run into the right field stands, giving St. Louis a lead that was safe because of the way Ole Pete Alexander was taming the Yankee bats. St. Louis won the game, 6–2, to even up the Series at a game apiece.

Southworth had the best World Series game he would ever have as a player. In the first inning, for the second time in his last three at-bats, he popped out to the catcher. Then he singled to left in the third inning, grounded out in the fifth, hit the game-deciding homer in the seventh and singled again in the ninth. He was 3-for-5 for the day, with two runs scored and three runs batted in. He had an easy day in the outfield with no fly balls hit to him.

Of course Billy was excited about hitting the home run and, more importantly, the Cardinals winning the ball game. But reflecting on the World Series almost 20 years later, he didn't consider his World Series home run as the hit that pleased him the most. "I always pointed back to that home run against the Giants as the high spot of my baseball career," he said. "It remains the greatest thrill of my playing days."[2]

The Series moved to Sportsman's Park in St. Louis where 37,708 fans showed up on a rainy day to see their Cardinals play a home game for the first time since before they clinched the pennant in New York on Sept. 26. Hornsby sent Jesse Haines to the mound. The Yankees countered with Dutch Reuther.

Haines, 33, had been spent his entire career with the Cardinals and was known as "Pops," partly because of his age, 33, but also because of his penchant for taking young ballplayers under his wing and helping them adjust to the big leagues. His fastball had always been his money pitch, but as he got older, he developed a knuckleball that he relied on more and more.

The ballgame was scoreless for the first three innings. After a 30-minute rain delay, Haines set the Yankees down in the fourth. In the bottom of the fourth, Les Bell singled to lead off the inning. Hafey sacrificed him to second. O'Farrell walked. The speedy Thevenow hit a double play ground ball to Lazzeri at second. He fired to shortstop Mark Koenig covering second for one out, but Koenig's throw to first was off the mark and got by Gehrig. Bell raced home with the first run. Haines then belted a two-run homer, the first one he had hit since 1920 and he would only hit four in his entire career. The Cardinals added a run in the fifth inning and Haines held the Yankees at bay the rest of the way for a 4–0 St. Louis win. It was only the fourth time all year the Bronx Bombers had been shut out. The Cardinals now led the Series, two games to one.

Southworth had another good game, singling to center in the first inning, laying down a sacrifice bunt in the third, and singling to left in the fifth before grounding out in the seventh inning. He was 2-for-3 with a run scored and played flawlessly as usual in right field.

One of the factors that was stifling the Yankees was Babe Ruth's lack of production. Through the first three games of the World Series, the Bambino was 2-for-10 and hadn't hit anything close to a home run. He took care of that with his first swing of Game Four on a pitch from the Cardinals' Art Reinhart. The ball cleared the right field roof to give the Yankees a 1–0 lead.

The Cardinals tied it in the bottom of the first but Ruth broke the tie in the third with another towering home run, this one clearing the bleachers in right center field and breaking a window of a Chevrolet dealership on Grand Avenue across from the ballpark. The Cardinals clawed their way back and actually had a 4–3 lead after four innings. Ruth's homer in the fifth put the Yankees ahead for good but he wasn't done. In the sixth inning, he hammered his third homer of the game, this one off reliever Hi Bell to straight-away center field. The Cardinals won, 10–5, to even the Series.

One bright spot for the Cardinals in the loss was Southworth's continued torrid hitting. He singled his first three times up and wound up 3-for-5. He was the Cardinals' leading hitter with eight hits in 16 at-bats in the first four games, including the three-run homer in Game One.

Game Five saw a rematch of the opening

Babe Ruth was a menace to pitchers in the World Series but he made the last out of the 1926 World Series against the Cardinals when he was thrown out trying to steal second base (Library of Congress).

game starters, lefties Sherdel and Pennock and once again, they locked into a great pitchers' duel. Before nearly 40,000 fans in the last game to be played at Sportsman's Park, the Yankees pushed across a run in the sixth, the Cardinals got runs in the fourth and seventh innings and had a 2–1 lead going into the ninth inning. Gehrig led off with a pop fly that dropped between Thevenow, Hafey and center fielder Wattie Holm and Gehrig legged it out for a double. He scored the tying run when Ben Paschal singled, pinch-hitting for Dugan. In the tenth inning, with both starting pitchers still toiling, the Yankees scored again on a single, a walk, a sacrifice bunt and a sacrifice fly. It was all they needed for a 3–2 victory, taking a 3–2 Series lead going back to Yankee Stadium. One of the things Pennock was able to do was stifle Southworth, who went 0-for-4.

Alexander took the mound as the Series returned to Yankee Stadium with the Cardinals facing elimination with one more loss. Ole Pete was staked to an early lead when St. Louis scored three runs in the top of the first inning against Bob Shawkey. They got another run in the fifth and sewed up the game with a five-run seventh inning. Meanwhile, Alexander threw another complete game, allowing two runs on eight hits. If there was any doubt about his contributions during the pennant race, there was no question of his value in the World Series. The Cardinals were heading into the championship game with Alexander notching two of their three victories. Les Bell was the hitting hero in Game Six with three hits including a homer and four runs batted in.

Southworth had another great game. He had three hits in five at-bats, a single, a double and a triple and drove in a run. He was now 11-for-25 for the Series, a .440 batting average. Billy the Kid had a good day in the field too. In the eighth inning, the Yankees had runners on first and second when Southworth caught a line drive for the second out of the inning and fired to second to double-up the runner and end the inning.

The seventh game was played on another rainy day in New York with Waite Hoyt taking the mound for the Yankees and Jesse Haines for the Cardinals. The game was scoreless until Ruth hit his fourth home run of the Series to give the Yankees a 1–0 lead in the third inning. In the fourth inning, Bottomley got his 10th hit of the Series, a single to left. Bell hit a ground ball to short but Koenig bobbled it and everyone was safe. Hafey followed with a base hit but Bottomley held up at third, loading the bases. O'Farrell hit a routine fly ball to left, setting up what was likely to be a close play at the plate with Bottomley trying to outrun the great arm of Bob Meusel. But Meusel dropped the ball for the second Yankee error of the inning. Bottomley scored to tie the game. Then Thevenow singled to right and two more runs scored. The Cardinals led, 3–1. The Yankees pushed across a run in the sixth inning to close the gap, setting up a dramatic confrontation in the seventh inning that is part of baseball lore.

Earl Combs led off the Yankee seventh with a base hit and was sacrificed to second by Koenig. Ruth was intentionally walked. Meusel hit into a force play, leaving runners at first and third with two out. Haines walked Gehrig to set up a force play at any base. As Lazzeri stepped to the plate, Hornsby came in to talk with Haines. The pitcher's knuckles were reportedly bleeding. His manager decided to make a change. He called for Alexander to come in from the bullpen. After his sixth game win, Hornsby warned Ole Pete not to celebrate too much because he might be needed in the seventh game.

There are many conflicting reports about Alex's condition as he sauntered in from the bullpen to take the mound. Some of his teammates say he stashed a bottle in the bullpen and enjoyed some alcoholic refreshment during the game. The bullpen was covered and sheltered from view. Others say he was asleep when he got the call. Still others say he was just hung over.

Whatever the case, his task was to retire Lazzeri and preserve the Cardinals' fragile 3–2 lead. The sequence of pitches added to the drama. First pitch, curve ball, missed the outside corner. Ball one. The next pitch hit the corner. Strike one. The third curve got more of the plate than Alex wanted and Lazzeri tore into it and hit it deep into left field. The ball hooked foul by a couple of feet — the difference between being a hero or a bum, Alexander would say later. He abandoned the curve on the next pitch and threw a fastball on the outside corner. Lazzeri lunged at it and missed. Strike three. Inning over. Alexander then mowed the Yankees down in the eighth and ninth innings.

With two out in the ninth, he walked Ruth, creating more conflicting reports on the strategy. Some observers said Alex knew what he was doing, walking the Bambino who could have tied the game with one swing. But the

Grover Cleveland Alexander (left) struck out Tony Lazzeri with the bases loaded to end a Yankee threat and help the Cardinals win the 1926 World Series (National Baseball Hall of Fame Library, Cooperstown, New York).

walk came on a 3-an-2 count and Alex said later he chided the umpire for not giving him the benefit of the doubt on a pitch that could have been called either way. With Meusel at the plate, Ruth broke for second and was thrown out trying to steal on a great throw from O'Farrell behind the plate. The Cardinals were the world champions for the first time in their history.[3]

Southworth went hitless for only the second time in the Series but his contributions in getting the Cardinals to the Series and helping them win it were enormous. He hit .345 for the Series with 10 hits in 29 at-bats, including a double, triple and home run, four runs batted in and six runs scored. He tied with Bottomley and Thevenow for most hits in the Series.

But the Series hero clearly was Alexander with two wins and a save. He would go on to have two more good years with the Cardinals, winning 21 in 1927 and 16 in 1928, but his behavior off the field was becoming more and more erratic, fueled by alcoholism and bouts of epilepsy. By 1930, he was out of the big leagues and most of the headlines he was to make in subsequent years had to do with embarrassing circumstances surrounding his drinking.[4]

Hornsby left immediately after the Series to attend his mother's funeral in Austin, Texas. He probably didn't realize that Game Seven of the Series was the last one he would ever manage in a Cardinals uniform.

Soon after the World Series ended, baseball owners started making managerial changes. On October 11, George Sisler was relieved of his duties with the St. Louis Browns although he would remain a player with them. On October 20, Stuffy McInnis replaced Art Fletcher as manager of the lowly Philadelphia Phillies. Two days later, Lee Fohl resigned as manager of the Boston Red Sox.

On November 3, three ball clubs made changes. Ty Cobb resigned as Detroit manager and was replaced by an umpire, George Moriarty. Dan Hawley was named to succeed Sisler as manager of the Browns. The Chicago White Sox announced they were replacing their manager, Eddie Collins, with Ray Schalk. On November 29, Tris Speaker resigned as manager of the Cleveland Indians. The next day, Boston named Bill Carrigan to succeed Fohl as manager of the Red Sox. On December 11, Jack McAllister was picked to follow Speaker as manager of the Indians.

While the managerial shuffling was occurring at a torrid pace in the off-season, much of it wasn't surprising because in many cases the teams involved hadn't lived up to expectations. But the next change to take place was a surprise to most baseball observers.

Sam Breadon, the Cardinal owner, was ecstatic with his World Series championship but not with his manager. He and Hornsby had always had a less than comfortable relationship in part because they were both strong willed but also because Hornsby seemed to ignore the fact that Breadon was the boss.

Cardinal fans were shocked five days before Christmas when Hornsby, the greatest right-handed hitter in National League history at the time, and a championship-caliber manager, was traded to the New York Giants for infielder Frankie Frisch and pitcher Jimmy Ring.[5]

Sportswriter Fred Lieb wrote, "It was one of those things which was simply unbelievable. St. Louisans were wondering if their eyes were deceiving them, or were those glaring headlines in the newspaper some sort of prank."[6]

It was no prank. The beginning of the end of the Breadon-Hornsby professional relationship occurred in early September when the Cardinals were about to make their eastern swing that resulted in their pennant-winning drive. Early in the season, Breadon had struck a deal with George Weiss, owner of the minor league team in New Haven, Connecticut, for the Cardinals to play an exhibition game in New Haven on an off-day.

As the National League pennant race got tighter, Breadon tried to cancel the arrangement. But Weiss told Breadon a deal was a deal and he had already spent $500 in advertising to promote the game. He told Breadon times were financially tough for the New Haven club and the Cardinals' appearance would be a big money maker for them. He said Breadon would understand it better if the situation was reversed and the Redbirds were falling on hard times but had a chance

Lida Southworth, Billy's first wife, with Billy Jr. in about 1925. Billy and Lida would later divorce (courtesy Southworth family).

to start to get out of the hole. But Weiss's main point, one that Breadon didn't think he could ignore, is they had signed agreement to play the game.

When Breadon informed Hornsby that the exhibition game must be played, Hornsby blew up, accusing his boss of being more interested in taking in a few bucks from an exhibition game than in winning a championship. That conversation was in early September but it was not forgotten, not even after the Cardinals won the World Series.[7]

To Cardinals fans, unfamiliar with all the behind-the-scenes discontent, the trading of their manager, who also happened to be the greatest hitter in the National League, was unthinkable. "St. Louis wasn't only stunned; it was wild with rage and indignation. Breadon's name was anethema. Boiling him in oil would have been light punishment."[8]

Fans threatened to boycott Cardinals games and one sportswriter, Jim Gould of the *St. Louis Star*, vowed never to attend another Cardinals game as long as Breadon owned the club. He kept that promise for years.

The animosity started to subside when Breadon named his popular catcher Bob O'Farrell as the new manager. O'Farrell had been a team leader ever since he joined the Cardinals and was inheriting a championship ball club with which he already had a terrific relationship. Soon, Cardinals management, players and fans began to focus on 1927.[9]

For Southworth, it meant he would be playing for his third manager in three years. He would have no way of knowing the managerial merry-go-round in St. Louis was in full swing and that in the not too distant future, he would join in on the ride.

But for now, in the winter of 1926, he was home in Columbus with Lida and Billy Jr. with time to reflect on what had been one of the best years of his big league career. He knew 1927 would be different, with Hornsby gone and Frisch, his old teammate from the Giants, on board.

Transitions

One of the things Southworth loved most about the offseason was going home to Columbus where he could relax, do a little hunting and fishing, follow Ohio State football and spend time with his family, especially with his son, Billy Jr. There had been a natural chemistry between the two ever since the boy was a toddler and held his first baseball. As each year went by, the agape love between father and son — boundless and unconditional — grew stronger.

Perhaps it was because as a ballplayer, meaningful friendships were hard to come by and sustain because they were mostly professional on the field and in the clubhouse or in hotels and bars after games and because at season's end everyone went their separate ways. With trades and other player transactions, the scene was repeated year after year with new teammates.

In Billy Jr., Southworth had a ready, appreciative, captive audience as they played catch out in the yard or Billy pitched underhand to his young son, teaching him the fundamentals of the game the boy would grow up to love, just as his father had. Billy Jr.'s boyhood was filled with times when his father would tell stories of the great men he had played with and against.

"There was plenty of time for story telling around the fireplace out in Ohio during the winter months. Old Billy had started with Cleveland and the great Larry Lajoie. He had played against Ty Cobb and Joe Jackson when they were tops and he had swung his none-too-menacing stick against the stream of liquid fire Walter Johnson used to spray hitters with."[1]

And of course there were his experiences with McGraw — the locker room tirade, the inevitable trade that sent him to the Cardinals, the tip he gave Billy about the Yankee Stadium outfield before the World Series; and Hornsby, one of the greatest hitters of all time who delayed his mother's funeral for the love of the game but who was dispatched out of town by an irate owner.

Billy told his son of how Lajoie was so popular in Cleveland that the team was called the Naps and how Jackson, perhaps the best pure hitter in the American League, was booted out of baseball in the Black Sox scandal. Surely he told his son about Hugo Bezdek, the football coach who managed the Pirates for a while and of Honus Wagner, the most popular of the Pirates. Southworth could mesmerize adults with his baseball tales. It is no wonder his 12-year-old son grew up with dreams of becoming a big league ballplayer like his dad.

Southworth's best adult friend was Bob Hooey. They had known each other from their sandlot days in Columbus. Hooey was a sportswriter who became the sports editor of the *Ohio State Journal*, a major daily newspaper in Columbus. He also was a regular contributor to *The Sporting News*, the weekly sports newspaper that was headquartered in St. Louis. Hooey followed Southworth's career as a friend and as a journalist and frequently wrote glowing accounts of his career for both publications.[2]

Billy left for spring training in 1927 with the high hopes that all ballplayers have as they head south and prepare for another season. Spring training is a time of optimism, of renewal, when every ball club is starting fresh with an attitude of "maybe this will be our year." For the Cardinals, they fulfilled their spring training dreams the previous year and were the defending World Series champions.

But 1927 would be different. Hornsby was gone to the Giants. Frisch was the new kid on the block for the Cardinals. And there were questions. Could O'Farrell be both an effective manager and an effective catcher? Could Rhem duplicate his 20-win season of 1926? Did Alexander have any gas left in his tank — and would he behave? And could Southworth himself, at age 34 and coming off one of the best seasons of his career, put together two good years in a row, something that had become a challenge in recent years?

Hornsby was still in the headlines in the 1927 pre-season because he still held stock in the Cardinals. National League President John Heydler ruled that since he was now a member of the Giants, Hornsby had to divest himself of the stock. After months of haggling, Hornsby sold the stock for $100,000 and the Cardinals paid all the legal fees involved in the transaction.

The regular season got off to a rocky start when the Cubs got to Alexander early and often on opening day, beating the Cardinals, 10–1. Three days later, Sherdel, in his first start of the season, threw a two-hitter, but one of the hits was a homer by Hack Wilson and the Cubs won, 1–0.

On May 14, the Cardinals witnessed a tragedy in Philadelphia. During a game against the Phillies, a section of the right field stands at Baker Bowl collapsed. Debris and people tumbled, causing multiple injuries. There was one reported death and that was the result of a stampede of fans trying to rush to safety. The ballgame was called with the Phillies winning, 12–4.

On July 16, the Cardinals split a doubleheader with Brooklyn, with reliable Jess Haines winning his 14th game against only four losses. St. Louis was 48–35 for the season, in third place behind the Chicago Cubs and the Pittsburgh Pirates.

For Southworth, his tendency to get hurt, which made McGraw wary of him years ago, struck again when he suffered a rib injury in the second game of that doubleheader and it kept him out of action for most of the rest of the season. He appeared in only 92 games. It was the fifth time in 12 years he played in fewer than 100 games. Filled with such high hopes when the season began, Billy hit safely in the first 11 games of the season and 15 out of the first 16. He did not know then that his best days as a player were over. He hit .301 for the season but would get only six more hits in his major league career.

Southworth received good news from two directions in the fall of 1927. Back home in Columbus, Lida was pregnant with twins. Young Billy Jr., an only child for 11 years, would have two siblings before he was a teenager. Lida was due in May, when Billy thought he would be on the road with the Cardinals.

But the other winter surprise came in a telegram Southworth received at his Columbus home. The sender was Branch Rickey, the Cardinal general manager, who requested that Billy meet him in Cincinnati the following day. The telegram gave no explanation. Had he been traded? Was he going to be asked to play another position next year, perhaps one where he wouldn't be so injury prone? Billy had no idea.

Cardinal general manager Branch Rickey gave Southworth his first major league managing job and then gave him a second chance many years later (National Baseball Hall of Fame Library, Cooperstown, New York).

His mind was still racing the next day as he approached Rickey, a stout man with thick glasses, half-inch eyebrows, bow tie and usually a cigar in the corner of his mouth. He looked more like a crusty banker than an old ballplayer but he was the mastermind of a system that made the Cardinals a dominant force for many years to come. For it was Rickey who developed baseball's first farm system in which St. Louis would acquire minor league teams in cities throughout the country and groom young players on how to play "Cardinal baseball." And on that wintry day in Cincinnati, Rickey offered Billy the Kid the job of managing the Cardinals' minor league team in Syracuse.

Southworth accepted the offer without hesitation. It kept him in the game, it kept him with the Cardinals and it was a step up in his career. There were still some details to work out so the official announcement did not come until December 11. Billy signed a three-year contract to manage Syracuse, replacing Burt Shotton, who had resigned to become manager of the Philadelphia Phillies. As it turned out, Billy never managed a day in Syracuse. Before the season started, the Cardinals moved the franchise to Rochester.

Had Billy remained with the Cardinals, he would have played for yet another manager as Breadon continued to use the ball club's organization like a checkerboard, making moves and jumps at his whims. "[He] changes managers as another man changes his ties" is how one writer described it.[3]

Hornsby's club won the World Series in 1926 but he couldn't get along with Breadon so he was out. O'Farrell's club was beset with injuries throughout 1927 and finished second so he was out. Now it was Bill McKechnie's turn to take the wheel in 1928.

An incident that occurred during the 1926 pennant race put Southworth on Breadon's front burner as possible managerial material. The Cardinals were battling Cincinnati and Pittsburgh for the top spot when trouble started brewing in the Cardinal clubhouse. A spat developed between two players to the point where they were no longer speaking to each other. As the dispute wore on, teammates began taking sides and it was causing great division on the ball club.[4]

Southworth, who had only been with the team for about six weeks, saw the harm all the arguing was doing and decided to step forward. It happened prior to a game when there was some rumbling in the clubhouse that was the result of the ongoing troubles. Southworth stood up on a bench and addressed his teammates. O'Farrell, Bottomley, Rhem, Haines, Alexander, Hornsby and others listened as Billy said, "Let's cut out this petty squabbling and get out there and play ball. We can win that pennant. I want to win and there are other fellows here who want to win. If you fellows who are fighting over nothing will throw half of that fight against the other clubs, we'll finish in front. I'm going out there and fight myself. How many are going with me?"[5]

That locker room speech seemed to settle things down. The feuding stopped and the Cardinals went on to win the National League championship and the World Series. Word of Southworth's leadership made its way to Breadon who hadn't forgotten about it. When the right circumstance came a year and a half later, he acted on it.

Rochester was a good fit for Billy. He was to spend parts of five seasons there as player and manager and from the very start, he took to the city and the city took to him. In 1928, he seemed to be rejuvenated as a player, perhaps because he went through the season injury free and perhaps because he was facing minor league pitching every day. At age 36, he compiled the highest batting average of his professional career, .361 and, as a manager, he was putting together a team that was hard to beat.

Managing in the minor leagues is different than managing at almost any other level because the best players, the ones who can bring a championship, will not be there long; the big league club will call them up. Many of the remaining players are young, inexperienced and, if they have the skills and work hard, will also one day advance to the big leagues. In some cases, a minor league club is also a pit stop for former major league players who have been sent down to sharpen their skills or whose skills and speed have diminished to the point where they will never play big league ball again.

Southworth's Rochester team had a mix of young and old, ranging in age from 41-year-old Del Gainer to 22-year-old Ira Smith. Gainer, five years older than his manager, was an outfielder/first baseman who played on pennant winners with the Boston Red Sox in the days when their top pitcher was Babe Ruth, but hadn't played in the majors since 1922. Smith was a fuzzy-cheeked third baseman whose professional career would never hit a higher level than Southworth's Rochester club.

A factor that probably helped Billy in his managerial debut year was that Rochester was well stocked with former teammates. Among them were Hi Bell and Vic Keen, former Cardinal pitchers, Specs Toporcer, the bespectacled Cardinal infielder who would one day succeed Billy as the Red Wings manager and 38-year-old Hank Gowdy, the old Giants catcher who tripped over his mask trying to catch the foul ball in the 1924 World Series.

The Red Wings got off to a good start and so did Billy. On opening day, Rochester defeated Jersey City, 3–1, in 12 innings with Hi Bell going the distance to get the victory and Southworth hitting a triple in the 12th inning to drive in the decisive runs. A pre-season poll of International League writers had predicted a last-place finish for Rochester but early on they played way above their expectations under their new manager.

In May, Billy got a call to come home to Columbus immediately. He was about to become a father again. Billy Jr. was about to have companions. The Southworth home was about to be a little more crowded. But when he arrived in Columbus, he learned there were complications, serious ones. On May 21, the Southworth twins both died at birth and Lida Southworth lay seriously ill. Billy remained in Columbus for two weeks.

There can be no more devastating blow to a parent than the death of a child, and for the Southworths, the grief was multiplied. The two most important things in Billy's life were his family and his job and he had to find a way of dealing with his despair, caring for his family and returning to work. In time, his answer was to immerse himself in his work.

The Sporting News reported on June 14, "Everything seems to have gone against Billy Southworth in his debut as a manager. First it was injuries, then some of the pitchers went bad, and finally a serious illness to Mrs. Southworth caused him to hurry home to Columbus."[6]

The Red Wings, who had played in the Little World Series the previous year, had trouble getting on track in 1928 but better days seemed to lie ahead. "Perhaps the reason for the change for the better lies in none other but Skipper Southworth. The dash and pepper exhibited by the manager took hold on the members of the club and they started after things with a do-or-die attitude."[7]

Rochester continued its winning ways and won the International League pennant with a record of 90–74. Charlie Gelbert, who would be the Cardinals regular shortstop in 1929, was the hitting star for the Red Wings, with a .340 batting average and 195 hits, including 21 home runs. Bell won 21 games, Keen won 12 and Art Decatur, who would also one day be in the majors, chipped in with 15 victories.

It had been a year of ups and downs for the Red Wings. They got off to the great start, then the tragedy with the Southworth babies, then more great baseball, then a freak accident with just weeks left in the season. In Montreal, a taxi cab carrying seven Red Wing players collided head-on with another car. Several players received cuts and bruises but Bob Morrow, the starting catcher, incurred some broken bones and was out for the rest of the season. The Red Wings got some welcome offensive help from Rip Collins, who had just joined the ball club and hit four home runs down the stretch.

Going into the last day of the season, Rochester was in a virtual tie with

Buffalo for the league championship. Buffalo was playing a single game. The Red Wings had a doubleheader against Montreal. If Buffalo won, Rochester had to sweep the doubleheader to win the championship.

The Red Wings won the opener, 5–2, behind the pitching of Hi Bell, whose nickname was Wheezer. Word reached the clubhouse that Buffalo had won. For Rochester, the championship was on the line in the second game. There was some doubt as to who Billy the Kid would choose to pitch.

As the players mingled around, Specs Toporcer finally said, "Who will it be, skipper?" Billy looked around and then put his arm on Bell's shoulder. "Wheezer," he said, "you're the one to sew up the championship for us. Change your sweatshirt and stand them on their heads."[8]

The Red Wings helped out their fatigued pitcher by scoring four runs in the first inning and Collins hit a home run later as Rochester coasted to a 5–0 victory and the International League championship. It was the closest race in league history. Rochester finished at 90–74, a .549 percentage. Buffalo was second with a .548 percentage.

For Southworth, it was a thrilling time. In his first year as a manager, his team was going to the Little World Series to take on Indianapolis. The stakes were as high as they could get.

But tragedy struck once again. Before the opening game of the Series, as Billy stood in the dugout and watched his team work out, a messenger came down and handed him a telegram. It read: "Come at once. Billy has been shot."[9]

Southworth raced to find the nearest phone to call home. It had been just a little over four months since he and Lida had suffered the loss of their twins. The thought of possibly losing Billy was unbearable.

The phone call brought the details. A group of neighborhood kids in Columbus had been in one of the kid's backyards watching him trying to shoot blackbirds flying overhead. The boy with the rifle was having trouble firing it. He turned away from the group as he pulled the trigger but pointed it in the direction of where young Southworth had just opened a gate and was coming into the yard. Billy was hit in the stomach and fell to the ground.

"I lived through hell on the way back to Columbus," said his father, reliving that day years later. "Just the knowledge the little guy had been shot was frightening enough but the fear he might have been critically shot was almost more than I could stand. He was only 12 but I kind of looked at him as the closest man friend I had."[10]

Southworth said that while he and his boy always enjoyed a close relationship, it had never been particularly emotional. There weren't a lot of hugs, he said, because Billy Jr. liked to play as if they were both grown-ups. "But this was one time I wanted to pick him up, hold him close and cry over him," he said.

Instead, when he entered his son's hospital room, he looked down at the boy and said, "How ya doin', pardner?" Billy Jr. looked at his dad and said, "I'm all right. Don't even hurt now." Then the youngster paused and said, "How'd ya do?" Billy told his son Rochester lost, 5–3, to which the lad replied, "You know what they say — you can't win 'em all." It was a tender moment of a 12-year-old boy with a gunshot wound consoling his father over losing a ballgame.[11]

As it turned out, the bullet that struck young Southworth had glanced against a button on his shirt, diverting its course and causing it to miss vital organs and the boy recovered without any serious effects.

Indianapolis won the 1928 Little World Series but Rochester's successful season made Southworth a popular figure. "The fact the Wings went on to lose the World Series to Indianapolis mattered little. The town was smitten with the job Southworth had done and was looking forward to the 1929 season," according to Rochester baseball historians.[12]

E.J. Lanigan reported in *The Sporting News*, "He's quite a manager was the word passed along by all players who had come in contact with Southworth. And their reports often came from men who couldn't do well enough to stick in Double A. There wasn't a man who blamed Southworth for their failure to stick."[13]

Lanigan said that frequently ballplayers who are cut from a team or demoted blame the manager for not giving them a fair chance or playing them at the wrong position or simply not knowing what they were doing. But Lanigan heard none of that with respect to Southworth. "Each Rochester player I met this year sang the praises of Southworth as a leader and from a Jersey City player there came the boost for Billy that he had just the right temperament for a manager and could inspire his men to work their heads off for him," he wrote.[14]

Meanwhile, in St. Louis, Sam Breadon was restless again. His Cardinals had evolved into a National League powerhouse, capturing two National League championships and a World Series title in two out of the last three seasons and finishing second in the other year. But for Breadon, success just created the desire for more success and his method of achieving loftier goals was to keep looking for just the right person to lead the Cardinals.

Hornsby won the World Series with the Redbirds in 1926; O'Farrell's club had a good year but not good enough to overtake the Waner brothers and Pittsburgh in 1927; and McKechnie led the Cardinals to the promised land in 1928. But Babe Ruth had a huge World Series and St. Louis lost four straight games to the New York Yankees. That was a humiliation for Breadon and in his mind clearly a sign that a change in managers was needed.

The change came that winter and it was yet another surprise for the Cardinals' loyal fandom. Billy Southworth, with one year experience as a minor league manager, was named to replace the veteran McKechnie in St. Louis — and McKechnie was sent to Rochester to replace Southworth.

Some sportswriters were wary of the latest change. "With a team of aging stars to reconstruct and keener competition among his league rivals than has existed in years to face, Billy will have to develop plenty of managerial horsepower," wrote John Wray in the *St. Louis Post Dispatch*.[15]

James J. Long, in the *Pittsburgh Sun Telegraph*, wrote about speculation that Breadon might have wanted a manager with a little tougher disposition than the congenial McKechnie. "As contradicting the determination to get a team leader of the aggressive, two-fisted variety, it is pointed out that Rogers Hornsby was a general on that order, one who ran the team to suit himself regardless of any preferred advice, yet he was fired after he won a pennant and the world championship in 1926," wrote Long.[16]

Hooey, in *The Sporting News*, noting what had happened to Hornsby, O'Farrell and McKechnie in the previous three seasons, said there was some concern in St. Louis about Southworth's new role and it wasn't about the thought of him failing. Given the fate of his predecessors, Hooey wrote: "Fans are asking: What will happen to Southworth if he wins?"[17]

◆ 8 ◆

"Every species of discouragement"

Billy the Kid had a world of experience to draw on when he went to spring training in 1929 as the youngest manager in the National League, but none of it as a big league skipper. His year at Rochester, filled with personal misfortunes, was hugely successful at the ballpark where Southworth had blended hardcore, tobacco-chewing, beer-guzzling old veterans with wide-eyed, innocent kids and delivered a championship.

He inherited a Cardinal team that had been in the World Series two out of the last three years, a team where just two years ago, he had been one of the boys, hitting with them, fielding with them, eating with them, drinking with them. Many of them probably expected him to be their pal. Breadon expected him to be their boss.

And while Southworth had achieved success in Rochester by being a mentor to some, leading by example to others, and always with a pat on the back and a smile, his experience with successful big league managers had been quite different. Joe Birmingham at Cleveland, Fred Mitchell at Boston, John McGraw with the Giants and Hornsby with the Cardinals were all no-nonsense men, each with an obsession of winning ballgames no matter who was stepped on, literally or figuratively.

Cullen Cain, a sportswriter who became publicity director for the National League, wrote in *The Sporting News*, "Since Billy Southworth has been called to lead the Cards this season, there has been more or less humorous speculation on how long he will hold the job. Even Billy's friends, and they comprise about 90 percent of the folks interested in baseball, do not think he will last long."[1]

Part of the skepticism was because Billy was known to be such a nice guy, a pal, and therefore would have trouble leading his old teammates. There was also the stigma of working for Sam Breadon, who was providing the ball club with its fourth manager in four years and who obviously had no trouble pulling the plug on a manager, even in seemingly the best of times.

Breadon had this answer for the skeptics: "I know Southworth better than a lot of people and I watched him pretty close last year. He's been on my payroll three years now and I ought to know something about him. He has plenty of character and firmness for the job."[2]

Cain pointed out the difficult year Billy had at Rochester in 1928, concluding "his brains and his heart carried him through against every species of discouragement" and that he was up to the next challenge of his career.[3]

The Cardinals players got an inkling in spring training of what kind of manager they were going to have and many were not pleased. They trained at Avon Park, Florida, a town of less that 10,000 residents about 175 miles north of Miami, where the presence of the Cardinals every spring was a huge boon to the local economy.

Bottomley, Hafey, Rhem, Haines and others had done well for themselves, having collected two World Series checks and, while coming to Florida to train, also wanted to have some time to enjoy the sights. Many had purchased automobiles and had driven to spring training, bringing their wives with them.

As the team prepared for a trip to Miami for an exhibition game, Southworth wanted to impress upon them the importance of going places as a team. "We go to Miami tomorrow and we go by train," he told them in a clubhouse meeting. "There won't be any riding in automobiles with your family and friends. I hope everybody gets that."

Some of his old buddies, like Bottomley and Hafey, snickered. Jimmy Wilson, a backup catcher to O'Farrell, wasn't laughing. "Billy, Mrs. Wilson is down here and she has been looking forward to that Miami trip ever since we landed in Florida. I, for one, am driving to Miami."

Southworth was taken aback. "Is that so?" he said. "Well, so long as you've gone on record, I'll go on record, too. You can drive to Miami but if you do, it will cost you $500." When the meeting broke up, Billy the Kid had become "Billy the Heel" in the words of Wilson and others did not disagree.[4]

There were other problems too, such as the time Billy thought two of his players had broken curfew and burst into their hotel room only to find them both in bed. Despite the friction between the young manager and his ballplayers, the Cardinals got off to a good start and proved themselves worthy of perhaps repeating as champions.

Old Jess Haines, using his knuckleball to baffle batters, won his first five starts before losing the first game of a doubleheader to Pittsburgh. The Redbirds, after going 7–5 in April, won 19 of 29 games in May and then hit a streaky June. On June 4, they won their seventh straight game but then lost four in a row before Haines stopped Brooklyn, 3–1, to increase his record to 7–1. They lost four more and then reeled off six straight victories. They reached their high level mark on June 17 with a record of 35–21.

Then the roof caved in. They had a disastrous road trip that contributed to a two-week spell in which the Cardinals lost 14 out of 15 — a four-game losing streak, then a win, then an 11-game losing streak. In the midst of all that was a tie-game, so they actually went 12 games without a win. Billy the Kid was not only having managerial woes but the strain was having an effect on his hitting, which had always been something the Cardinals could depend on.

On July 22, Breadon had seen enough. With the Cardinals at 43–45 and Southworth hitting .188, Billy was fired but given his old job back in Rochester. McKechnie, the manager who had been demoted to Rochester after losing the World Series in four straight to the New York Yankees, was brought back to lead the Cardinals.

It was not a bad deal for Billy. Breadon could have shipped him off to oblivion but he didn't. Instead, he returned him to the city where he was considered a hero for winning the International League championship the year before. The bad experience he had managing the Cardinals would provide lessons that he would use to great advantage in the future.

The St. Louis experience was a tough challenge for a first-year manager. He had been successful in Rochester by being congenial with his players, treating with respect both the old-timers on their way out and the kids on their way up. But when he got the call to manage the Cardinals, he was thrust into a situation in which the owner wanted someone with a harder edge than McKechnie had with the ballclub. So Billy had to try to show some authority over players who had been his drinking buddies just two years earlier, and it didn't work.

As author Jerome M. Mileur observed, "His style, modeled after that of McGraw and other tough managers for whom he had played, grated on the players and produced a near mutiny."[5]

Historian Fred Lieb said the problem in St. Louis stemmed from the days when Billy the Kid was one of the boys, playing with them, singing with them, imbibing in liquor at a time when Prohibition forbade it. They won a pennant together and they let the good times roll. It was Billy and his pals. "But in a varied major league career, he had been under some tough managers, Joe Birmingham in Cleveland, George Stallings [sic] in Boston, John McGraw in New York and Rogers Hornsby in St. Louis. A fellow with a naturally sweet disposition, he felt like he had to emulate these men — to be tough with his fellow former players to command their respect."[6]

Bob Hooey, the Columbus sportswriter and Southworth's good friend, said Breadon usually waited until the end of the year to fire his manager, as he had with Hornsby, O'Farrell and McKechnie. In firing Southworth in July, Breadon was ahead of schedule, Hooey wrote in a piece for *The Sporting News*.[7]

The Cardinals were in fourth place when Southworth and McKechnie traded places and that's where they finished. When Billy got off the train in Rochester, he was back in familiar territory, in a city he enjoyed — and which enjoyed him, with ballplayers who, in many cases, he had helped groom the year before, and perhaps most appealing of all, his club was in another hot pennant race. So in many respects, it was as if he was picking up where he left off in Rochester.

Southworth got his first shot at managing in the big leagues with the Cardinals in 1929, but he only lasted a half-season (courtesy Southworth family).

He had a good ball club to work with — it was the nucleus of what would become a great team. Branch Rickey had created the first farm system for major league teams and he did his best to stock as many teams with potential major leaguers as he could — players who would learn "Cardinal baseball" from the ground up. That was a better fit for Southworth than trying to appease major leaguers. Many of Southworth's Red Wings would one day be part of the famed "Gas House Gang" in St. Louis.

Rip Collins played the full season for the Red Wings, and hit 38 home runs. He was one cog in a remarkable infield defense that played a part in turning 225 double plays, smashing the professional baseball record of 194 set by the Cincinnati Reds. The Red Wings were so adept at turning double plays that opponents accused Rochester pitchers of walking batters semi-intentionally just to set up a double play situation.

Billy the Kid, never afraid to try anything he thought would give his team an advantage, said the semi-intentional walk only happened once. "We had made 193 double plays and the boys wanted to tie the big-time record set by Cincinnati," he said. In the middle of a ballgame where the Red Wings were comfortably ahead, some of the players in the dugout started suggesting that Wheezer Bell walk the lead-off batter in the next inning.

"Nothing doing," said Southworth, but after a little cajoling, he gave in. Bell walked the first batter and, sure enough, the next batter hit into a double play and Rochester had tied the record. Later in the same game, center fielder George Watkins made a spectacular shoestring catch and doubled a runner off second to set the all-time double play record. The Red Wings also pulled off two triple plays that year.[8]

The pitching staff was solid, anchored by Tex Carleton and Paul Derringer, who would go on to have stellar major league careers. They were both 24 with live arms. Southworth knew he wouldn't have either one of them for very long. Within two years Carleton was in the major leagues where he won 100 games, pitching primarily for the Cardinals. Derringer had a 15-year career in which he won 223 games, pitching for several clubs. He had four seasons in which he won 20 games or more.

Under Southworth's guidance, the Red Wings won 43 and lost just 27 and once again the team won 103 games overall and earned another spot in the Little World Series. They lost to Kansas City, five games to four, but the final game ended in a controversy that dragged on for months.

Kansas City won the game, 3–2, in 10 innings. In the bottom of the ninth, with the score tied at 2, the Red Wings mounted a rally. Specs Toporcer came to bat with two men on and two out. With a 3-and-2 count, he thought he checked his swing but umpire John Goetz called him out on strikes. Toporcer argued vigorously, so vigorously in fact that a report on his rage was sent to the International League office. The league's executive committee ruled that Toporcer be suspended for the entire 1930 season, that he be fined $200—and Southworth was fined $500, apparently for not restraining his ballplayer.

Rochester sportswriters and fans were outraged. They deluged the league office with letters and calls protesting the harsh action. Toporcer spoke on his own behalf at a hearing. Among other speakers was Branch Rickey who felt compelled to defend his player and his manager. The next day, the committee dropped the suspension, upped Toporcer's fine to $500 and reduced Southworth's to $200.[9]

That bit of business out of the way, Billy the Kid and his boys could start looking to the 1930 season. It would be hard to top the 1929 record of 103–65 under the combined leadership of McKechnie and Southworth, so no one could have foreseen that the Red Wings taking the field in 1930 would be remembered as one of the greatest teams in professional baseball history.

The pitching staff was led by Derringer who won 23 and lost only 11. Jack Berly was 16–8 and Carleton was 13–13. Berly never reached the major league prominence that awaited Derringer and Carleton. He won 10 games over four years in the big leagues before retiring. Ira Smith, still one of the youngest Red Wings, chipped in with a 12 and 7 record.

Rip Collins and Specs Toporcer were back at their familiar positions at first and second base with Joseph Brown handling most of the chances at third base and Charlie Wilson doing the same at shortstop. John "Pepper" Martin, Bob "Red" Worthington and Ray Pepper were in the outfield and Southworth inserted himself into 66 games. Paul Florence was the catcher.

The ball club had six pitchers who won 10 or more games, seven batters who hit over .300, four who scored more than 100 runs and four who drove in more than 100, including Collins, who set an International League record with 180 RBIs.

Rochester baseball historian Bill McCarthy summed up the talent. "You could wear your adjectives thin writing about Billy Southworth's 1930 Rochester Red Wings and not do the club half justice," he wrote. "Those boys had spark and spring, a wealth of class.... Those Wings of 1930 could have zoomed to the top of either major loop."[10]

One of the reasons for the Red Wings' good fortune came in part as a result of yet another Southworth injury — the nemesis that haunted him years ago and made a skeptic of John McGraw. In spring training, Billy was working with a Red Wing pitcher and was struck on the hand by a line drive, breaking his finger in two places. Not long before that, Red Worthington chipped a bone in his elbow and was out indefinitely. With one starting outfielder and the top reserve outfielder on the shelf, Red Wings general manager Warren Giles contacted Branch Rickey to send some help. The Cardinals had a kid named John Martin, nicknamed "Pepper," who wasn't going to see much big league action so Rickey dispatched him to Rochester.

Martin was a fiery, never-say-die ballplayer, who belly-flopped his slides, made circus catches in the outfield, ran to first base even when he drew a walk and his attitude and style invigorated the entire ball club. Southworth took an immediate liking to him because Martin played the game the way Southworth thought it should be played. The manager and player hit it off immediately.

But even more important, Martin brought added punch to the already powerful lineup. He hit .363, and banged out 33 doubles, 18 triples, 20 homers and drove in 114 runs. Martin had bounced around in the minor leagues for several seasons but this would be his only season in Rochester and his last in the minor leagues. In 1931 he was back with the St. Louis Cardinals to stay and, along with Dizzy Dean and others, was part of the "Gas House Gang" of ballplayers who knew how to have fun on and off the field.

However, his one year under Southworth made a lasting impression on him. "As far as I'm concerned," said Martin, "Billy Southworth will always be the greatest manager of all time. A fellow who didn't break his neck for Billy was no good at heart. Our gang just outdid ourselves for the grandest man I know."[11]

Despite all the hype about the 1930 Red Wings, they sputtered at the start of the season, partly because of the spring training injuries. They were in the second division most of the first half of the season. On May 31, they lost a game to Montreal when reserve outfielder Gene Bailey, playing in place of Worthington, dropped a fly ball, let another one drop in front of him and butchered a ground ball base hit, allowing base runners to advance.

The usually patient Southworth bristled on the bench, figuring he could do better with a broken finger. That night, Billy took an old catcher's mitt and cut a hole in it that would secure his injured finger. The catcher's mitt provided much more padding than a fielder's glove. The next day, at Toronto, he inserted himself in the lineup and sought permission from Toronto manager Steve O'Neill to use the makeshift glove. O'Neill agreed although he told Billy he didn't think it was a good idea to be playing with a broken finger. The Red Wings won that afternoon and Southworth made a diving catch in the outfield to save the game. Word spread around the league about the special glove and he was prohibited from using it any more.

But the determination of Billy, the infectious spirit of Pepper Martin and the slugging of Rip Collins started to take hold in July. The Red Wings put together some winning streaks and by August seemed unbeatable. In a crucial Series with Baltimore in late August, Rochester swept the three games, two of them in extra innings and the last two with Southworth back at the hotel battling the flu.

Scouts for major league teams started cherry-picking the Red Wings roster. Worthington was signed by the Boston Braves and Berly was snatched up by the New York Giants. Despite the depletion of star players, the Rochester bandwagon continued to roll. The Red Wings finished with a record of 105–62, the second straight year they topped the 100-win mark. They went on to defeat Louisville, five games to three, in the Little World Series.

For the season, Collins hit .376, Worthington hit .375, Martin hit .363,

Pepper hit .347, Joe Brown hit .313, Specs Toporcer hit .307 and Southworth hit .370 in limited action. Derringer was 23–11 with a 2.89 earned run average and Berly was 16–8 with a 2.49 earned run average.

In a sense, this team was almost too good to last, for Rochester, like all minor league teams, was a training ground, a stepping stone to the big time. By 1931, Collins, Martin and Derringer were all up with the St. Louis Cardinals, and Joe Brown and Toporcer were both sold to Jersey City. Delker was playing for Columbus, another Cardinals farm team, and Carleton was shipped to Houston where he joined another up-and-coming pitcher by the name of Dizzy Dean.

Branch Rickey naturally wanted to bring the cream of the crop to the Cardinals but he also wanted to stock his farm system with good ballplayers. While Rochester was a great team, some of the Red Wing players would make other Cardinals farm teams more competitive, and that would increase attendance and earnings in the other cities. It was a great system for the organization overall, but it had pretty well plucked most of the feathers off of Southworth's Red Wings.

Billy was used to working with young, untested talent and mixing them with veterans, and 1931 would be no different. One of his veterans now was Ira Smith, the youngest player on the team when Billy took over in 1928, who had won 12 games for the 1930 champions. Paul Florence was still there as the starting catcher and Ray Pepper was still patrolling the outfield. Wheezer Bell, hero of a previous Red Wings team, was back after a stint with the Cardinals.

But two key player transactions helped propel the Red Wings to yet another sensational season. A pitcher named Carmen Hill had a 10-year major league career in which he won 49 games, 22 of them with the Pirates in 1927. After a couple of unproductive seasons with the Cardinals, Hill was dispatched to Rochester. Ray Starr was a hurler sent over from Houston, where he never reached the potential the Cardinals saw in him when they signed him.

Perhaps because of his own experience trying to satisfy John McGraw, Southworth was able to relate to Hill and especially to Starr. Hill seemed to be rejuvenated in Rochester and won 18 games while losing 12. Wheezer Bell won 16 and lost 11. Smith, now 25 years old, turned in a record of 15–9.

But the big surprise of 1931 was Starr. He had been frustrated in previous years, feeling at times he was ignored or unappreciated. Billy knew the feeling and tried to make sure Starr knew he was needed. The young pitcher responded by winning 20 games while losing 7. Southworth showed his confidence in Starr by starting him in both games of doubleheaders three different times during the season. He won both games of a twin bill on July 19 against Jersey City, which also marked the day Toporcer returned to the Red Wings, another boost in Rochester's quest to remain a championship team. On August 9, he again worked both ends of a doubleheader again against Jersey City, losing 2–1 in the opener before winning 6–1 in the nightcap. On August 20, he started and won both games against Reading.[12]

The biggest gift Rickey bestowed upon Southworth in 1931 was the signing of George Sisler, one of the greatest hitters in American League history, who at age 38 was in the twilight of his career. He wasn't going to play in the major leagues again and he had never played minor league baseball. But he didn't want his career to end and Rickey needed a star to help Southworth, to fill the gap left by the departure of first baseman Rip Collins and to satisfy the Rochester fandom, hungry for another championship.

Sisler, who hit over .400 twice in the big leagues and set the all-time, single-season record for most hits with 257 in 1920, had a lifetime major league batting average of .340. He proved to be the catalyst in the batter's box that Starr was on the pitcher's mound. He hit .303 for the season as the Red Wings won more than 100 games for the third consecutive season (101) and captured another championship. In Sisler's great career it was the only time he played on a championship team.[13]

The Red Wings defeated St. Paul, five games to three, in the Little World Series. Sisler reaggravated a pulled muscle in his first at-bat and did not play the remainder of the Series.

For Billy Southworth, it had been a great run in Rochester, winning 399 games in four years, including 100 or more three years in a row and having four pennant winners and two Little World Series championships. He was on top of the minor league baseball world as the 1932 season beckoned.

Down and Out

Athletes know when their skills are diminishing, when the bat speed isn't what it once was, when the run from home to first is a step slower than it used to be, when the ground ball that whizzed by wouldn't have whizzed by a few years ago. Frequently it is the legs that are the tell-tale sign or for a pitcher, it's the arm — the fastball that isn't as fast, the curve ball that's losing its bite, the arm that gets weary too soon. It is often more difficult to pinpoint the time in which the personal life starts going downhill. In the case of Billy Southworth, it might have been the aftermath of when he and Lida lost their twins at birth in 1928. Or it might have been all of Billy's traveling and being away from home for such long periods of time. Or it might have been his drinking in which one beer always seemed to lead to two and would sometimes cause Billy the Kid to act "out of character."[1] For all the success he had on the field for four years in Rochester, his life off the field was starting to become erratic. The closeness he and Lida felt in the early days in Portland was not there anymore. When Billy had time off, he seemed more intent on getting home and spending time with his boy than with his wife.

Sportswriters of the era tended not to mention ballplayers' behaviors off the diamond unless their antics were cause for disciplinary action by the ball club, such as in the cases of Babe Ruth and Grover Cleveland Alexander who incurred suspensions for their off-the-field transgressions.

Bob Hooey, the Columbus sportswriter and Southworth's great friend, wrote an in-depth biographic series of stories about Billy for *The Sporting News* and never mentioned any personal problems in Billy the Kid's life other than his disagreements with John McGraw.

Arthur Daley, the famed sports columnist for the *New York Times*, touched on the drinking problem in a retrospective of Billy's career, but it was hardly an indictment. "As a ballplayer, Southworth was popular and convivial," Daley wrote. "If he was too convivial at times, it didn't seem to affect his work."[2]

The mystery year of 1932 started with Southworth again at the helm in Rochester, coming off four consecutive pennant-winning seasons, three straight seasons of 100 wins or more, enjoying the most successful run in professional baseball. His ball club faced the challenges it always had, with its best players being promoted to the big leagues, some big leaguers in the waning years of their careers signing with Rochester in hopes of hanging on for a little while longer, and with a fresh crop of youngsters hoping to make it at all.

The Red Wings sputtered at the start of the season but that was nothing new. What was new was the Cardinals' decision to make a managerial change in July. Southworth received word that Lee McPhail, owner of the Columbus ball club in the American Association, had fired manager Harry Leibold and that Billy was to replace him. It meant he was returning to his hometown and in fact, being in a ballpark not far from where he had played sandlot ball as a kid. It also meant he would be leaving the city where he had achieved his greatest professional success at the very time he had reached the pinnacle of that success. Specs Toporcer was named his replacement in Rochester.

The fans in Rochester were surprised, even shocked by the news, but in Toporcer they were getting a veteran ballplayer who would be a playing manager and was hugely popular in the city, just as Southworth was. In Columbus, the fans were getting a hometown boy who had made good and was now coming back home to lead the troops. He guided the Redbirds to a second-place finish, their highest placement since 1918.

Then another strange development occurred. At the end of the season, Southworth was removed as manager. Bob Hooey had this take on it: "Billy, by this time, had established himself as a capable minor league pilot, worthy of another major league trial."[3]

Other accounts weren't so kind. "Billy started drinking heavily and the injury-bedraggled Redbirds finished second. The Cards fired Southworth," Jon Daly wrote in his biography of Southworth for the Baseball Biography Project of the Society for American Baseball Research.[4]

The Cardinals never said publicly why Southworth was dismissed so quickly. All of this was occurring during the Depression years and many ball clubs were looking to player-managers as a way of cutting expense and Billy's playing days were over. There was also the notion that Southworth had not brought the same managerial magic to Columbus as he had done in Rochester.

A bigger factor might have been that stories were circulating about Billy's drinking. While there had been no reports of anything serious happening because of it, he was nonetheless working for Branch Rickey, a man who didn't drink, didn't smoke, didn't go to the ballpark on Sundays, the day of rest, and wanted his managers to toe the line.

Billy's daughter, Carole Southworth Watson, acknowledged her father had a low tolerance for alcohol but insists he was not an alcoholic. She said events in his life in the late 1920s and early 1930s were starting to get the best of him. "He was going through tough times," she said. "He was losing Lida, he was drinking more heavily and his baseball career was going downhill. I still wouldn't call him an alcoholic but about once a week he'd get totaled. But he didn't do that before he was to take the field. He would never do that."[5]

In December, Bill Terry, Southworth's old teammate with the Giants who was now New York's manager, hired Billy as one of his coaches. It was a bittersweet situation for Southworth. It brought him back to the major leagues but with the organization in which he experienced his worst times. And Bill Terry was a tough, gruff individual, not unlike the man he was succeeding as manager, John McGraw.

The Giants trained in Arizona. The exhibition games gave Billy the chance to renew some acquaintances with men he played with and against, many of whom were now managers and coaches with other teams. But as a Giants coach, he was under the thumb of Terry, like he had been with McGraw, except now he was 10 years older and had enjoyed success being his own boss with a successful minor league team.

At the end of March, as the ball club was making its way back north, Southworth and Terry stopped in a diner to get something to eat. Friendly chatter between the two became teasing and the teasing became unpleasant and the reaction of both of them became physical. The next day, Terry was sporting a black eye and Southworth was no longer with the ball club.[6]

Sportswriter Tom Meany, who was traveling with the Giants, didn't see the skirmish but witnessed the aftermath. "We were playing an exhibition game at Galveston," he said. "We looked around and we couldn't see Terry and we couldn't see Southworth. We finally found Southworth in his street clothes in the grandstand. When Terry showed up, he had a beautiful black eye." Meany said both men denied Southworth had given Terry the shiner and Terry never provided an explanation as to how he got it. So from that standpoint, it was a mystery but Meany said it was no mystery that Southworth had an interest in "extracurricular activities," a not-so-vague reference to his drinking.[7]

No other team offered him a job. Just a year after he was the most successful manager in the minor leagues and for the first time in more than 20 years, Southworth was out of baseball. His fate was to return to Columbus to try to pick up the pieces in a career that had hit rock bottom and a family life that had been gradually falling apart. He was now a 40-year-old man living at 770 Linwood Avenue in Columbus, Ohio, and like so many other men and women of this era, he was looking for work.

He landed a job as a salesman for Capital City Products in Columbus, selling cottonseed oil. It was a difficult time for Billy and he yearned to get back into baseball, hopefully the big leagues, but if it was to happen, the journey would be long, almost like back in the days when he toiled in outfields of Portsmouth and Portland and Birmingham.

He worked for Capital City Products for two years and during that time struck up a friendship with Mabel Stemen, a pretty, 21-year-old bookkeeper who shared a lot of the same interests as Billy—sports, hunting, horseback riding. Southworth's marriage was on the rocks. Lida had moved to Portsmouth to be closer to her parents. Billy Jr., now 17, was a star athlete at East High School in Columbus with his eye on a football or baseball scholarship to Ohio State. He had been caught in the middle of the soured relationship between his parents and had been living, at least part of the time, with his Uncle Arley and his wife in Columbus.[8]

Southworth told interviewers many times that the Longfellow poem "The Village Blacksmith," recited to him by his father when he was a kid, was something he memorized and gave him inspiration as an adult. The resolve of his father, now an aging man in Columbus, and the words of Longfellow—"each burning deed and thought"—might have come to mind as Billy struggled to put his life back together.

> Thanks, thanks to thee, my worthy friend,
> For the lesson thou has taught;
> Thus at the flaming forge of life
> Our fortunes must be wrought;
> Thus on its sounding anvil shaped.

Whether he was inspired by ancient poetry is the subject of pure speculation but the inspiration and the will to succeed he drew from Mabel Stemen is permanently etched in the Southworth family history. "She straightened him out. She turned him around. There is no question about that," said Carole Southworth Watson, the daughter they would one day have together.[9]

On September 12, 1934, newspapers throughout Ohio printed a two-paragraph story that created a buzz as if it had been a banner headline across the state. Lida Brooks Southworth, wife of baseball legend Billy Southworth, had filed for divorce after almost 20 years of marriage. Not long after that,

Billy and Mabel were married. Daughter Carole was born in August 1935. Lida, whose health had never been the same since the death of the twins in 1928, died in 1936, reportedly of a brain hemorrhage.[10]

There were now two driving forces in Southworth's life, the desire to be a good family man and the itch to get back into baseball. Both depended on him changing some of his personal ways. One thing that never wavered over the years was the close father-son relationship between Billy and Billy Jr.

After being out of baseball for two years, in early 1935, the newly-married Southworth contacted his old boss, Branch Rickey, and pleaded with him to find him a job managing somewhere. "I won't let you down," he said, and then he uttered the words Rickey wanted to hear. "I've quit drinking."

Rickey was supportive but practical. "My boy," he said, "If you can prove to me that your reform is genuine, I promise you the best job in baseball. But all I can give you now is a Class B team at $300 a month. The rest is up to you." With that, Southworth became manager of the Ashville, North Carolina, Tourists in the Piedmont League in the low levels of the minor leagues. But he didn't care. His days selling cottonseed oil were over. He was back in baseball.[11]

Asheville was a small town in the mountains of North Carolina that was a small dot on the map of organized baseball. But its ball club's history dated back to the days of the Asheville Moonshiners before the turn of the century and had a loyal fan base. Its most famous brush with major league baseball came in 1925 when the New York Yankees and Brooklyn Dodgers journeyed to Asheville for an exhibition game.

As the Yankees' train arrived, dozens of fans waited to get a glimpse of the Bronx Bombers, especially Babe Ruth. They didn't know that the Babe wasn't feeling well. He was suffering from severe stomach cramps that at times doubled him up in pain. When the train arrived in Asheville and Ruth saw the crowd clamoring at the station, he made a valiant effort not to disappoint them.

When the train door opened and the Yankees began to exit, Ruth lumbered out and collapsed unconscious on the floor of the train station. It wasn't long before rumors spread that the Sultan of Swat had died. In reality, he was suffering from an intestinal abscess that laid him up in Asheville and required surgery when he got back to New York. But the Yankee front office was kept busy denying rumors of the Bambino's death. When the truth of the episode was finally known and accepted by the public, W.O. McGeehan of the *New York Times* referred to it as "the bellyache heard round the world." It became a permanent part of Asheville baseball history.[12]

For Southworth, managing in Asheville was different from any previous stints in the dugout. In St. Louis, where his tenure was short and some times tumultuous, he was dealing with tried-and-true major league ballplayers. At Rochester, he had a mix of youngsters on their way up and veterans who had seen better days — but at least they were veterans. But Asheville was the bottom rung on the ladder, the starting point.

Twelve of his 22 players were 22 years old or younger. A pitcher, Bill Curlee, was 18 and was 0–8 for the season with a 5.14 earned run average. Nineteen-year-old Herb Moore, also a pitcher, turned out to be the ace of the staff with a 21–5 record. Outfielder Cap Clark, at 28, was the graybeard on the club and also its best hitter. He finished with a .358 batting average. Seven of his players eventually made it to the major leagues but none reached stardom.

Southworth employed the same tactics that had served him well in Rochester, insisting on hustle, respect and adherence to the fundamentals, good defense and being good teammates. The Tourists led the league in 1935 with a record of 75–62 and won the league championship by defeating Richmond, four games to two, in the league playoffs.

Asheville won the championship again in 1936 but Billy was on the move again. In July, Tom Watkins, owner of the Class A Memphis Chicks, a New York Giants farm club, asked Branch Rickey if he would allow a deal in which Southworth would take over as manager of the last-place Chicks. Rickey thought Billy deserved a chance to move up a few notches on the managerial scale so he agreed on the condition that he could bring Southworth back into the Cardinal organization when he saw the need.

It was a move up for Southworth and, ironically, it came at about the time the Asheville ballclub signed a promising young outfielder from Columbus, Billy Southworth, Jr. Not yet 20 years old, unproven and untested as a professional ballplayer, young Southworth hit .253 in limited action with Asheville and was dispatched to Martinsville in the Class D Bi-State League where he would get more playing time. There he hit .340.

When Billy Southworth left Asheville, the team was struggling with a 29–59 record. But, just as years earlier, when a young Pepper Martin talked of how much Billy had meant to him in Rochester, Billy also left his mark on ballplayers in North Carolina, including one who never played for him there.

Enos Slaughter, who would go on to have a Hall of Fame career with the St. Louis Cardinals and New York Yankees, was just a kid playing for Martinsville, Virginia, in the Class D Bi-State League when Billy took notice of him. Branch Rickey had asked Southworth to venture over to Martinsville to have a look at some of the Cardinals' young farmhands.

He noticed Slaughter right away. He was hitting .275, a respectable batting average but no great shakes in Class D ball. But Southworth noticed more than half of Slaughter's hits were for extra bases so he thought he must be fast. Billy watched him on the base paths and noticed a surprising weakness. For all the skills Slaughter had and the potential to be a good ballplayer, Southworth thought he was too slow to ever be a big leaguer.

He took Slaughter aside and gave him some advice — to quit running flat-footed. He told him to go to the outfield before games and practice running on his toes, not on his heels. It wouldn't be easy at first, but if he ever wanted to make it to the major leagues, he was going to have to make that adjustment, Southworth told him. Slaughter, 19 at the time, took Billy's advice and practiced diligently this new way of running. He made the adjustment and credited Billy with turning him into an outstanding base runner. Four years later, Slaughter led the National League with 52 doubles on his way to a 19-year major league career.[13]

One of his pitchers at Memphis, Del Wetherell, had played for Billy at Rochester five years earlier. For Wetherell, it was a happy reunion. "It's a pleasure to pitch for Billy," he said. "If things don't go well, he comes out and asks you how you feel. If you feel all right, he just gives you a pat on the back, says something encouraging, and you'd be surprised how much that helps."[14]

Just as Asheville was struggling when Billy left the Tourists, Memphis was also floundering and Southworth didn't have time to right the ship that year. The Chicks were 21–35 under his guidance. In 1937 and 1938, the Chicks finished 88–64 in second place and 77–75 in fourth place, respectively, and lost in the first round of the league playoffs each year.

But Billy had proven himself once again to Sam Breadon and Branch Rickey. He had a knack for developing young ballplayers and, more importantly, he had straightened out his personal problems. He was a happily married family man whose favorite beverage was a Coke. Rickey decided to act on his agreement with Memphis that Billy could return to the Cardinals organization whenever they decided they wanted to pull the switch. The Cardinals top brass had yet another assignment for Southworth. It was time for him to go back to Rochester.

The city welcomed Billy back as if he was a hometown kid coming home. And Southworth had always felt a certain loyalty to Rochester. When he had been there before, the ball club had provided team members with tags to put on the handles of their suitcases with the Red Wing logo on them. Billy had never removed the tags. Now he replaced the old ones with a new set.

Ray Blades, his predecessor and former teammate, was now up in St. Louis managing the Cardinals. Billy inherited a Rochester team that was a group of underachievers with great potential. The roster was filled with past and future major leaguers including pitchers Si Johnson, who four years earlier, pitching for Cincinnati, struck out Babe Ruth three times in one game. The Babe retired a week later. There was also Elwin "Preacher" Roe, then an erratic lefthander who would one day have a stellar career with the Brooklyn Dodgers and other big league teams.

The Rochester shortstop was Marty Marion, who at age 21, was already starting his third season with the Red Wings, a launching pad for his Hall of Fame career with the Cardinals. The second baseman was Danny Murtaugh, who 20 years later would manage the Pittsburgh Pirates to a World Series championship over the New York Yankees.

One of the veterans on the ball club was 34-year-old Estel Crabtree, now in his seventh year with the Red Wings after spending parts of four seasons with the Cardinals and Cincinnati Reds. He would play parts of three more seasons with those clubs during the war years, when oldtimers helped teams fill gaps left by ballplayers going off to serve their country. For Rochester in 1939, Crabtree had his finest year in pro ball, hitting .337 with 14 home runs and 94 runs batted in.

Under Southworth, the Red Wings scrapped their way to a second-place finish in the International League with an 84–67 record and then polished off Buffalo, four games to one, in the first round of the league playoffs. This set up a championship match with the Newark Bears, a traditional International League powerhouse.

In the opening game of the Governor's Cup finals at Red Wing Stadium, Preacher Roe had a rough outing and lasted less than two innings, though he only gave up one run. Rochester got solid relief pitching and won the game easily, 8–1. Si Johnson, who many observers thought would be the opening game pitcher, was masterful in Game Two and the Red Wings won it 2–0. They headed off to Newark with a 2–0 lead in the Series with a goal of finishing it off in Newark. But it was not to be. The Bears won the next three games. So when the Red Wings returned to Rochester, they found themselves having to win the next two games.

In Game Six, the Red Wings staked Johnson to a 2–0 lead but he could not hold it. When the Red Wings came up in the bottom of the ninth, they were down, 6–2, and their first two batters were two quick outs. Dusty Cooke then drew a walk, pinch-hitting for pitcher Ken Raffensberger. As Newark pitcher Hank Borowy concentrated on the batter, Cooke took second base and then third base with no play on him. To the Bears, his run, if he scored, was meaningless. They focused on getting one more out.

Whitey Kurowski, another future Cardinal, singled to keep the inning alive as Cooke crossed the plate with Rochester's third run. Pitching carefully, Borowy then walked Harry Davis. That ended Borowy's night. Norman Branch was brought in to face Crabtree, who represented the tying run at the plate. Crabtree lined a homer into the right field stands to tie the game and put the Red Wings crowd — those who hadn't already left — into a frenzy.

Branch settled down and got the third out and then pitched scoreless ball for the next two innings. Southworth brought in Preacher Roe and he set the Bears down in the 10th, 11th and 12th innings. In the bottom of the 12th, Davis reached on an error that got him all the way to second base. Crabtree grounded out to first with Davis going to third on the play. After an intentional walk to set up a double play, Jim Asbell singled to left to drive in the winning run.

The win forced a seventh game but Game Six is a permanent part of Rochester Red Wings history. The drama of Game Six and the never-say-die attitude of the Red Wings were a reflection of their manager's will to win. Southworth said after the game, "I never blinked an eye when ol' Crabby put the wood to that ball."[15]

The euphoria for Rochester and the dismay of Newark may have carried over to the seventh game which Rochester won, 2–1, to capture the Governor's Cup. The next plateau was the Little World Series against upstart Louisville, which had compiled just a 75–78 record during the regular season. The magic ran out for the Red Wings as Louisville won the Series in seven games.

It was a disappointing end but it was also a great time for Billy and his relationship with the Cardinals, one in which his promise to Rickey to conform several years ago and Rickey's faith in him had paid off. Given a second chance to prove himself, Southworth was back in the good graces of his bosses.

In his five seasons at Rochester, the Red Wings had been in the playoffs every year, had won four pennants and captured the Junior World Series championship twice. Southworth's overall managerial record was stunning:

Year	Team	Record	Finish
1928	Rochester	90–74	First
1929	Rochester	43–23	First
1930	Rochester	105–62	First
1931	Rochester	101–67	First

Year	Team	Record	Finish
1932	Rochester	43–45	
	Columbus	42–25	Second
1935	Asheville	75–62	First
1936	Asheville	29–59	
	Memphis	21–35	Eighth
1937	Memphis	88–64	Second
1938	Memphis	77–75	Fourth
1939	Rochester	84–67	Second

The Red Wings got off to a fast start in 1940, winning 31 of their first 44 games. Meanwhile, in St. Louis, the Cardinals were underachieving and Sam Breadon, never known for his patience, decided a change was necessary. A call went out for Billy Southworth.

◆ 10 ◆

The Redbird Renaissance

When Billy managed the Cardinals the first time in 1929, he was young and inexperienced, particularly in his handling of his players. When he returned to the helm in 1940, he was 47, mature, confident and had a knack for instilling confidence in his players. In 1929, he had been part of Sam Breadon's managerial merry-go-round that started with the trade of Rogers Hornsby after the 1926 World Series. Then came Bob O'Farrell and Bill McKechnie in 1927 and 1928, Southworth and McKechnie in 1929 and Gabby Street in 1930—six managerial changes in five years.

In the early 1930s, there was some stability with Street staying until 1933 and Frankie Frisch taking the helm through 1938. Ray Blades had the team in 1939 and into the 1940 season. In 1939, the Cardinals were 92–61 for a second-place finish, four and a half games behind the champion Cincinnati Reds. But the Cardinals stumbled badly out of the gate in 1940 and had a 14–24 record when Breadon decided to make a change. Coach Mike Gonzalez handled the team for six games (1–5) when Billy got the call to take over.

He was in his hotel room in Newark where his Rochester club was to take on the Newark Bears. "I received a phone call to meet Mr. French (Red Wings owner) in the New Yorker Hotel," Billy told the press "And there was Sam Breadon. He told me Blades was through. And I accepted the job."[1]

In one of his first interviews, Southworth reflected on his previous stint as Cardinal manager, his abbreviated work in 1929 that ended in mid-season. He admitted his promotion to the top spot then might have been "premature" but pointed out the Cardinals had a .509 winning percentage when he was fired and finished the season with a .504 percentage.

"All I ask is a fighting chance to make good," he said. "I'm going up with an open mind. I plan no drastic changes. There is nothing wrong with that team that spirit and hustle can't fix. I'm ambitious and I like to be on a winner."[2]

The Cardinals' change in direction was immediate. They won their first six games under Southworth — all on the road — a four-game sweep of the Philadelphia Phillies and two wins against the Dodgers at Ebbets Field. Five of the six games were complete game victories by the pitching staff with Mort Cooper winning his first two games of the year during that stretch.

The rest of the baseball world took notice. "Billy Southworth, the St. Louis Cardinals' peppery new manager, is in danger of being tabbed the new 'Miracle Man' of baseball," Arthur E. Patterson wrote in the *New York Herald Tribune*. "The Redbirds haven't lost since he took over Ray Blades' job. Almost like magic Southworth has remolded the Cardinal pitching staff into the formidable corps it promised to be when the experts were experting in the merry month of March."[3]

The Redbirds' winning streak ended at six with a loss to Brooklyn and then they lost two out of three to Boston. Still, they had won seven out of 10 since Southworth took over. St. Louis writers took note of the .700 winning percentage and started speculating what it would take for the Cardinals to overtake Cincinnati and Brooklyn, the current powerhouses in the National League.

Southworth contended that the Cardinals would lose on the field from time to time but nobody would beat them in terms of their spirit and their will to win. He made himself easily accessible to the press and, therefore, to the fans, a stark contrast to Blades, who hardly even made appearances on the field when he was managing.

The Cardinals' rise in the standings was remarkable. When Southworth took over, the team was 15–29, a .341 percentage and was buried in seventh place in the National League standings. By mid-August, the Cardinals had won 32 out of 50 with Billy the Kid at the helm, a percentage of .640 — almost twice as good as when he took over. Many observers believed the difference was in his handling of the pitching staff.

Starting pitchers took a lot of pride in finishing what they started. They wanted the opportunity to work their way out of jams and they didn't look kindly on managers who they felt lacked confidence in their ability to finish the job. In 1939, the Cardinals had six pitchers who won 10 or more games, accounting for 82 of their 92 wins. But there were only 51 complete games among them, an oddity for that era in baseball, and one of their starters, Bob Bowman, had more than twice as many saves out of the bullpen (9) than he had complete games (4).

"There is no use taking pot shots at Ray Blades, the perplexed little chap who handled the club in the spring," opined *The Sporting News*. "Blades, jockeying his pitchers as he did last year, scarcely had a man who could go the distance, and the entire staff was demoralized."[4]

By season's end, the Cardinals had worked their way up to third place, 69–40 under Southworth, but not nearly good enough to catch a Cincinnati team that won 100 games. The die-hards believed Southworth just didn't have enough time to bring home a winner. The Cardinals offensive punch was supplied by Johnny Mize, a strapping, lefthanded first baseman who hit .314 with 43 home runs and 137 runs batted in. Another big contributor was Enos Slaughter, who five years earlier Southbridge took aside at Asheville and taught him how to run if he was ever going to make the big leagues. Slaughter hit .306 with 17 homers and 73 RBIs.

Terry Moore was a graceful, dependable outfielder, the team captain, who hit .304 and was the leader off the field as well. When players wanted to confide in another player, when they needed some advice and didn't want to bother the coaching staff, they came to Terry Moore. The Cardinals also had Pepper Martin, one of Southworth's stars at Rochester a decade earlier who became a sparkplug on the Cardinals' Gas House Gang in the 1930s. He proved in 1940 he still had one good year left in him as a player. He hit .316 in 86 games. At the end of the season, he was named manager of the Cardinals farm club in Sacramento.

Lon Warneke and Bill McGee were the aces of the pitching staff. Each won 16 games. Mort Cooper, who hadn't won a game when Southworth became manager in June, finished with 11 wins, an indication of the fine career he had ahead of him. Clyde Shoun was 13–11 and Max Lanier, another prospect with a bright future, chipped in with nine wins.

Marty Marion was the shortstop and Johnny Hopp played outfield and subbed for Mize at first base from time to time. Joe Orengo was the second baseman. One of the bright spots in the Cardinals organization was the vast farm system that Rickey had developed. In September, with the pennant race no longer in doubt, Rickey and Southworth looked to the future by bringing up three farmhands, lefthanded pitcher Ernie White and catcher Walker Cooper from Columbus, and Frank "Creepy" Crespi, a shortstop from Rochester. Cooper was the brother of Mort Cooper. In years to come, they would prove to be a powerful battery combination for the Cardinals with catcher Walker knowing how to settle his brother down when Mort got flustered on the mound.

As the 1941 season beckoned, it was evident Billy the Kid was a far different manager from when he first managed the Cardinals in 1929. Those were the days when a young, inexperienced Southworth felt the need to lay down the law, in the style of John McGraw, to the fellows who not that long ago were his drinking buddies. They were not impressed or intimidated by his hardline approach and either snickered at him behind his back, ignored him or begrudgingly went along with him.

Now Southworth was a man who respected his players and they respected him. He passed up no opportunity to compliment his players publicly and instill confidence in them. He was a stickler for fundamentals. His teams knew how to bunt, hit-and-run, be smart base runners, play good defense and never give up.

"We have a wonderful spirit within the club," he told an interviewer in April 1941. "The principal objective of every man in the organization is to win. It makes no difference who is playing that day; everyone on the bench is pulling for the men out on the field," he said.[5]

Southworth said there was no grousing in the dugout if a pitcher was having a bad day and no mumbling by a pitcher if one of the fielders made an error behind him. No one makes a mistake intentionally, he said. "We talk about our mistakes objectively, not in the spirit of criticism which might arouse resentment but with the idea of reducing future mistakes."[6]

The Cardinals players certainly knew of Billy's credentials. Many of them had played for him in Rochester. But they must have heard about his dictatorial, McGraw-like antics in his first tour of duty as St. Louis manager. If they were wondering what to expect with the new Southworth, they didn't have to wait long. Billy joined them when the club was on an eastern swing. They had played the Giants in New York and the next stop was Boston after an off day. Southworth met with his team and said, "I was thinking some of you boys might want to stay over in New York another night for the Louis-Godoy fight. It doesn't make any difference to me whether you sleep here or in Boston, so if you think it over and let me know how you feel about it, I'll have the secretary make train arrangements to suit your wishes." This, coming from the man who 11 years earlier wouldn't let his players drive their wives to Miami. (Joe Louis knocked out Arturo Godoy in the eighth round on June 20, 1940.[7])

When Billy wasn't talking about baseball, he was often talking about Billy Jr., his son, his pal, a handsome man who had embarked on a promising baseball career of his own. He was an exceptional athlete at East High School in Columbus who signed with the Asheville Tourists in 1936. He was joining the team at about the time his father was leaving it. He hit .253 in limited time at Asheville and was sent to Martinsville in the Class D Bi-State League where he hit .340. He played for Asheville again in 1937 and was with Kinston in 1938. In 1939, he had his best season in professional baseball. An outfielder for the Rome Colonels in the Class C Canadian-American League, he hit

.342 with 15 home runs and 85 runs batted in. He was named the league's most valuable player.

He moved up the next year to the Triple A Toronto Maple Leafs, where he started the season with five hits in his first 11 at-bats, giving both him and his father thoughts that the major leagues might be a part of his future. But he was unable to hit consistently well, was sent down to Class A Wilmington before returning to Toronto at the end of the season.

But young Southworth had more than just baseball on his mind. War was raging in Europe and he believed it was only a matter of time before America got involved. He told his father he thought it was his duty to enlist. On December 12, 1940, a little less than a year before the Japanese bombed Pearl Harbor, William Brooks Southworth enlisted in the Army Air Corps, becoming the first professional ballplayer to voluntarily enlist in the armed services in World War II.

On New Year's Day 1941, Billy Southworth, Sr., and his son left Columbus and drove 10 hours to Parks Air College in East St. Louis, Illinois, where Billy Jr. began his stint in the military. What a man and his son talk about on a 10-hour car ride can only be imagined. They surely talked about baseball and each of their careers. They might have relived moments of the past — their hunting and fishing together in the offseason, their many years of following Ohio State football. They may have even recalled the tragic day when young Billy was accidentally shot by a playmate. When they reached their destination at the air college in Illinois, the two men parted as men often do. "A firm handshake, and I was off," said Billy Jr.[8]

During the winter months, while the Southworths were preparing for Billy Jr.'s entrance into the military, Sam Breadon and the Cardinals were engineering some exits to put some cash in the coffers. It had actually started the previous summer when the Cardinals peddled their popular outfielder, Joe Medwick, to the Dodgers in a multi-player deal that included $125,000 for Breadon and company. On December 5, the Cardinals sent pitcher Bob Bowman and infielder Joe Orengo to the New York Giants and got $170,000 out of that deal. Not long into the 1941 season, the Cards unloaded another starting pitcher, Bill McGee, who also went to the Giants. The Cardinals reaped $20,000 out of that deal.

The baseball season opened with the depleted Cardinals winning three straight at Cincinnati behind the solid pitching of Warneke, Cooper and Lanier. Within six weeks, it appeared already to be a two-team race between Southworth's upstart Cardinals and Leo Durocher's Brooklyn Dodgers. The Redbirds put together a 10-game winning streak from April 26 through May

5 and by the end of May had a 31–11 record. But Brooklyn kept pace almost game for game and by month's end the Dodgers were 30–12, a game behind the Cardinals.

In June and July, injuries began to cripple St. Louis. Mize, their biggest offensive threat, broke a finger and then was out for several games with shoulder problems, Infielder Jimmy Brown broke his right hand sliding into a base and was sidelined for weeks. Walker Cooper broke both his collar bone and his shoulder blade. His brother Mort developed elbow trouble and didn't pitch between June 17 and August 3.

The injuries continued to mount. On August 10, Slaughter and Moore both went after a fly ball to right-center field and collided. Moore was shaken up but Slaughter, the Cardinals' leading hitter, broke his collarbone and was out for the rest of the season. Two weeks later, Moore was beaned in a game at Boston and was hospitalized.

Through all of the trauma on the field, the Cardinals continued to win, though their pace was slowed. Southworth had to make good use of his bench players, putting them in starting roles and Branch Rickey's farm system also came to the rescue. Estel Crabtree, Southworth's hero in Rochester, had one more fling in the big leagues and hit .341, playing about half the season. Hopp, playing several positions — wherever Billy needed him on a given day — hit .303. In the September stretch drive, Rickey brought up two kids from Rochester, Stan Musial and George "Whitey" Kurowski, who filled in admirably.

One of the things that kept the Cardinals in the race, despite all the injuries, was the solid performance by the pitchers. Ernie White, the lefthander, won 17 games including three in three days against the Giants and got a fourth win two days later. Rickey reached into the farm system and pulled up Howard Pollet, another lefthander, who was 20–3 with a 1.16 earned run average for Houston when he got the call to go to St. Louis. He was 5–2 for the Cardinals. Howard Krist, an unknown when he came up to the Cardinals from Houston, was 10–0. It was an amazing showing for a patchwork pitching staff that just a year ago was so problematic that it led to Ray Blades' dismissal.

At the end of June, Brooklyn and St. Louis were tied for first with 47–23 records. At the end of July, the Cardinals led the Dodgers by two games. Their records were 62–34 and 60–36, respectively.

As the pennant race heated up, *The Sporting News* did a piece on how it all was affecting Southworth's family. "Mrs. Bill has been through six years of managing with the Kid and she confesses that she gets a big kick out of trying to buoy up her husband's spirits after the Cardinals have lost a tough one," the article noted.

Mabel Southworth said they usually go out to dinner after a Cardinal win "and the food tastes better to both of us." Then they go home and usually do some reading before retiring for the night, she said. "But if the Cards lose, that's all off. Nothing appears to be very interesting," said Mrs. Southworth.

She said when Billy is on the road, her constant companion is their six-year-old daughter, Carole, who she described as a "Daddy's girl" who has a pony, a dog and a goat "and she has the time of her life," Mabel Southworth said.

There was a 19-year age difference between Billy and his wife but she said their shared interests helps fill the age gap. She said she loves to go hunting and fishing with her husband and they try to never miss attending an Ohio State University football game in the fall.

The interviewer told Mrs. Southworth she didn't seem to have any problems. "Not as long as the Cardinals keep winning," she said with a grin.[9]

As September rolled around, the teams were in a virtual tie for first place, St. Louis at 81–45, Brooklyn at 82–46. The Dodgers went on a tear in September, winning 18 and losing only 8, finishing the season with 100 wins. The Cardinals played well, winning 16 out of 27, but on September 25, Brooklyn clinched the National League championship. The Cardinals gallant run fell short by 2½ games. The final standings:

	W-L	GB
Brooklyn	100–54	...
St. Louis	97–56	2.5
Cincinnati	88–66	12
Pittsburgh	81–73	19
New York	74–79	25.5
Chicago	70–84	30
Boston	62–92	38
Philadelphia	43–111	57

For Southworth, perhaps his redemption as a big league manager was complete when, eight years after he had been tossed overboard and was selling cotton seed oil in Columbus, *The Sporting News* named him the National League's Manager of the Year.

Billy went home to Ohio to work on the home he was building for his family on an acreage in Sunbury, about 20 miles southwest of Columbus. It would be a year before the house was built, a perfect spot for the Southworths, close to the big city and yet a get-away, a place for Mabel to establish her special brand of homelife for Billy, for six-year-old Carole and there would be a room for Billy Jr. for when he came home, filled with his books, his sports awards, his memorabilia. And not far from the family home, there would be places to hunt, fish and horseback ride.

Billy began hauling 104 loads of stone from a nearby quarry on December 7, 1941, a quiet, not-quite-winter Sunday afternoon when the people of Sunbury and across the nation were shaken by the news that the war had reached American territory. On this day, "a day that will live in infamy," as President Franklin D. Roosevelt called it, the Japanese bombed the U.S. naval base at Pearl Harbor, killing and injuring thousands of Americans. Within 24 hours, the United States declared war on Japan.

Billy's mind and his heart had to be racing. Where was Billy Jr.? Would he be cast into battle? Would he be safe?

And what would this mean to America, to the God-fearing, peace loving people of Sunbury and their brothers and sisters all across the country?

And what would this mean for baseball which was, next to his family, the heart and soul of Billy's countenance?

Baseball's commissioner, Judge Kenesaw Mountain Landis, who had been the czar of the game for more than 20 years and who had overseen the rebirth of the game after the Black Sox scandal of 1919, would now have to see the sport through another troubling time. Landis, a lifelong, die-hard Republican who detested President Roosevelt and had said so publicly, now wrote to the commander in chief, the nation's most prominent Democrat, pledging baseball's support to the war effort, whatever sacrifice that might mean, including cancellation of the upcoming baseball season.

Roosevelt responded with what has come to be known as the "green light" letter. On January 15, 1942, he wrote to Landis, saying the ultimate decision concerning the upcoming baseball season was up to the owners. So he would offer a personal, rather than an "official" point of view.

"I honestly feel it would be best for the country to keep baseball going. There will be fewer people unemployed and everybody will work longer hours and harder than ever before. And that means they ought to have a chance for recreation and for taking their minds off their work even more than before ... if three hundred teams use five thousand or six thousand players, these players are a definite recreational asset to at least 20 million of their fellow citizens — and that in my judgment is thoroughly worthwhile."[10]

◆ 11 ◆

A Special Year

When the Cardinals arrived in Florida for spring training in 1942, Johnny Mize was not among them. For six years, he had been the Redbirds' most potent power hitter, driving in more than 100 runs each year and leading the National League in home runs in 1939 and 1940 with 28 and 43, respectively. In 1941, his home run production dropped to 16 and he was beset with injuries.

During one of those periods where he missed several games because of injuries, he stayed in his street clothes and watched the action from the grandstand rather than suiting up and sitting on the bench with his teammates. That did not go unnoticed by Southworth who had instilled an "all for one and one for all" spirit on the ball club — and that meant those who were not playing were expected to be in the dugout rooting for those who were. On December 11, 1941, Mize was traded to the New York Giants for Bill Lohrman, Johnny McCarthy, Ken O'Dea and $50,000.

While Mize's attitude annoyed Southworth, his drop in production led Rickey to believe that he might have peaked as a player, one of the few times Rickey misjudged a player's abilities. In addition to that, Mize was slow afoot whereas the Cardinals were putting an emphasis on speed.[1]

The Cardinals were the youngest team in the National League. They had not yet been hit hard by the war and their youthfulness was also served by so many of them coming up through Rickey's farm system rather than coming over in trades. When the season began, all eight position players (besides pitchers) were products of Rickey's farm system; two starters, Stan Musial and Whitey Kurowski were rookies; two of their pitchers, Johnny Beazley and Murray Dickson, were rookies; only two players on the ball club had five years experience or more; and four members of the pitching staff had been in the big leagues two years or less.

The reality was it was a team full of youth but lacking experience. Southworth's spring training camp had two purposes: work the players into such shape that they would not wilt in the dog days of summer; and drill them on fundamentals in every aspect of the game. Billy knew how many games could be decided by a player making the right move at the right time or, conversely, losing a game because of the inability to execute a fundamental. His practices were well organized and rigorous, with attention given to the smallest detail and to players giving their best effort. Billy wasn't the drill sergeant that he had tried to be in 1929; he was more on the order of a scoutmaster leading his troops with passion, loyalty and a desire to teach them the right way to do things.

"There wasn't any uncertainty about what to do in Southworth's 1941 camp," wrote St. Louis sportswriter J. Roy Stockton. Cardinals players moved from one drill to another on a split-second schedule devised by Southworth to make sure every man got the practice he needed, the conditioning he needed and the guidance he needed. Nothing was left to chance.

Southworth had made a chart, dividing the players into two groups. There were three copies of the chart, one posted in the clubhouse, one at the hotel, and Billy had one with him at all times. "He probably slept with it," said Stockton.[2] The idea was for each player in both squads to know what he was to be doing every minute of the camp. No excuses. "Batting practice pitchers stepped on the mound by the clock. As one stepped off after his stint, another took his place and began pitching to the next hitter without any time-wasting warm-up. That had been done on the sidelines with a catcher assigned to the task by Billy's chart."[3] While that was going on, as one infield group finished its fielding practice, the next moved in. Coaches hitting ground balls hardly had to hesitate as one group left the field and the next group ran on.

Billy had a theory that batters never got tired of hitting; in fact, they got stale if they were inactive too long. But pitchers could get tired of pitching and in fact could hurt themselves if they threw too much. Southworth and Rickey thought there had to be a way of reconciling the desire of batters to keep on hitting without destroying the pitching arms of the hurlers.

The solution came in the form of an automatic pitching machine developed by a Cardinal fan. The amazing machine was engineered to project pitches at about the same speed as a major league hurler would throw them, and from the same distance, and within the strike zone. The machine was so accurate it was given the nickname "Ole Pete," which was the nickname of Grover Cleveland Alexander, the former great Cardinal pitcher.[4]

Another technique Southworth emphasized and the players practiced was sliding. Billy believed there was an art to sliding just as there was to base running, as he had taught Enos Slaughter years ago, and a good slide could be the difference between winning and losing a ball game. Not only that, players could get injured by sliding improperly. So Southworth had sliding pits installed at the camp, pits of sand with a base in them for players to learn the skill and practice it.

"Many a game may be won or lost on a slide. I will drive and drive and talk to all our players. I know some never will be sliders but I must make them be able to take care of themselves. It is so important," said Billy.

He said a good slide could put fear in the hearts of a shortstop or second baseman taking a throw. A bad slide could cause serious injury. He thought Jimmy Brown injured himself in the 1941 pennant race because of a bad slide and Southworth said he broke his ankle back in 1914 because he didn't know how to slide.

Another part of Southworth's spring training regimen was pepper games, in which fielders would stand side by side, and as a batted ball was hit to one of them, he would quickly field it and flip quickly to another, who would just as quickly flip to another until the ball was finally dropped. Most of the players found it to be fun, a break from the regular exercises and training, but Southworth believed it was sound conditioning for quickness and testing the reflexes.

"With hard work, we can let every player in on the secrets of baseball. The good ones will keep these secrets in their hearts and help us. The poor players will never learn them," he said.[5]

Billy had a method of showing respect for his older players, who might not have the value they once had, and his younger players, who might have questions about their own value. Southworth put the veterans to the task of working with the new players. Gus Mancuso, the veteran catcher, worked with the pitchers and with the Cardinals up-and-coming catcher, Walker Cooper. Lon Warneke, whose background on the hill included two one-hitters, was assigned to provide guidance to young pitchers like Murray Dickson and Howie Pollet. Southworth saw to it that everyone in camp knew they had a purpose.

The Cardinals finished the spring training exhibition season with a 20–9 record, with the only major disappointment being the .199 batting average of rookie outfielder Stan Musial. When he had come up with the Cardinals in September 1941, he opened some eyes hitting .426 in 12 games, with 20 hits in 47 at-bats, with four doubles, a home run and seven runs batted in.

The Cardinals had high hopes for their young rookie and the start of the season seemed to rejuvenate him as Musial rapped out six hits in 14 at-bats in a three-game Series against the Cubs to open the season. The Cardinals took two of three from the Cubs but entered a stretch where they couldn't get the big hit when they needed it, losing four games in a little more than a week by one run. At the end of April, they found themselves with a 7–7 record, in fourth place, 5½ games behind Leo Durocher's Dodgers.

The personalities of Durocher and Southworth couldn't have been more different. Both had an obsession for winning. Whereas Southworth touted almost constant enthusiasm and encouragement, Durocher, 12 years younger than Southworth, was brazen, dictatorial and mouthy. Whereas Southworth played under managers like McGraw and Hornsby, Durocher came up with the Yankees with Miller Huggins at the helm and Ruth and Gehrig as teammates. In the mid 1930s, when Billy had dropped out of the major leagues because of his personal problems, Durocher hit it big with the Cardinals' famed Gas House Gang, a nickname he reportedly gave them because of their scrappiness on the field and their love of life off the field. He became the playing manager of the Dodgers in 1939, a year before Southworth took over the Cardinals.

As the 1942 season got under way, true to form, Durocher was ejected from Brooklyn's opening day game against the Giants at the Polo Grounds. His talented Dodgers ball club, loaded with veterans compared to Southworth's crop of kids, had a great month and won 10 out of their last 11 headed into May. The Dodgers were 14–3, clearly establishing themselves as the team to beat.

The inability of the Cardinals to get the big hit showed up statistically. After getting six hits in his first 14 at-bats, Musial got six hits the rest of the month for an average of .158 after the opening Series. Shortstop Marty Marion, perhaps the best fielding shortstop in the major leagues, was not so adept at the plate. He was hitting .128. Captain Terry Moore was hitting .260—and was one of the top hitters with that mark. Sportswriters and St. Louis fans began wondering whether the loss of Johnny Mize was going to cripple the Cardinals.[6]

The Cardinals had particular difficulty against lefthanders. On May 2, Lou Tost of Boston handcuffed them, 1–0, in a game called at the end of six innings because of rain. Three days later, Larry French of the Dodgers hooked up with Cardinals lefty Howie Pollet in a game won by feisty Brooklyn, 3–1, in 11 innings in which the go-ahead run was on base as a result of an error. On May 9, at Cincinnati, the Cards lost a 5–2 decision to Johnny Vander Meer, giving them an 0–5 record for the season against southpaws.

11. A Special Year

Southworth watches spring training action with young rookie Stan Musial in 1942 (courtesy Southworth family).

The next day, the Redbirds dropped a doubleheader to Cincinnati and didn't score a run all day. The following day, they scored two but lost to the Reds, 3–2, putting them under .500 at 12–13. The rest of the month provided some hope for Southworth and legions of Cardinals fans as they put together a streak in which they won 11 of 15 games, including a stretch where they won five in a row and six out of seven. Included in that was a 7–4 win over Boston in which the Cards finally beat a lefthander, Lou Tost, who had shut them out on May 2.

Heading into June, the National League standings looked like this:

	W-L	GB
Brooklyn	32–13	...
St. Louis	25–18	6
Boston	25–22	8
New York	23–23	9.5
Cincinnati	22–22	9.5
Chicago	21–24	11
Pittsburgh	19–27	13.5
Philadelphia	14–32	18.5

One of the surprise teams in the first two months of the season was the Boston Braves, in third place, trailing second-place St. Louis by just two games. Boston was managed by Casey Stengel, someone with whom Southworth had a long history. Billy got called up to the major leagues with the Pittsburgh Pirates in 1918 when Stengel, a Pirate outfielder, joined the Navy. Five years later, when Southworth was with Boston and Stengel with the New York Giants, they were traded for one another. Now they were managing against one another.

The Cardinals had gotten over their early season sluggishness and now were moving almost stride for stride with Brooklyn. Musial and Slaughter were the leading hitters, spraying the ball all over the place. Whitey Kurowski was contributing clutch hits. Catcher Walker Cooper, shortstop Marty Marion and center fielder Terry Moore anchored a defense that assured the Cardinals of being strong up the middle. With Musial, Moore and Slaughter, the Redbirds had the fastest outfield in the league.

Moore, the team captain, could be counted on to hit .280 or better and to catch anything within his reach in center field. "If it's hit in the air, he'll get it," said Durocher. Moore was also great at keeping his teammates on their toes, praising them for their good plays, pinching them on the back of their necks and admonishing them when they lost their concentration. The pitching staff was solid with Mort Cooper, Howie Pollet, Ernie White, Lon Warneke, Max Lanier and rookie Johnny Beazley leading the way.[7]

But the thing that made the Cardinals stand out — what sportswriters, fans and even players on other teams noticed — was their hustle. They ran onto the field; they ran off the field. They ran out routine ground balls. They made wide turns on the bases, always ready to take the extra base. Their energy seemed boundless. It was if they got out of bed running in the morning and never stopped the rest of the day.

The Cardinals won nine out of their first 11 games in June and had a six-game winning streak as they headed to Ebbets Field for a five-game Series with the league-leading Dodgers. As hot as the Cardinals were, they still found themselves in second place, 4½ games behind Brooklyn. As the Redbirds took batting practice on June 18, the first day of the Series, Southworth talked to writers about the pennant race.

There had been rumors that St. Louis might sell Mort Cooper to the Giants so the Cardinals could get some cash and start thinking about next year. "Now wasn't that silly?" said Southworth. "I mean for a second-place club to quit on June 15? Why, we've got almost two-thirds of the race ahead of us. Anything can happen."

He recalled when the Pittsburgh Pirates had a seven-game lead in 1921 and the Giants overtook them in the last two weeks of the season. Then he rattled off the names of his players who were doing well. "Slaughter and Moore and Musial. Kurowski is playing a good game for us at third base. Jimmy Brown is a real ballplayer no matter where he is stationed. Look at Marion's runs-batted-in total and you'll be surprised. And if Johnny Hopp isn't hitting often, he is getting in his licks when they count the most."

It was a typical Southworth oration. Players reading the newspapers the next day would see the confidence their manager had in them. As for the five-game Series coming up with Brooklyn, Billy the Kid was not worried. "I cannot see this Series with the Dodgers as crucial," he said.[8]

The opening game had a 7 P.M. start, a twilight game, or as Dodger executive Larry MacPhail called it, a "twight game." It would begin in daylight and end under the lights at Ebbets Field. Starting pitchers were two lefties, Larry French for the Dodgers and Max Lanier for the Cardinals. Each had a win over their opposing team earlier in the year.

The Cardinals took the early lead when Walker Cooper doubled in the second inning and came home on Coaker Triplett's triple. Triplett started in left field in place of Musial to get another righthanded bat in Southworth's lineup. Each team pushed across a run in the third inning.

In the sixth inning, the Dodgers got aggressive — a little too aggressive as far as the Cardinals were concerned — although they were just playing Durocher's kind of ball. Joe Medwick, the former Cardinal, walked, and when a pitch was bobbled by Cooper behind the plate, Medwick took off for second but was thrown out easily by Cooper who had recovered the ball quickly. Even though shortstop Marion was poised to make the tag for the easy out as Medwick approached, he slid into Marion with his spikes high. Marion knocked his feet down and then the two of them grappled and punches were thrown. Second baseman Crespi ran over and threw Medwick to the ground and Hopp ran over from first base to join in the fray. Dolph Camilli, who was at-bat at the time, and Dixie Walker who was on deck, raced out to help their teammate and Whitey Kurowski was now in the pile-up, running over from his position at third base.

When the umpires restored order, about 20 minutes after the melee began, Medwick and Crespi were tossed out of the game, Kurowski had a shiner and Walker limped off with a sore ankle and a sore jaw. When play resumed, the Dodgers tied the game with a walk and a couple of hits. It remained tied until the bottom of the eighth when Brooklyn scored on a squeeze bunt and then French helped his own cause by hitting a double, driving in two runs. When the dust settled on the long night, Brooklyn had taken the opener, 5–2, to increase their lead to 5½ games over the Cardinals.

In the second game of the Series, Ernie White, making his first start in almost a month, went up against veteran Brooklyn hurler Whitlow Wyatt. The Dodgers got two runs early on a home run by Johnny Rizzo, an ex–Cardinal and spot starter for Brooklyn. In the sixth inning, Pete Reiser stole home for a third Brooklyn tally. By the ninth inning, the Dodgers held a 4–2 lead. St. Louis scored one off Wyatt in the ninth but could not push the tying run across. Brooklyn left the field with a swagger and a 6½ lead over the Cards.

In Game Three of the Series, Lon Warneke took the hill for St. Louis while the Dodgers countered with Curt Davis, who had already won nine games. Both teams scored twice in the third inning and again twice in the fifth inning. But Brooklyn scored four in the seventh and two more in the eighth while the Cardinal bats turned silent. The 10–4 Brooklyn victory now put them 7½ games ahead.

The Series ended with a Sunday doubleheader. Southworth urged his boys to go out and play with the same vigor with which they had started the Series, though their confidence level had to be shaken. Mort Cooper was given the task of righting the ship. He pitched brilliantly and the Cardinal hitters awakened. Musial had a homer and double, Crespi had a double that was, remarkably, his first extra-base hit of the year, the club as a whole had 14 hits and St. Louis won, 11–0.[9]

In the second game, the Dodgers earned a split for the day, winning 5–2. As the Cardinals left the field, having lost four out of five to the first-place Dodgers, the Ebbetts Field organist gleefully played "St. Louis Blues." The Cardinals had come into Brooklyn 4½ games out. In the unlikely chance of a sweep, the Redbirds could have left town in first place. Instead, they were now 7½ back and even the most ardent fan would have to admit Durocher's Dodgers had made a statement.

"Durocher's Dandies beat the Cardinals four out of five which was a rude shock to little Billy Southworth and his hired hands," gloated John Kiernan in the *New York Times*. "So instead of hauling the Dodgers back, the Cardinals themselves were knocked down and trodden upon."[10]

The Cardinals went on to Boston where Stengel's troops hung two more losses on them before Mort Cooper tossed a shutout for his 10th win against 3 losses. The next stop was Philadelphia where they lost a 2–1 heartbreaker in 15 innings. The losing pitcher was young Krist, who had won 13 straight going back to his 10–0 year in 1941. They won the second game behind Warneke 3–1 and closed out the month with a 4–2 win over Pittsburgh as Cooper won his 11th. Going into July, the standings were:

Southworth with one of his coaches, Mike Gonzalez, during the glory years with St. Louis when the Cardinals won three consecutive National League pennants (courtesy Southworth family).

	W–L	GB
Brooklyn	48–20	...
St. Louis	38–27	8.5
Cincinnati	39–32	10.5
New York	37–35	13
Chicago	36–38	15
Pittsburgh	32–36	16
Boston	33–43	19
Philadelphia	19–51	30

To put the National League standings in perspective, the Cardinals were 8½ games out of first place and just 7½ games ahead of sixth-place Pittsburgh. After a strong start, Stengel's Braves won just eight games in June and were mired in seventh place. In short, Brooklyn was on the verge of running away with the National League pennant. As Kiernan pointed out in the *New York Times*, "The strange situation today is the Dodgers have a larger lead in the National League than the New York Yankees have in the American League."[11]

The Redbirds showed some signs of life in July, combining good hitting and pitching with what was now their trademark — opportunistic base running. Between July 4 and July 25, they won 18 out of 22 games, including taking three out of four from the Dodgers at Sportsman's Park. On the field, they acted like a team that still felt like it was in a pennant race. Off the field, management made some moves that were more common in teams that had thrown in the towel. On July 8, the Cardinals sold Lon Warneke to the Chicago Cubs for the waiver price of $75,000.

Skeptics in the press wondered why the Redbirds would dispose of a veteran pitcher unless they had all but conceded the pennant to the Dodgers and Sam Breadon took advantage of a chance to fatten his wallet. Warneke was 6–4 in 12 starts for the Cardinals. Breadon said St. Louis had a lot of young pitchers who needed work to gain experience and Warneke's departure would give them more opportunities.

The young pitchers came through in July with the help of the bats of Musial, Slaughter, Marion and Kurowski. Rookie Johnny Beazley won five of his six starts during the month and Howard Krist also picked up five victories while losing only one, giving him a record of 15–1 over the past two seasons.

When the Dodgers came into St. Louis on July 18 for back-to-back doubleheaders, they still had a healthy 8-game lead in the standings despite the Cardinals' hot streak. The four-game Series might not have been do-or-die for St. Louis, but time was starting to be a factor if they were going to make a move.

The Redbirds won the first game of the series, 7–4, in a contest in which a line drive off the bat of Musial broke the finger of Dodger starter Hugh Casey and tore off the nail on his little finger. Ed Head replaced him and gave up a run in typical Cardinal fashion: Kurowski doubled, went to third on a passed ball and scored on a suicide squeeze bunt by Marion. In the second game of the doubleheader, Dolph Camilli hit and triple and a home run to help Brooklyn to a 4–3 victory. At the end of the day, there was no change in the standings, an obvious advantage to the Dodgers.

The next day, the biggest crowd of the year poured into Sportsman's Park as the two teams met in their second consecutive doubleheader. In the opener, Mort Cooper didn't have his best stuff but the Cardinal bats were humming, highlighted by Hopp's bases-clearing triple and a solo homer by Kurowski. The final score was 7–5. In the nightcap, Beazley, the Cardinals sensational rookie, took the mound against the Dodgers veteran righthander Kirby Higbe. Both starters got banged around and weren't around at the finish. The game went into extra innings with the score tied, 6–6. In the 11th inning, Slaughter hit a line drive to deep center field. Pete Reiser, Brooklyn's fearless center fielder, gave chase and almost caught the ball. It glanced off his glove as Reiser crashed into the wall and collapsed. Slaughter circled the bases for an inside-the-park, game-winning home run. St. Louis had taken three out of four from the Dodgers, gaining two games in the standings. And Brooklyn had suffered two key injuries, to Casey and Reiser.

The Cardinals were playing good baseball but they seemed to be spinning their wheels. After losing three out of four to the Cardinals in St. Louis, the Dodgers won six out of their next seven and took two out of three from St. Louis later in the month at Ebbets Field. The standings heading into August:

	W-L	GB
Brooklyn	69–29	...
St. Louis	60–36	8
Cincinnati	52–44	16
New York	52–47	17.5
Chicago	47–54	23.5
Pittsburgh	43–52	24.5
Boston	41–61	30
Philadelphia	27–68	40

The Cardinals had won 22 and lost only 9 in July but had gained only a half-game in the standings. But they had managed to separate themselves from the rest of the league. It was now clearly a two-team race—if there was to be a race at all. To Southworth, the race was still on. "We're going to keep hitting and hustling until our string runs out," he said. "Nobody's going to coast to any pennant as long as we're in the league."[12]

To many observers, Billy's words may have seemed hollow, considering the mountain the Cardinals would have to climb. His optimism may have been considered more as "just Billy being Billy" because the numbers were clearly against him. And seven days into August, the numbers got worse. Brooklyn was 74–30. The Cardinals were 63–40, 10½ games off the pace—and neither team was giving any indication of changing directions.

But something happened at about that time that occurs every once in a while with sports teams. It's as if all the intangibles, the things that don't show up in box scores, start to kick in. And suddenly—just as it is when a player breaks out of a slump and all of those line drives he's been hitting all year start to drop in, or when a pitcher who has been having trouble with his control finally finds it—sometimes that kind of thing embraces an entire team. It is the whole equaling the sum of its parts and creates a feeling of invincibility. The result is momentum.

On August 8, the Cardinals and Pirates battled into the darkness in a 5–5 game that was stopped after 16 innings. The Redbirds won two out of the next three at Pittsburgh. Then it was on to Chicago where they won three out of four.

They came home to Sportsman's Park and swept a four-game Series with Cincinnati. The Cubs came into town for one game and the Cards won that one. Then they beat the Pirates twice to extend their winning streak to eight games.

In the space of about two weeks, since the 5–5 tie at Pittsburgh, the Cardinals won 13 out of 15, which included a stretch of winning 11 out of 12 and the eight-game winning streak. St. Louis won 25 games and lost only 8 in August. The Cardinals were 6–0 in one-run games, including two thrillers with the Dodgers in which they won 2–1 in 14 innings and 2–1 in ten innings on consecutive days.

Musial, Slaughter and Marion, three players who would eventually be in the Hall of Fame, were all hitting their stride. Musial was expected to put up big numbers and he was producing. The rookie pitcher Beazley continued to impress. He was 6–0 in August to bring his season record to 17–5. Mort Cooper picked up five wins in August and was 17–7 for the year. Lefty Max Lanier won six in August to double his win total for the year.

The turnaround of the Cardinals was stunning. Frank Graham, a columnist for the *New York Sun*, tried to explain it to his audience. "Part of the determination with which the St. Louis players are pressing their pursuit comes from within themselves, of course," he wrote. "But part also is due to the influence of Southworth. A ball club usually, although not always, reflects the character of its manager. Here is one that reflects it perfectly."[13]

J. Roy Stockton in the *St. Louis Post Dispatch* had a similar view: "Despite all the bad breaks and the discouraging lead the Dodgers took early and have held tenaciously, the Cardinals have kept their morale high. That is where Southworth has shown his managerial ability. It would have been easy for the Cardinals to lose heart. Southworth stands as one of the greatest keepers of morale the game has known."[14]

More important than all the individual accomplishments and impressive team statistics in August was the fact that since that 5–5 tie game on August 5, they had trimmed 6½ games off the Dodgers' lead. The standings going into September:

	W-L	GB
Brooklyn	88–40	...
St. Louis	85–44	3.5
New York	70–58	17.5
Cincinnati	63–64	24
Pittsburgh	58–66	27.5
Chicago	60–72	29.5
Boston	51–79	37.5
Philadelphia	36–87	49

The Dodgers and Cardinals each started September with victories. On September 2, Brooklyn beat Cincinnati while the Giants were pasting the Cardinals, 8–2. The Dodgers' lead over St. Louis was now 4½ games. It stayed that way the next day when veteran old-timer Bobo Newsom, making his first start with Brooklyn, shut out Cincinnati, 2–0. But Howie Pollet of the Cardinals, young enough to be Newsom's son, also threw a shutout, blanking the Giants, 7–0.

The next day, the Dodgers were idle. Beazley won his 18th game, downing Cincinnati 5–3, trimming Brooklyn's lead to 4 games. On September 5, with the Cardinals beating the Reds again, this time 3–2, and the Giants downing Brooklyn, 7–6, the lead was down to 3 games.

The next day, Mort Cooper won his 19th game as St. Louis beat Cincinnati for the third straight time, 10–2. The Dodgers split a doubleheader with the Giants, winning, 6–2, then losing the nightcap, 4–2. At the end of the day, the Cardinals had pulled to within 2½ games of Brooklyn. Both teams split doubleheaders on September 7. The following day, the Cardinals were idle and Brooklyn beat Pittsburgh, 4–0, moving their lead on St. Louis back up to three games with less than three weeks left in the season.

Both teams enjoyed an off day on September 9. The next day, the Cardinals beat the Giants, 5–1, while the Cubs beat the Dodgers, 10–2. Brooklyn's lead was down to just two games on the eve of a two-game Series with the Cardinals in Brooklyn. The Series couldn't have been more crucial for either team. If they split, the Dodgers would escape unharmed and the clock would start running out for the Cardinals. If Brooklyn swept, they would have a four-game lead. If the Cardinals swept, there would be a tie for first place with exactly two weeks left to play.

"What P.T. Barnum would give, were he alive, to have the opportunity of staging this grand melodrama," sportswriter James Murphy wrote in the *Brooklyn Eagle*.[15]

Arriving at Ebbets Field, Southworth knew how high the stakes were but he was brimming with his usual optimism. "We've been making up for lost time because we have a club full of youngsters. Now that we're going full speed, we don't expect to stop until after we've played the Yankees in the World Series," he said.[16]

It was typical Southworth hyperbole, probably said not only with the intention of keeping his players' hopes high but also to rankle Durocher and the Dodgers a little. Here was a manager whose team was two games out of first, about to play the first-place team on their home turf—and he was already talking about the World Series.

In the first game of the Series, Mort Cooper, who normally wore uniform number 13, had a number 20 on his back when he took the mound for the Cardinals, a reminder that he was on a quest for his 20th victory. The Dodgers countered with their veteran, Whitlow Wyatt. The two hurlers had faced each other twice earlier in the season with Cooper coming out the winner both times in close games, 1–0 and 2–1. But Wyatt was a clutch performer who a year ago had stifled the Cardinals in a 1–0 victory when St. Louis was once again advancing on the Dodgers in the pennant race.

Both pitchers were sharp in this latest encounter. The game was scoreless after five innings. In the sixth inning, Mort Cooper singled, was sacrificed to second and scored on Slaughter's single to right. In the eighth inning, Cooper once again got things started, this time with an infield hit. Jimmy Brown then doubled down the left field line with Cooper stopping at third. Terry Moore brought them both home with a base hit. Meanwhile, Mort Cooper handcuffed the Dodgers on three hits to gain his 20th victory, his seventh straight win and his eighth shutout. More importantly, the Cardinals were now just one game out of first place.

In the final game of the Series, Durocher chose rookie lefthander Max Macon as his pitcher, perhaps hoping to still the bats of Musial and Slaughter. Southworth went a lefty of his own, Max Lanier. The Cardinals took a 2–0 lead in the second inning on a two-run homer by Kurowski. The Dodgers got one of the runs back in the bottom of the second after which both pitchers settled down. Lanier was aided by a great defensive play by Jimmy Brown at second base and circus catches in the outfield by Slaughter and Musial. The Dodgers put runners on first and third in the bottom of the ninth but could not score. Lanier had persevered, the Cardinals won, 2–1, and were now tied with Brooklyn for first place in the National League, both with records of 94–46.

The next day, September 13, St. Louis split a doubleheader with the Phillies, but the reeling Dodgers lost two to Cincinnati, putting the Cardinals in first place for the first time since April. On September 14, Brooklyn was idle while the Cardinals beat the Phillies, 6–3, to move 1½ games ahead. The margin increased to two games on September 15 when St. Louis won again and the Dodgers did not play. Both clubs won on September 16, but the Cardinals moved up yet another game the next day when they beat Boston, 6–4, while Pittsburgh was beating Brooklyn, 3–2. St. Louis had its biggest lead in the standings, three games up on the Dodgers.

After both teams had an off day, Brooklyn beat Philadelphia, 5–4, on September 19 while the Cardinals were idle, so the St. Louis lead was down to 2½ games. It stayed that way for five days as each team split a doubleheader and then won four games. On September 25, Brooklyn beat Boston, 6–5, while the Cardinals were off, trimming the lead to two games, and then to 1½ games the next day with another Brooklyn win while the Cardinals did not play.

The National League pennant race came down to the last day of the season. Brooklyn needed to beat Philadelphia and the Cardinals needed to drop a doubleheader to the Cubs for the Dodgers to win it. St. Louis needed just one win to cinch it, regardless of how the Dodgers fared. Brooklyn beat Philadelphia, 4–3, but the Cardinals took care of the Cubs, not once but twice to lock up the championship. They beat the Cubs, 9–2, in the opener for the clincher and Beazley won his 21st game in the nightcap, 4–1. The final National League standings:

	W-L	GB
St. Louis	106–48	...
Brooklyn	104–50	2
New York	85–67	20
Cincinnati	76–76	29
Pittsburgh	66–81	36.5
Chicago	68–86	38
Boston	59–89	44
Philadelphia	42–109	62.5

The Dodgers did not wilt after losing the two-game set to the Cardinals that was the pivotal Series in the pennant race. In fact, Brooklyn finished the season with eight straight victories — but the Cardinals won 10 of their last 11.

Since August 7, when St. Louis was 63–40, 10½ games out of first place, the Cardinals won 43 and lost only 8. From August 5 on, they played in 14 one-run games and won 13 of them. Three of the one-run victories were over the Dodgers. Mort Cooper, the veteran, won 22 games on the season and Johnny Beazley, the rookie, won 21. Musial, the rookie outfielder, finished with a .315 average with 10 home runs and 72 RBIs. Slaughter hit .318 and led the club with only 13 homers but drove in 98 runs. Moore, the captain, hit what everyone expected him to hit, .288, and Walker Cooper hit .281.

The World Series, against the Joe DiMaggio-led New York Yankees, turned out to be a microcosm of the regular season. The Cardinals lost the first game and looked all but dead through most of the game. Then that certain something happened, that jelling that occurs when everything seems to go right, like what happened to the Cardinals beginning in the first week of August in the regular season.

It was the National League's turn to have the Series opener and the home field advantage if the Series went the distance. Mort Cooper, Southworth's 22-game winner, took the hill for the Cardinals, matched up with Charles "Red" Ruffing, who was appearing in his eighth fall classic.

The teams traded zeroes for the first three innings. The only real excitement was Yankee manager Joe McCarthy badgering the umpires, first about Cooper's delivery and then to challenge what he believed was a wide strike zone of the home plate umpire. The Yankees got to Cooper in the fourth on an RBI single by Buddy Hassett. They added a run in the fifth when the Cardinals failed to execute an inning-ending double play, allowing a run to score. The Bronx Bombers added two more in the eighth, aided by a miscue when Slaughter dropped a fly ball in the outfield.

Meanwhile, some drama was building. Ruffing mowed down the Cardinals in the first seven innings without allowing a hit. He was six outs away from recording the first no-hitter in World Series history. He got the first two Cardinals out before Terry Moore, the captain, the team leader, laced a clean single to right to keep Ruffing from the baseball record book. Slaughter then flied out to end the inning.

In the top of the ninth, Lanier relieved Cooper and the Yankees scored two more, helped by two Lanier errors. Ruffing had a one-hitter and the Yankees had a 7–0 lead going into the bottom of the ninth. Who knows what words of encouragement might have come from Southworth at that point. His team was losing by seven runs, they had just one hit and had committed four errors — all in front of a capacity crowd in their home ballpark.

After Musial fouled out for the first out in the bottom of the ninth, Walker Cooper beat out an infield hit for the Redbirds' second hit. Hopp popped out for the second out. Sanders pinch-hit for Kurowski and walked. Marion followed with the Cardinals' third hit, a triple into the right field corner, scoring Cooper and Sanders. Ken O'Dea batted for Lanier and singled, driving in Marion. Then Brown singled to short center, causing pinch-runner Creepy Crespi to stop at second.

Spud Chandler relieved Ruffing but could not stop the sudden Yankee bleeding. Moore singled up the middle, his second hit in two innings, scoring Crespi with the Cardinals' fourth run. Slaughter hit a grounder to short that took a bad hop and hit Rizzuto in the face. It was ruled a hit. Suddenly, the Cardinals, now down by only three runs, had the tying runs on base and the winning run at the plate in the person of Musial. Stan the Man stroked a ground ball to first that Hassett handled and flipped to Chandler covering the bag for the third out of the inning. The Yankees won the game, 7–4, but the Cardinals felt a sense of rejuvenation by their ninth-inning rally.

Johnny Beazley, the Cardinals 21-game winner, took the mound in Game One. New York went with Ernest "Tiny" Bonham, who led the Yankees in wins during the regular season with 21. The Cardinals jumped on him with two runs in the first inning coming in on a Walker Cooper double. The score remained that way until the bottom of the seventh when Johnny Hopp singled and was brought home on a Kurowski triple into the left field corner.

Beazley had been sailing along and the 3–0 lead seemed safe. But in the eighth inning, Roy Cullenbine and DiMaggio both singled and Charlie Keller launched a three-run homer to tie the game. With two out in the bottom of the eighth, Slaughter doubled and went to third when shortstop Phil Rizzuto bobbled the throw in from the outfield. Musial then got his first hit of the Series, a single to center, scoring Slaughter with the go-ahead run. The Yankees threatened in the ninth but did not score. The Cardinals won, 4–3, evening the Series at a game a piece as the two teams headed for New York for the next three games.

A crowd of over 69,000 gathered at Yankee Stadium, a place most of the Cardinals had never seen, as Spud Chandler took the mound for New York against St. Louis lefty Ernie White. Southworth had employed a strategy all year of playing for one run. He didn't have the luxury of waiting for a three-run homer to bail him out, as the Yankees had done by way of Keller's blast in Game One. For Southworth, the strategy was to get a man on and move him around any way possible. There was no better example than what happened in the third inning. Kurowski walked. Marion hit a dribbler between the pitcher's mound and third and beat Chandler's throw to first. White then laid down a sacrifice bunt, moving the runners to second and third. Brown then stroked a ground ball that second baseman Joe Gordon snared and threw to first for the out, but Kurowski scored on the play. No further damage was done, but Billy the Kid's troops had scored without hitting the ball out of the infield—a typical Cardinal rally.

Another Southworth trademark was good defense and White benefited from it in the eighth inning when Slaughter and Moore each made terrific catches in the outfield. Moore's was the most spectacular. Joe DiMaggio hit a line drive into the gap in left center field. Musial and Moore both gave chase. At the last moment. Musial dove to the ground to give Moore a clear shot at it. Moore tumbled over Musial but made a backhanded catch to rob DiMaggio of at least a double. Again, it was typical Cardinals baseball.

The Cardinals added a run in the ninth and White set the Yankees down without much trouble for a 2–0 victory — the first time the Bronx Bombers had been shut out in a World Series game since 1926 — and they had played in eight World Series since then. Sportswriters marveled at Southworth's style of play. Tommy Holmes of the *Brooklyn Eagle* asked, "Since when has it become good strategy to play for one run in the first inning?" He exaggerated just a little — the manufactured run occurred in the third inning — but it could have just as easily happened in the first, given Southworth's approach.[17]

Billy sent Cooper, his 22-game winner, to the mound for Game Four. The Yankees went with Hank Borowy, their 15-game winner. The Yankees scored a run in the first and the score remained 1–0 until the fifth inning. That is when yet another tool in the Southworth arsenal came into play, team speed. Musial led off the inning with a bunt single. Cooper then singled to center and Musial scampered to third, just beating DiMaggio's throw. Cooper took second on the throw. Hopp walked, loading the bases. Kurowski then singled home two runs. Borowy then walked Marion to once again load the bases. Mort Cooper then helped his own cause by singling to right, scoring two more runs and causing the exit of Borowy. The Redbirds scored two more times before the inning was over to take a commanding 6–1 lead. But Cooper could not hold it. Buoyed by a three-run homer by Keller in the sixth inning, the Yankees came storming back. Gumbert replaced Cooper but could not still the Yankees bats. Two more runs scored before Howie Pollet, the third Cardinals pitcher of the inning, finally got the third out. But the Yankees had tied it, 6–6. St. Louis didn't wait long to get back on the board. They scored two in the seventh and one in the eighth to notch a 9–6 victory and take a 3–1 lead in the series.

This was unfamiliar territory for the Yankees. Since losing to the Cardinals in the 1926 World Series, they had won World Series titles in each of the next eight they competed in — 1927, 1928, 1932, 1936–1939 and 1941 — and had only lost a total of four games in that entire stretch. Now they were in danger of losing four straight to a bunch of upstarts whose leading power hitter had 13 home runs for the season.

Prior to the game, while Yankee players sat somberly at their lockers, the Cardinal clubhouse was full of life. Creepy Crespi was talking nonstop to whoever would listen. White was singing in the shower. Moore was walking around talking quietly and confidently to his teammates. And Southworth was talking to the press about his running Redbirds. "I've always wanted a running ball club. I have one now," he said.[18]

The Yankees took a quick 1–0 lead in Game Five when Rizzuto launched a Johnny Beazley pitch into the left field stands. The score remained 1–0 into the fourth inning when Slaughter hit a solo home run off Yankee starter Red Ruffing. It was the Cardinals' first home run of the Series. The Yankees took the lead right back in the bottom of the fourth on an RBI single by DiMaggio. The Cardinals tied the game in the sixth on a Walker Cooper sacrifice fly. The score remained tied through the next four innings, though Beazley was aided by two catches by Slaughter and one by Musial, both running hard to snare them.

In the top of the ninth, Walker Cooper singled, was sacrificed to second by Hopp and then came home on a long home run by Kurowski. The Yankees began the bottom of the ninth with two straight hits, putting the tying runs aboard. With Jerry Priddy batting and being expected to bunt, Beazley threw a fastball high and inside. Marion, the shortstop crept over to second base as Joe Gordon, the base runner, leaned toward third. Walker Cooper fired the ball to Marion who put the tag on Gordon for a pick-off. Beazley got the next two batters and the Cardinals had accomplished the unthinkable — winning the World Series by beating the Yankees in four straight games, and winning the finale with a burst of power: two home runs.

It was a most improbable season — the uncertainty of it all at the beginning because of the war; the 43–8 finish to overtake Durocher's Dodgers; and capping it off with the disposal of the Yankees in the World Series.

Billy was once again named the National League Manager of the Year but he said what meant more to him was a comment Commissioner Landis made to him during the World Series locker room celebration. Landis said, "Mr. Southworth, I want to congratulate you on having a team of champions — and also a team of gentlemen."[19]

Privately and inwardly, Southworth was experiencing a personal victory. "Rickey told me it takes one year to stop drinking but ten years for the world to stop tagging you for it," he said. "My 10th anniversary rolls around soon."[20]

Two months after the season was over, the Cardinals pulled yet another surprise on the baseball world, this one from the front office. Rickey, the man who had given Billy Southworth his first chance — and his second chance — at managing the Cardinals, and the man who masterminded and developed the farm system that produced the championship ball club, quit the Cardinals to become president of the Brooklyn Dodgers.

Many wondered how a man who devoted his life to the Cardinals could suddenly jump ship. There was all sorts of speculation. Some in the press said Breadon and Rickey led differing lifestyles and didn't like each other but both knew how they could be successful professionally working together. There were reports that Breadon hired Southworth without consulting Rickey and, though it obviously worked out well, Rickey never got over not being consulted on such a big decision.

Rickey offered no complicated or controversial explanation. He simply said he was presented with an offer too good to pass up. Southworth may have been disappointed in seeing his old mentor leave, but four years later Billy the Kid would do the same thing for the same reason.

◆ 12 ◆

Two More Just Like It

Southworth returned to his home in Sunbury, Ohio, on October 9, 1942, as the nearby city of Columbus was planning a big reception for their hometown hero. But the reception would have to wait. Two days after returning home, Billy flew to Bangor, Maine, to visit his son, Billy Jr.—Captain Billy Southworth of the U.S. Air Corps.

The younger Southworth most recently had been stationed in Michigan and kept close tabs on the Cardinals by listening to radio broadcasts as often as he could. His father thought he was in Michigan when he received a phone call at his New York hotel room after the third game of the 1942 World Series. Young Billy told his father he was in Bangor and the two made arrangements to get together after the World Series was over. His son didn't say so directly, but his father got the idea Billy Jr. was about to be shipped out.

So when Billy the Kid returned to Columbus, he participated in a huge dinner in his honor but his thoughts most certainly drifted to where his son might be and what he was doing.

Columbus had good reason to celebrate. Not only was Southworth a product of the city, but many of the Cardinals ballplayers played for Columbus on their way up to the big leagues, including Terry Moore, Enos Slaughter, Mort and Walker Cooper, Max Lanier, Ernie White, Ray Sanders, Harry Walker, Coaker Triplett and Murray Dickson.[1]

Billy enjoyed talking about "the greatest team that ever stepped on a ballfield" and what made the team so great. In a long article he wrote for the *Saturday Evening Post*, one of the most popular magazines in the country, Southworth gave several examples of how team dynamics were always more important than individual glory for his players.

"We stress emotional steadiness on the Cardinals because it is our most important factor in team success," he wrote. "Cohesive thinking and coordinated movement of an intelligent team will always beat a team of individual stars."[2] While he didn't say so specifically, Southworth knew Johnny Mize didn't fit that philosophy; when he declined to sit in the dugout with his teammates when he was injured, he was considered expendable despite his home run power.

Similarly, in the magazine article, Southworth explained why the Cardinals passed up the chance to get veteran hurler Bobo Newsom when the pitcher was put on waivers in the height of the pennant race. "Being both a veteran and an individualist, he simply wasn't our type of player," said Southworth. "We try to assemble youth and speed but above all, we always demand complete subordination of solo ambitions."[3]

One of the reasons the Cardinals succeeded in 1942 was they were not hit as hard as other teams with players going off to war. Many of their players were young fathers and therefore were not the highest priority for Uncle Sam. But as the war intensified, more soldiers were needed. In the winter of 1943, Beazley, the 21-game winner, Slaughter, the team's leading hitter, Moore, the team captain, and Crespi, the versatile infielder, all went into the armed services. During the 1943 season, the Army also reached out and grabbed pitchers Murray Dickson and Howie Pollet and second baseman Jimmy Brown.

Though Rickey was gone, the Cardinals were going to have to depend on the farm system he developed if they were going to make any kind of showing in the National League race in 1943. Harry Walker, brother of Brooklyn's Dixie Walker, was brought up to take Moore's place in center field. Lou Klein, another of the Columbus ballplayers, laid claim to second base, replacing Brown. Two other pitchers from the Columbus ball club, Harry Brecheen and George Munger, also got the call to the big leagues as did Alpha Brazle, a hurler on the Redbirds' Sacramento farm team.

In effect, the 1942 championship team, winner of 106 games and the World Series, had been decimated, albeit for a good cause, one far more important than baseball. It was up to Southworth to take this mishmash of rookies and veterans and try to produce a winner, the same challenge he faced in Asheville, Rochester, Memphis, Columbus and when he took over the Cardinal reins in 1940.

The opening day lineup featured Sanders, a holdover, at first base; newcomer Klein at second; and Marion and Kurowski at their spots at short and third. Musial was in left, Walker was in center where Moore had patrolled for years and Coaker Triplett started the season in Slaughter's old position in right field. In mid-season, the Cardinals peddled Triplett and two lesser players to the Phillies for outfielders Danny Litwhiler and Earl Naylor. Southworth moved Musial to right field and Litwhiler started in left field. Walker Cooper was in his familiar spot behind the plate.

Though the loss of Beazley on the pitching staff was significant, St. Louis still had a stable of capable hurlers, most notably Cooper, their 22-game winner the year before. Also returning were Lanier, Krist, Dickson and Gumbert. Pollet started the season with the Cardinals and was 8–4 when Uncle Sam paged him.

St. Louis opened the season the way it frequently did, looking just average. They displayed their usual good pitching but their hitters acted as if they left their bats in Florida. In the first two games of a four-game series at Crosley Field in Cincinnati, Cooper and White turned in sterling pitching performances, but both lost, 1–0, the first game in 11 innings, the second game in 10. In the third game, the Cardinals scored their first run of the season in the sixth inning, added another one later and won, 2–1, behind another strong pitching performance, this one by Gumbert. The fourth game featured two lefties, Pollet and Johnny Vander Meer. In this one, the Cardinals scored only one run but Pollet threw a shutout, giving the Cardinals a 1–0 victory.

So after the first four games, St. Louis had scored just three runs, were shut out twice and already had put together a two-game winning streak and a two-game losing streak. The Cardinals boarded a train and headed west for their home opener at Sportsman's Park while Southworth pondered how to generate some offense.

Cooper pitched the home opener against Paul Derringer and the Cubs. The game resulted in yet another shutout but this time the Cardinals were on top. They broke out of their slump with five runs in the first inning on their way to a 7–0 victory. They split the next two games and ended April with a 4–3 record. In the first seven games, all three of their losses were by shutout and two of their wins were by shutout. And they had already played three extra-inning games.

Meanwhile, Durocher's Dodgers started the season winning five out of their first six so the Cardinals found themselves in familiar territory in the early season — trailing Brooklyn by a game and a half.

In May, the Cardinals began to get in synch. The pitching remained consistently good and the offense was enhanced by the emergence of Musial as one of the best hitters in the National League. He had learned to hit left-handers, which had been a weakness in the past. He hit with occasional power and he sprayed the ball to all fields. He possessed one of Southworth's staples — speed — and when he hit a ball to left-center or right-center, a double was a sure thing and a triple was a possibility. With that kind of dangerous hitter in the lineup, it had a positive effect on those hitting ahead of him and behind him. Not yet 24 years old, Musial was becoming the embodiment of Cardinal baseball, a position he would hold for the next 20 years.

St. Louis put together strings of little winning streaks in May, two games, three games, four games, without ever losing more than two in a row. The result was an 18–9 month and a record of 22–13 for the season. In the same time frame, Brooklyn won 20 and lost 12 and maintained a 1½ edge over the Cardinals, heading into June.

As was the case in 1942, the two ball clubs showed they were clearly the teams to beat and a third straight down-to-the-wire pennant race looked like it was in the offing. At one point in June, Brooklyn stretched its lead to 3½ games. A week later, the Cardinals led by a game. On June 30, after the Dodgers took two from the Giants, they retook the lead by one game.

The Cardinals regained first place on July 2 in a 4–3 win over the Giants with Gumbert besting Carl Hubbell. It was the second win in what would be a five-game winning streak. Later in the month they would win six straight. And between July 21 and July 27, the Redbirds put together a 10-game winning streak. Those streaks accounted for 21 of the 22 games they won in July, losing only 8. In the meantime, the Dodgers hit their first big slump of the year and it proved to be fatal. On the day the Cardinals' 10-game winning streak ended, the Dodgers went on a 10-game losing streak. By August 8, Brooklyn had slipped to third place, 16 games behind St. Louis. Cincinnati had moved into second place, 13 games off the pace.

By now, Southworth was fielding a team far different in individuals from his 1942 championship club but nearly identical in character. They had great team speed, always looking to take the extra base — to force an opposing outfielder to make a great throw. They executed fundamentals — bunting, stealing bases, hitting to the opposite field, executing double plays. Now they had an established star in Musial but they played Billy the Kid's game of team performance over individual accolades. Musial was the only .300 hitter, but nobody in the starting lineup hit lower than .279.

From mid–August, the pennant was never really in doubt but the Cardinals poured it on, winning 17 of 18 during one stretch in September and finished with 105 wins, one short of what the 1942 club had accomplished. Second-place Cincinnati finished 18 games out of first place.

Mort Cooper won 21 games. Lanier, Krist and Gumbert won 15, 11 and 10, respectively, Munger and Brecheen each won 9 and Dickson, Pollet and Brazle each contributed 8 wins. Pollet, Lanier and Cooper ranked first, second and third in the National League in earned run averages with 1.75, 1.90 and 2.30, respectively.

Musial finished with a league-leading batting average of .357 and also led the league in hits with 220, doubles with 48 and triples with 20. He also contributed 13 home runs and 81 runs batted in and was voted the National League's Most Valuable Player. Cooper hit .318 with 9 homers and he also drove in 81.

While they were the two main catalysts, the rest of the lineup was amazingly consistent in what it contributed: Walker hit .294; Klein and Kurowski each hit .287; Sanders and Marion each hit .280; Litwhiler, acquired in mid-season, finished at .279 — just a 14-point difference in the high and low batting averages in those six starters. That meant Southworth knew pretty much what he was going to get out of his lineup, day in and day out.

In the American League, the Yankees once again coasted to the championship with a 13½ game lead over second-place Washington, setting up a rematch of the 1942 World Series. The Yankees, like the Cardinals, had lost some big names to the armed services, notably Joe DiMaggio and Red Ruffing, but still produced a great ball club. Charlie Keller and Joe Gordon provided much of the pop, with 31 and 17 home runs, respectively — not Ruthian in numbers but dwarfing the Cardinals' "slugger," Musial, with his club-leading 13 homers. The Yankees' best newcomer was Nick Etten, acquired from the Philadelphia A's, who led the team in RBIs with 107.

The Yankees had strong starting pitching with Chandler, Tiny Bonham and Hank Borowy. Southworth was respectful but not awed by the Yankee hurlers. "Chandler is a good pitcher," he said. "We expect to see good pitching in the World Series. The Yankees wouldn't have won the pennant without good pitching, but the same is true of our club," he said.[4]

The World Series opened October 5 before 68,676 fans in Yankee Stadium with Lanier and Chandler the starting pitchers. The Cardinals struck first with a run in the second inning but Lanier gave up two runs in the fourth inning. The Cardinals came right back to tie in the fifth but the Yankees broke it open in the sixth with two runs on three singles and a wild pitch. It was all they needed in the 4–2 New York victory in a sloppy game in which both teams made two errors.

In the early morning hours of October 6, Mort and Walker Cooper were awakened by an urgent phone call. Their father, Robert Cooper, a mailman in Independence, Missouri, had died. Southworth consoled his two ballplayers and told them they could go home. But much like Rogers Hornsby who mourned the death of his mother during the 1926 World Series, the Cooper brothers elected to stay, saying their father would have wanted it that way. So Mort was the starting pitcher and Walker was behind the plate in Game One.

The Cardinals had an unexpected power surge when Marion and Sanders both homered off of Tiny Bonham. Mort took a 4–1 lead into the bottom of the ninth when the Yankees rallied for two runs but the Cardinals held on to win, 4–3. Walker Cooper went 1-for-3, a single, and also laid down a sacrifice bunt.

With the Series tied at a game apiece, Brazle took the mound against Hank Borowy and held the Yankees in check for seven innings. The Cardinals grabbed the lead on a two-run single by Litwhiler in the fourth inning. Clinging to a 2–1 lead, the roof fell in during the eighth inning, aided by two Cardinals errors. The Yankees scored five and won the game, 6–2. Uncharacteristically, the Redbirds hurt their cause by making four errors.

In Game Four, Lanier made his second Series start. Manager Joe McCarthy chose Marius Russo as his mound opponent. Russo had been a spot starter for the Yankees for six years and had won 14 games for them in two different seasons. But in 1943, he was just 5–10. Perhaps McCarthy was looking ahead, to set up his best starters for games five, six and seven if it came to that. Or perhaps he was just playing a hunch. Whatever the case, Russo pitched his best game of the year, allowing one run on seven hits in a 2–1 Yankee victory. He also doubled and scored the winning run in the eighth inning.

Southworth was frustrated with the ball club. He felt the Yankees were pushing them around, literally, on the base paths, causing his infielders to hurry their throws and not handle throws they were receiving very well. The usual sure-handed Cardinals had made nine errors in the four games. Usually tolerant of the press, even in defeat, after this ballgame, Billy the Kid told reporters, "Ask your questions in a hurry and get the hell out of here." The next day, the clubhouse was closed to the press before the game.[5]

The Yankees hoped to do to the Cardinals what the Redbirds had done to them a year earlier — knock them out in five games. Each manager sent his top pitcher to the mound, Chandler for the Yankees, the still grieving Cooper for St. Louis. The Cardinals sprayed 10 hits all over Sportsman's Park, but all of them were singles and none of them scored. Cooper pitched well but made one mistake, a two-run homer to Bill Dickey. The Yankees prevailed, 2–0, to win the World Series in five games, just as the Cardinals had done the year before.

It was a difficult time for the Cardinals and their fans. For the past two years, they had become accustomed to everything going pretty much their way. And then there was the question of Breadon and how he would react to the dismal performance in the World Series. Fifteen years earlier, he demoted his manager Bill McKechnie for that exact reason. That's how Southworth got his first big league managing job. Now, ironically, it might be his job that was on the line. Breadon settled that in a hurry. "He won two pennants with a total of 211 victories. Could anyone ask more of a manager?" he asked.[6]

After the Series was over, Southworth did his best to make amends with reporters he had whisked out of his clubhouse. "So long as I am manager of the Cardinals, our clubhouse door never again will be closed to baseball writers," he said. Looking back on the World Series, Southworth said, "We simply never played our game. We never got started. In baseball you've got to take the sour with the sweet. Well, last year we enjoyed the sweets — so this year we've got to take the sour."[7]

Within days after the Series ended, Billy got a visit from his son, home for a few days from flying bombing missions over Europe. He told his dad he nicknamed one of his bombers "Bad Check," because it always returned, and "Winning Run," partly because his bombing runs were so successful, but mostly as a tribute to his father.[8]

As the 1944 season approached, the war in Europe was taking more and more able-bodied men from major league rosters. The Cardinals, who had already lost Johnny Beazley, Terry Moore, Enos Slaughter, Jimmy Brown, Howie Pollet and Murray Dickson to the armed services, also lost Moore's replacement, Harry Walker, Brown's replacement, Lou Klein, and pitchers Brazle, White and Krist prior to opening day in 1944. Breadon was sympathetic to the war effort but lamented he might have a better team in the Army than he did in St. Louis.

Billy still had a pretty good nucleus with Musial, Marion, Walker Cooper, Kurowski, Sanders and Litwhiler in the lineup and Mort Cooper, Brecheen, Lanier and Munger on his pitching staff but there were definitely holes to fill if the Cardinals were to "three-peat." One person who didn't feel sorry for the Cardinals was Branch Rickey, now with Brooklyn, because he created the Cardinal farm system and knew that Southworth could pluck some good youngsters up from the minors and play competitively in the wartime major leagues.

Every ball club was scrambling for players and even the good teams such as the Cardinals needed depth if they were going to contend. The clubs not only had to have reserves ready in case starters got injured but also had to be ready in case any more players were called to the war.

Billy the Kid loved to build his teams around youth, speed, attention to fundamentals and team success above individual glory. He also liked to have some veterans around, not only to work with the young players but to be examples for them on and off the field.

Southworth needed depth, experience and leadership and he found it all in one of his old friends from back in Rochester—Pepper Martin. At age 40, Pepper came back to help the manager he loved and appeared in 40 games for the Cardinals. Emil Verban, an infielder who was 4-F (disqualified from the military) because of a perforated eardrum, was called up from Columbus to help out. And when the Army plucked Munger, who was 11–3 at the time, Southworth put a rookie, Ted Wilks, into the starting rotation. Wilks was as much of a surprise in 1944 as Beazley had been in 1942, winning 17 games and losing only 4.

Southworth seemingly pushed all the right buttons in 1944 as the Cardinals romped to another National League title, winning 105 games for the second year in a row, and topping 100 wins for a third straight year.

Second-place Pittsburgh finished 14 games out. For a while, the Cardinals had a chance to tie or break the all-time win record of 116, set by the 1906 Chicago Cubs, but a slump in which they lost 15 out of 20 games in late August and early September took care of that.[9]

The Cooper brothers came through again. Walker hit .317 with 13 homers and 72 runs batted in. Mort won more than 20 games for the third straight year with a 22–7 record. Johnny Hopp had his best year, hitting .336 and Sanders hit .295. Kurowski was the top power hitter, slugging 20 home runs. And Musial had another great year, hitting .347 with 51 doubles, 14 triples, 12 home runs and 94 runs batted in. In addition to Mort Cooper's 22–7 mark and Wilks finishing at 17–4, Lanier also had another good year, winning 17 and losing 12 and Brecheen had his best year at 16–5.

The biggest surprise in major league baseball in 1944 occurred in St. Louis but it wasn't the Cardinals. It was their American League counterpart, the Browns, who won their first championship in a race that went down to the wire with the underdogs sweeping a four-game Series from the Yankees to clinch it. Going into the Series, the Browns were in second place, one game behind Detroit. The sweep catapulted them into the championship. Had the Yankees swept, they would have been the champions again.

Both the Browns and the Cardinals had Sportsman's Park as their home field during the regular season, one team using it while the other was on the road. So every game of the World Series would be played in the same stadium. One minor detail needed to be worked out. Billy and Luke Sewell, the Browns' manager, shared the same apartment during the season when they were never there at the same time. For the World Series, Billy found temporary housing with a friend.

Southworth and St. Louis Browns manager Luke Sewell pose with Ohio governor James Bricker before a 1944 World Series game. Bricker was a guest of Billy's at the Series (courtesy Southworth family).

The Cardinals knew only too well the importance of momentum — that certain something that catches a team on fire. They had it '42 when they won 43 of their last 51 games to wipe out a 10½ game Dodger lead and then bowled over the Yankees in the World Series. They got a taste of it themselves when the upstart Browns, fresh off their pennant-winning drive, took two out of the first three games of the World Series.

In the opener, Mort Cooper was brilliant, allowing just two hits, a single to Gene Moore followed by a homer by George McQuinn. Denny Galehouse, the Browns' starter, had a shutout for eight innings, spoiled in the ninth when Marion led off with a double and scored on two infield outs. Final score: Browns 2, Cardinals 1.

Mabel Southworth, daughter Carole and longtime friend Fred Blum pose as Carole holds a pillow heralding the Cardinals 1944 World Series title. Blum was a batboy for Billy in Rochester (courtesy Southworth family).

The Cardinals won the second game, thanks in large part to the relief effort of little-used pitcher Blix Donnelly, who Southworth summoned in the seventh to snuff a Browns rally. He did and held them scoreless through the 11th inning when the Cardinals scored the winning run on an RBI single by pinch-hitter Ken O'Dea.

Wilks, the rookie 17-game winner, was the Cardinals Game Three starter, opposed by Jack Kramer of the Browns. St. Louis scored in the first inning but Wilks gave up five straight hits in the third inning, sending him to the showers. The Browns eventually won it, 6–2. The next day, Musial had his best World Series game ever, with a single, double, homer and walk in five at-bats. Meanwhile, Brecheen tamed the Browns' bats in a 5–1 Cardinal victory.

With the Series even at two games apiece, Cooper and Galehouse once again went at it in Game Five. Both were brilliant. Cooper struck out 12 Browns while Galehouse fanned 10 Redbirds. The only two runs in the game came on solo homers by Sanders and Litwhiler for a Cardinal 2–0 victory. Cooper ended the game by striking out three Brown pinch-hitters in the ninth inning. The 22 strikeouts amassed by both pitchers set a World Series record.

The Cardinals now had a three-games-to-two lead with a chance to clinch it in six. Southworth sent Lanier to the mound. Nelson Potter got the call for the Browns. The Cardinals grabbed a 3–1 lead but Lanier got in trouble in the sixth and Southworth pulled him for Wilks, who had gotten pummeled in Game Three. On this day, he retired the side in the sixth — and in the seventh, eighth and ninth innings as well. The 3–1 victory gave the Cardinals their second World Series championship in the three years.

Billy had taken an ever-changing roster and mixed and matched for the past three years, winning more than 100 games each year. In the modern era, only Connie Mack's 1929–1931 Philadelphia A's had ever done that.[10]

Billy went home to Sunbury to hunt and fish, go horseback riding with Mabel and their 10-year-old daughter Carole, plan his next meeting with Billy Jr. and look forward to the opportunity to go to the World Series for a fourth straight time in 1945. He had never felt more secure in his life.

◆ 13 ◆

William Brooks Southworth

On the eve of the 1944 World Series, Southworth attended a gathering at the Hotel Chase in downtown St. Louis and began chatting with an old newspaper buddy, Tommy Holmes of the *Brooklyn Eagle*, who was in town to cover the Series.

They exchanged pleasantries with Browns manager Luke Sewell, who was also there, and in the course of the conversation, Holmes asked Billy how his son was doing. "He's here," said Billy, motioning across the room and then led the writer over so he could introduce him to Major William Brooks Southworth, better known as Billy Southworth, Jr. Holmes said he was immediately struck by how handsome the young man was — several inches taller than his father with dark hair, a wisp of a moustache and a resemblance to Clark Gable, one of Hollywood's leading men at the time.

Young Southworth said he was on leave and had a chance to take in the World Series and didn't want to pass up the opportunity. He recalled how two years ago, when the Cardinals were playing the Yankees, he got as close as Bangor, Maine, and arranged to meet his dad there after the Series. As he was flying into Bangor, he was listening to the fifth game of the Series on the radio. Kurowski was at-bat when the radio went dead. It wasn't until after he landed that he learned Kurowski had homered and the Cardinals had won. During the '43 World Series, he was in England and could only hear portions of some games. He said the last time he saw his dad in a World Series was as an outfielder with the Cardinals in 1926, when he was 10 years old.

Holmes took particular notice of how, as the conversation went on, the two Southworths kept grinning at one another, not the kind of grin that comes with the telling of a joke, but the kind that comes from mutual adulation.[1]

Billy Jr. was born in Portland, Oregon, on June 20, 1916, while his father was playing for the Portland Beavers in the Pacific Coast League. Eventually, the family settled in Columbus where young Southworth was a star athlete at East High School, earning letters in football, basketball and baseball. He attended Ohio State University but did not participate in sports because he had signed a contract to play semi-pro baseball.

After Billy's first wife Lida divorced him, father and son spent many nights together on the minor league circuit, Billy the Kid managing, Billy the Kid's kid hanging out, shagging fly balls, arranging bats in the bat rack and the two simply enjoying each other's company.

In 1936, Billy Jr. signed with the Asheville Tourists of the Piedmont League, a team his father was managing at the time. He played in 29 games before being sent to Martinsville in the Bi-State League. In 1937, he began the season at Asheville but was optioned to Kinston where he remained for two years. In 1939, playing for the Rome Colonels in the Canadian-American League, he improved to .342 with 15 home runs and 85 RBIs. That led to his promotion to the Toronto Maple Leafs in 1940, a step away from the big leagues. He spent part of the season there, then went to Wilmington, then returned to Toronto to finish the season.

Billy Jr. had always had an interest in aviation, from the time he built model airplanes in his bedroom at home and he also had a keen interest in world affairs. At the end of the 1940 baseball season, he made the decision to enlist in the Army Air Corps because he sensed American involvement in the war in Europe was imminent and he had a duty to do his part.

He was the first professional ballplayer to enlist and it wasn't long before he had hit it big as a pilot. He joined the new 303rd Bomb Group in 1942 and took command of his first Boeing B-17 Flying Fortress later that year. It was a four-engine heavy bomber used to hit German industrial and military targets. Soon he was promoted to first lieutenant. He and his father wrote to each other constantly — sometimes daily — so they could keep up with one another's activities.

On January 21, 1943, *The Sporting News* reported, "When the history of baseball's part in the war is written, there will be no more stirring chapter than the achievements of Billy Southworth, Jr."[2]

On the same day, The *Ohio State Journal* reported, "Young Southworth, once the star of Columbus East High's athletic teams, is making history on a bigger field, blasting Nazi installations with regularity and precision as pilot of a Flying Fortress engaged in numerous bombing missions over Germany and France." The newspaper reported that Southworth wore a St. Louis Cardinal baseball cap on his bombing missions as a tribute to his father. He said the lightweight cap also made it easier to fit on the headgear pilots had to wear to receive radio traffic.[3]

Fred Blum, sportswriter Bob Hooey, Billy Jr. and Billy Sr. pose by the Southworth garage in 1943 (courtesy Southworth family).

On January 23, two days after those newspaper accounts, Southworth flew his seventh mission and was over France when Bad Check was fired upon, causing an engine to fail. The plane also encountered German cannon fire. Billy was forced to pull back with a crippled aircraft and managed to land at the Exeter airfield in England. Four days later, in a different B-17, Southworth led the first American bombing mission into Germany. By the time he ended his tour of duty as a bomber pilot, he had completed 25 missions without any injuries to himself or his crew. "I was just another Joe, occupying a lucky seat with a fine crew," he said. "I tried to manage 'em like Dad manages the Cardinals."[4]

In August 1943, Southworth Jr. was awarded the Distinguished Flying Cross for his missions as pilot of the Flying Fortress that was named The Winning Run, in honor of his father. The citation accompanying the medal said Southworth "displayed great courage" and "set an inspiring example." Earlier in the year, he earned an Air Force medal with three oak clusters.[5]

When he came back to the states, he was assigned to the Santa Monica, California, Air Force Distribution Center while he awaited his next assignment. One night, he ventured over to Hollywood to take in a boxing match. Someone recognized him and had him come into the ring where he was introduced to the crowd as a war hero. In the audience was Hunt Stromberg, a movie producer, who was struck by Southworth's good looks and presence. They met several times later and even talked about a possible movie deal when the war was over.[6]

He was promoted to major and became a bombing crew instructor and then a deputy commanding officer of a special task force. He had experienced an extraordinary military career that included the 25 successful bombing missions, leading dozens of young men into war and developing administrative skills of a military officer. All during his time in service, he had kept a diary as a way of recording his thoughts before and after flying into harm's way and having a written history of what was going on that would be a great memento once the war was over. Time and again, he would mention his father in his diary entries:

> December 17, 1942 — I have to date completed more missions than any other pilot.... Hitting 1,000 percent; Little worried. Dad was sick as of last writing and letter is overdue...
> June 7, 1943 — We in this theater have lived on our luck and our skill or have had death as our fate. Too many of those swell guys are gone. Had five letters from Dad in two days. Words can't express what I think and feel for that guy.
> June 30, 1943 — A great man wrote that story the article in the *Saturday Evening Post* about his 1942 Cardinal team, which, it is obvious, is one of our greatest baseball minds — to me, he's far the greatest. To me, he's the greatest guy who ever pulled on shoes.[7]

In October 1944, Southworth Jr. got some time off so he could come to St. Louis for the World Series. As he and his father stood in the Hotel Chase, chatting with Luke Sewell, Tommy Holmes and others, it would have been easy for observers to get caught up in and relish the baseball atmosphere, the excitement of a city that was about to experience an all–St. Louis World Series. It had never happened before and would never happen again.

Yet Holmes, the veteran sportswriter, came away with a different lasting impression. He kept noticing the non-verbal, non-physical connection between Billy Southworth and his son — the grins, the eye contact, the pride each had for the other. "It was sort of a pleasant thing to see," Holmes wrote. "I never saw a father so proud of his boy and a son so proud of his Dad."[8]

Billy hadn't wanted his son to enlist, or at least not right away. In 1940, the boy had a promising baseball career ahead of him, the world was about to be in turmoil and the father wasn't sure it was the right time or the right thing to do. He and Billy Jr. talked about it one December night in front of the fireplace in the Southworths' Sunbury home.

Carole is atop Midge with Billy Jr. and Billy Sr. on each side with their dogs as they prepare to go small-game hunting (courtesy Southworth family).

Billy Jr. said he thought his dad was looking at it selfishly, that legally he didn't need his dad's permission to enlist — but he wanted it. Billy admitted he was looking at it selfishly — that he just wanted the best of everything for his son and he wasn't sure this was it. As the two men retired for the evening, the situation between them was amicable but unresolved.

The next morning Billy got up early, awakened Mabel and told her he wanted to have a special breakfast for the whole family that morning — bacon and eggs, sausage, fruit, muffins, juice, the whole works. As Billy and his wife and Billy Jr. and Carole sat at the breakfast table, Billy looked out the window and said to his son, "It's a beautiful day. You'll never have a finer day to enlist." Billy Jr. replied with two words, saying only, "Thanks, Dad."[9]

Billy couldn't have known it then that he had just given permission for what would become an outstanding military career — but in the Hotel Chase four years later, the proud papa passed up no opportunities to show off his kid.

After the World Series, young Southworth went back to work and came home to Sunbury on November 28 to spend some time with his family before

Billy Jr. managed to play some baseball while a member of the armed forces. Billy, standing at left, was at Norland Air Base when this picture was taken (courtesy Southworth family).

taking on his latest assignment in Grand Island, Nebraska, site of a training center for heavy bomber crews. He and his father attended the Ohio State-Michigan football game at Columbus.

On the afternoon of Thursday, February 15, 1945, bombers of the U.S. Air Force and British Royal Air Force conducted four bombing raids on Dresden, Germany, causing mass casualties and destroying 15 square miles of the city. There was a time in the not too distant past that Major Southworth might have been leading the raids. But on this day, he was on a much more peaceful venture, piloting a B-29 on a routine flight from New York to Florida. He was training pilots to fly the B-29 Superfortress.

As he took off from Mitchel Field in New York, Major A.L. Anken, one of his crew, noticed smoke coming out of one of the engines. He alerted Southworth who answered, "Keep an eye on it." At 3:50 P.M., Southworth radioed the control tower at LaGuardia Airport to prepare for an emergency landing. With one engine dead, he tried to maneuver the aircraft, which weighed about 75,000 pounds, to a safe landing but he overshot the runway and the plane flip-flopped into Flushing Bay and burst into flames.

Rescue workers battled through the raging fire and managed to save five crew members in the back of the aircraft. But the front section, where Southworth and four other crew members had been sitting, broke off and sank in 30 feet of water. Their bodies could not be found.

Back home in Sunbury, Billy Southworth, Sr., received the dreadful news. He and Mabel headed immediately for New York where rescue efforts were continuing. When they arrived at Flushing Bay, Billy, speaking in a cracked voice, asked someone to point out where the plane had gone down. He gazed at the site, said nothing, and became overcome with emotion. A few minutes later, he asked about the condition of the survivors and seemed relieved that the five who had been rescued were hospitalized but were expected to live.[10]

Billy and Mabel stayed in New York for weeks, accompanying search parties on barges that went out into Flushing Bay daily. Inevitably, the rescue mission became a recovery mission but the Southworths held out hope, as any parents would. And they were grateful for all of the efforts made to find their son.

Billy told reporters, "It has been my privilege to go aboard the ship from which the search is being made. The close personal contacts that I have had with the officers and men conducting the search was most gratifying. Every officer and man is doing a heroic job. Their loyalty to lost comrades is present in their every act."[11]

Messages of condolences poured into the Southworths from all over the country. One was from Hunt Stromberg, the movie producer, who wrote, "I can truthfully say that I never met a young man I liked as richly and completely as your son. I told him one day that I wanted to adopt him as one of my sons. That is how much I cared for him."[12]

St. Louis was stunned by the tragedy. "This couldn't have hit me harder if it had been my own son," said Cardinal owner Sam Breadon.[13]

The upcoming baseball season seemed inconsequential by comparison and Billy was still in New York when his ball club began spring training. Eventually, he rejoined the club and threw himself into his work to try to stave off the grief that wouldn't go away. It was going to be a long season for the Cardinals anyway because Stan Musial and Mort and Walker Cooper had all been called into the armed services.

On August 4, the Cardinals were in Pittsburgh where rookie second baseman Red Schoendienst drove in two runs with a base hit as St. Louis edged the Pirates, 6–5. Harry Brecheen won his sixth game of the year and the Cardinals improved their record to 58–41, five games behind the first place Cubs.

After the game, Southworth received a phone call. He was to come to New York immediately. A body had washed ashore at Long Island Sound. It was believed to be his son. Dental records confirmed the identity but Billy also spotted a scar on the torso of the corpse, the result of the bullet wound from the accidental shooting of so long ago.

Major Billy Southworth, Jr., came home to Columbus where he was buried on August 7, 1945. It was closure in the fact that Billy Jr. was finally laid to rest, but for Billy Sr. there was a gaping wound to his soul that would never completely heal. He had lost his son, his pal, his best friend on earth. He would struggle with those thoughts for most of the rest of his life.

Carole Southworth Watson was 10 when her step-brother was killed. Her father struggled for years after that, she said. "Every once in a while, he would be out splitting wood and something would make him think of Billy Jr. It was tough, especially tough the first Christmas after it happened."[14]

"Every father of a son yearns desperately to be that boy's constant companion, intimate confidant and pal," wrote Arthur Daley in the *New York Times*. "Unfortunately, few of them ever attain such lofty objectives. But one of those rare and beautiful relationships was that which existed between Billy Southworth and Billy Jr. The father worshiped the son. The son idolized the father."[15]

The Cardinals finished second to the Chicago Cubs in 1945, another remarkable accomplishment for Southworth, all things considered. Stan Musial had gone into the military and was lost to the Cardinals the entire season. But Billy had been juggling lineups for three years to make up for players going to war. Many observers believe Southworth would have won his fourth straight championship, establishing a true dynasty, had it not been for the tragedy that preoccupied his thoughts most of the season.

The loss of Musial to the army could be overcome by simply finding a temporary replacement. The loss of a son was a chunk taken out of a man's heart that could not be replaced.

"Major Billy Southworth is gone," wrote Daley, "and gone with him is the light from his father's life."[16]

◆ **14** ◆

Brave New World

In October 1945, Billy went to Detroit to watch World Series games between the Detroit Tigers and Chicago Cubs. It was the first time since 1941 that he was a spectator at the World Series but he was certainly not lost in the crowd. Old baseball friends from around the country who had not seen him for a while greeted him, shook his hand and many expressed their condolences over the loss of his son.

One of the people who approached him was Louis Perini, one of the owners of the lowly Boston Braves, who had not won a pennant since the "Miracle Braves" of 1914. One thing led to another in their conversation and Perini asked Billy if, for the right price, he would consider becoming the manager of the Braves.

It was a stunning proposition. Southworth had been affiliated with the Cardinals for 20 years, except for his brief foray into cottonseed oil sales. He was the most successful manager in the major leagues and owed his success to the Cardinals organization that had given him a second chance when he was down on his luck. He had never thought about leaving St. Louis, but Perini offered him a $50,000 salary, considerably more than he was making with the Cardinals.

Beginning with his minor league managing career in Rochester, he had been successful where ever he went, consistently winning championships. In that regard, there wasn't much more he could accomplish with the Cardinals. The Braves, on the other hand, were perennial losers who needed someone who could instill the will to win in them and show them how to do it. Perini knew that's what his baseball team needed, and he was willing to pay for it. Southworth decided to accept the challenge.

There was one sticking point. Billy had one more year left on his contract with the Cardinals. With his permission, Perini contacted Sam Breadon to see what could be worked out. Breadon told him he would hate to lose Southworth but wouldn't stand in the way of a good opportunity for him.

National League of Professional Baseball Clubs

UNIFORM MANAGER'S CONTRACT

Parties   The............**National League Base Ball Club of Boston**............

herein called the Club, and............**William H. Southworth**............

of............**Sunbury, Ohio**............, herein called the Manager.

Recital   The Club is a member of the National League of Professional Baseball Clubs. As such, and jointly with the other members of the League, it is a party to agreements and rules with the American League of Professional Baseball Clubs and its constituent clubs, and with the National Association of Professional Baseball Leagues. The purpose of these agreements and rules is to insure to the public wholesome and high-class professional baseball by defining the relations between clubs and their employes, between club and club, between league and league, and by vesting in a designated League President and Commissioner broad powers of control and discipline, and of decision in case of disputes.

Agreement   In consideration of the facts above recited, the parties agree as follows:

Employment   1. The Club hereby employes the Manager to render skilled service as such in connection with all baseball activities of the Club during the year 8........ 19....*....; and the Manager covenants that he will perform with diligence and fidelity the service stated and such duties as may be required of him by the Club. * **1948, 1949, 1950, 1951, 1952**

Salary   2. For the service aforesaid the Club will pay the manager an aggregate salary of $**50,000**. ....**per year**............as follows:

In semi-monthly installments after the commencement of the playing season covered by this contract, unless the Manager is "abroad" with the Club for the purpose of playing games, in which event the amount then due shall be paid on the first week-day after the return "home" of the Club, the terms "*home*" and "*abroad*" meaning, respectively, *at* and *away from* the city in which the Club has its baseball field. If the Manager is in the service of the Club for part of the playing season only, he shall receive such proportion of the salary above mentioned, as the number of days of his actual employment bears to the number of days in the Club's playing season.

Loyalty   3. (a) The Manager pledges himself to the American public to conform to high standards of personal conduct, of fair play and good sportsmanship.

(b) The Manager represents that he does not, directly or indirectly, own stock or have any financial interests in the ownership or earnings of any Major League club, except as hereinafter expressly set forth, and covenants that he will not hereafter, while connected with any Major League club, acquire or hold any such stock or interest except in accordance with Major League Rule 20(e).

Service   4. The Manager shall not render baseball service during the period of this contract otherwise than for the Club.

Above and opposite: Southworth signed a five-year contract with the Boston Braves for $50,000 a year, covering 1948 to 1952 (Boston Braves Historical Society).

Agreements and Rules	5. (a) The National League Constitution and the Major and Major-Minor League Agreements and Rules, and all amendments thereto hereafter adopted, are hereby made a part of this contract, and the Club and Manager agree to accept, abide by and comply with the same and all decisions of the League President or Board of Directors and of the Commissioner, pursuant thereto.
Publication	(b) It is further expressly agreed that, in consideration of the rights and interest of the public, the Club, the League President, and/or the Commissioner may make public the record of any inquiry, investigation or hearing held or conducted, including in such record all evidence or information given, received or obtained in connection therewith, and including further the findings and decisions therein and the reasons therefor.
Special Covenants	6. This contract is subject to Federal or State legislation, regulations, executive or other official orders, or other governmental action, now or hereafter in effect, respecting Military, Naval, Air or other governmental service, which may, directly or indirectly, affect the Manager, the Club or the League; and subject also to all rules, regulations, decisions or other action by the Major Leagues, the Commissioner, the Major or Major-Minor League Advisory Council, or the League President, including the right of the Commissioner to suspend the operation of this contract during any National emergency.
	7. The Club and Manager covenant that this contract fully sets forth all understandings and agreements between them, and agree that no other understandings or agreements, whether heretofore or hereafter made, shall be valid, recognizable, or of any effect whatsoever, unless expressly set forth in a new or supplemental contract executed by the Manager and the Club (acting by its president, or such other officer as shall have been thereunto duly authorized by the president or Board of Directors, in writing filed of record with the League President and Commissioner—and that no other Club officer or employe shall have any authority to represent or act for the Club in that respect), and complying with all agreements and rules to which this contract is subject.

This contract shall not be valid or effective unless and until approved by the League President.

Signed in duplicate this 6th day of October, A. D. 1947.

(SEAL) NATIONAL LEAGUE BASE BALL CLUB OF BOSTON, Inc.
(Club)

Witness:
[signature] (President)

[signature] (Manager)

Sunbury, Ohio
(Address of Manager)
R.F.D. #1

On November 6, 1945, the baseball world absorbed some shocking news—Billy Southworth was leaving the Cardinals. "Such opportunity knocks at the door of a baseball man only once in a lifetime," Billy told the press. He wanted to assure everyone there were no hard feelings between him and Breadon "with whom I've never had a harsh word. I want to assure you that I'm glad Mr. Breadon is such a thorough gentleman that he put not the smallest obstacle in my way to improve myself."[1]

In typical Billy the Kid fashion, he then began to talk about what he wanted to do with his new ball club, cautioning his listeners not to expect miracles overnight. He then went into detail about how he manages a team, striking themes that were familiar to anyone who had observed his success over the years in St. Louis.

"It's a challenge to me to bring up a team with spirit, hustle and ability," he said. "I never criticize players before their mates. We do not toss around harsh words in defeat.

It gives me great satisfaction to see them improve when they play for me. I shall continue along those lines in Boston."[2]

Baseball analysts were puzzled as to how and why Breadon let Southworth go. He was the most successful manager in baseball and, whatever price Perini was willing to pay, Breadon surely could have met it. From Southworth's standpoint, he had security in St. Louis and although the salary he was offered in Boston might have been more, he was certain not to get any World Series checks with the Braves, not for a while at least. There had to be more to the story than Billy the Kid leaving St. Louis for more money and Breadon letting him go.

One of the writers trying to figure it out was Tommy Holmes of the *Brooklyn Eagle*, the man who had chatted with Billy and his son in the Chase Hotel prior to the 1944 World Series. Holmes wrote that a baseball insider, who he didn't name, had a theory. His thought was that Perini first approached Breadon about purchasing some good ballplayers such as Musial, Kurowski, Marion and Walker Cooper. Any of those players would vastly improve the Braves and the Cardinals had so many players coming home from the war — Musial, Slaughter, Moore, Beazley and others — that they were going to have to unload some players anyway.

As this man's theory went, Breadon wanted a lot more money for his players than Perini was willing to pay. Somewhere in the discussions, Southworth's name came up. Perini was willing to pay top dollar for Southworth; Breadon would get a fistful of cash and wouldn't have to part with any players. Beyond that, in the summer of 1945, the Cooper brothers demanded more money from Breadon. Walker Cooper went in the service. Mort Cooper staged a brief walkout. He was traded to Boston. Walker Cooper would be returning to a situation in St. Louis in which his brother was gone and he was on bad terms with Breadon. So, the theory went, Walker would probably want to be traded to the Braves and Breadon would accommodate him. If all this worked out, Perini would get the game's best manager and an all-star catcher out of the deal; Breadon would keep his ball club intact and have more money in the coffers.³

On January 5, 1946, Breadon indeed peddled Walker Cooper, but to the New York Giants rather than the Braves, for $175,000. The Cardinal owner had accomplished a lot in one transaction. He got rid of his unhappy catcher; he got a lot of money in return; and he didn't appease Cooper or Perini by sending him to Boston.

Lawton Carver, sports editor for the International News Service, sized up Southworth's challenge in Boston: "He rises or falls on his own. His owners have told him to spend money as if it were water running down a drain. But get a winner."⁴

The Braves finished sixth in 1945, winning just 67 games. Bob Coleman was the manager at the start of the season but departed with his team at 42–51. Coach Del Bissonette took over on an interim basis and guided them to a 25–34 mark the rest of the way, giving them an overall record of 67–85.

They had one established star, outfielder Tommy Holmes (no relation to the sportswriter) who hit .352 with 28 home runs and 117 runs batted in. Third baseman Chuck Workman contributed 25 home runs. Outfielder Carden Gillenwater hit .288. No one else in the lineup hit higher than .274.

The top pitcher on the staff, Jim Tobin, won only 9 games while losing 14 and ended the season with the Detroit Tigers. Tobin was at the end of a career in which he had thrown two no-hitters for the Braves, both in 1944, and was often used as a pinch-hitter. He had a lifetime batting average of .230 and hit 17 home runs.

Mort Cooper was 7–4 for the Braves after coming over from the Cardinals and represented someone whom Southworth knew well from all the successful years the two of them had in St. Louis. Ed Wright won 8 games for the '45 Braves and Bob Logan and Nate Andrews each won 7.

It was going to be an uphill climb for Billy, something he had experienced in the past when he took over several minor league teams and then was elevated to the Cardinals in 1940. But he approached the job with his typical optimism and vigor and expected the same from his ballplayers. His method of success had not changed — the Braves would work relentlessly on fundamentals, working as a cohesive unit, rooting for one another rather than focusing on individual accomplishments. They would bunt, hit behind the runner, hustle, take the extra base whenever possible, play good defense and always hit the relay man, and play for one run at a time.

Another Southworth trademark was finding the right mix of veterans and young ballplayers so he would always have a steady stream of older players willing to teach and youngsters willing to learn. That formula had served him well all the way back to his days in Rochester.

As it turned out, the Cardinals helped him out in that regard. In the next few years, the Redbirds and Braves established a pipeline in which the Cardinals unloaded players who no longer fit into their plans, the Braves picked up some veterans who would meld nicely with their young ballplayer and Breadon pocketed handsome sums of cash. It actually started before Southworth arrived when Mort Cooper was traded to the Braves on May 2, 1945, for pitcher Red Barrett and $60,000. That was Breadon's response to Cooper's demand for more money.

After Southworth's arrival the following transactions occurred:

> February 5, 1946: All-purpose player Johnny Hopp was traded to the Braves for infielder Eddie Joost and $40,000.
> April 15, 1946: First baseman Ray Sanders was sold to the Braves for $25,000.
> May 14, 1946: Pitcher Ernie White was released by the Cardinals and signed by the Braves for an undisclosed amount.
> June 9, 1946: Outfielder Danny Litwhiler was sold to the Braves for an undisclosed amount.

In a separate move, on January 5, 1946, the Cardinals sold Walker Cooper, the other half of the unhappy Cooper brothers to the New York Giants for $175,000. Breadon had disposed of Cooper but did not reunite him with his brother at Boston.

The result of all the transactions was, halfway through the 1946 season, Southworth had Mort Cooper, Hopp, Sanders, White and Litwhiler, all of whom he knew very well; Breadon had more than $250,000 in cash with which to try to build another dynasty; and Perini and the Braves had a fresh new look.

Mort Cooper joined a staff that had a great righthander in Johnny Sain and an up-and-coming lefty named Warren Spahn. Tommy Holmes anchored a lineup that also featured Connie Ryan, a journeyman second baseman, who didn't hit for much average but played Southworth's kind of hustling baseball, and Phil Masi, a catcher who helped provide another Southworth staple, a team that would be strong up the middle.

Johnny Hopp played in 129 games at several positions and led the Braves in hitting in 1946 with a .333 average. Holmes hit .310 and led the team in RBIs with 79. Litwhiler appeared in only 79 games but hit .291 and led the team in homers with 8. It was a team without much punch but Sain won 20 games while losing 14, Mort Cooper was 13–11, Ed Wright was 12–9, Bill Lee, at age 36 and nearing the end of good career, chipped in 10 wins while losing 9 and Spahn was 8–5.

In Southworth's first year, the Braves were far from great — they weren't even good yet — but they clawed their way to an 81–72 record, moving up from sixth to fourth place in the National League and winning 16 more games than they had in 1945.

Southworth with Mort Cooper, his pitching ace in St. Louis, who came over to the Boston Braves toward the end of his career. They pose for the camera in 1947 (courtesy Southworth family).

In the offseason, the Braves continued to try to put the pieces together. They purchased the contract of a strapping young slugger, Earl Torgeson, from Seattle in the Pacific Coast League. And the pipeline to St. Louis continued. On December 9, 1946, the Cardinals sold pitcher Red Barrett to the Braves, the same Red Barrett who had gone from the Braves to the Cardinals 18 months earlier in the Mort Cooper deal. On April 18, 1947, St. Louis sold pitcher Johnny Beazley, one of the stars of the 1942 championship team, to the Braves.

But the biggest acquisition for 1947 came on September 30, 1946. The Braves acquired third baseman Bob Elliott from the Pittsburgh Pirates along with catcher Hank Camelli for aging third baseman Billy Herman, pitcher Elmer Singleton, outfielder Stan Wentzel and shortstop Whitey Wietelman.

Southworth hoped Elliott would be the catalyst to get the Braves' engine chugging. His nickname was "Mr. Team" because of his unselfishness on the field and for his leadership, qualities Southworth cherished. And he was a good hitter. He drove in more than 100 runs three years in a row, 1943–1945, and showed speed on the base paths by hitting 10 or more triples four times during his days with the Pirates. Pittsburgh had given up their best ballplayer but they had a youngster coming up named Ralph Kiner who they thought would provide even more punch than Elliott. But the key to the deal from Pittsburgh's standpoint is they wanted 37-year-old Herman as their manager.

The Braves got off to a good start in 1947 in what looked to be another typical National League year with Brooklyn and the Cardinals fighting to the finish (they tied for first in 1946, with the Cardinals winning a playoff) and perhaps the Cubs making a run. But Boston, unspectacular but steady, hung around and on June 15 took over first place in the standings. It had been a long time since the leaderboard looked like this:

	W-L	GB
Boston	30–22	...
New York	28–21	0.5
Chicago	29–22	0.5
Brooklyn	27–25	3
Cincinnati	26–29	5.5
St. Louis	24–28	6
Philadelphia	24–30	7

Southworth was becoming the sage of Boston just as he had been in St. Louis and Rochester. As the Braves sat on top of the standings, New York sportswriter Bob Considine marveled at the turnaround of the team.

"Southworth has done this with a band of semi-spavined cast-offs, rejects, almost, never-quites and wet-eared youngsters," Considine wrote. "As for

Southworth himself, the man is making a great comeback, the second of a life that has not been easy. Years ago, his personal problems were such that he thought his baseball career was at an end." But, Considine wrote, he got a second chance with the Cardinals. "He sat on top of the baseball world only to have his security and even his stomach for living pulled from under him" with the death of his son. "To blot out that tragedy," he wrote, "Southworth has thrown himself into his Boston job with everything that's in him."[5]

In the *New York Post*, Leonard Cohen also wrote about Southworth's resiliency. "The Billy Southworth story is still the same," he wrote, "though the setting has changed from St. Louis to Boston. No matter where Southworth may go, the tale will be unchanged, the motif unvaried. Billy Southworth is that kind of guy. He'll give any job all he's got, no matter where he is."[6]

Southworth was the toast of the town when he took over as Boston Braves manager in 1946. He was featured on the front of the Braves scorecard (Boston Braves Historical Association).

Cohen said spending time with Southworth is an instant energy source, even for sportswriters, so he could easily see the effect it would have on his players. And Billy's philosophy hadn't changed from the days when he was inspiring Pepper Martin in Rochester or encouraging rookie Stan Musial in St. Louis.

"He can forgive any error, every mistake in judgment if the man involved was trying and giving it his best," Cohen wrote. Billy told him, "We want no second-guessing or post-mortems. All we ask is that every man give his best effort. We never quit. We keep trying. The opposition has got to beat us. We refuse to concede defeat."[7]

He gave an example of a game in Chicago in which the Braves were down, 5–3, with two outs in the ninth inning. Elliott and Frank McCormick then hit back-to-back home runs to tie the game and the Braves went on to win it in 11 innings. "Effort pays off," he said.[8]

At the end of June, the Braves were 37–27, clinging to a first-place lead by a half game over Brooklyn, a game and a half over the Giants, 4½ over the Cubs and Cardinals and six games ahead of Cincinnati. Six of the eight teams were still in the National League race going into the last three months of the season.

In July, Boston cooled off, not with any extended losing streak but without a sustained winning streak either. The Braves won 13 and lost 18 for the month. But the Dodgers caught fire, going 25–8 during the same stretch. The result was Brooklyn taking over the lead and Boston plunging to fourth place, 10½ games back. It was simply too big a hill to climb in the next two months. At season's end, the Dodgers were the champions but the Braves had climbed into third place with an 86–68 record.

Under Southworth, they had steadily improved, moving from 65 wins the year before he took over to 81 wins his first year and now 86. The Braves were moving in the right direction — and attendance at Braves Field was 1.2 million. Like Southworth and his players, the Boston fans had become believers too.

One obvious difference from previous years was the presence of Elliott. He played in 150 games, hit 22 home runs and drove in 113 runs and was the National League's Most Valuable Player. He tied with Holmes for the team lead in games played with 150, was second to Holmes in hits with 176, and led the club in runs scored with 93, doubles with 35, home runs with 22, RBIs with 113, batting average with .317 and walks with 87. Always-dependable Holmes hit .309 and struck out only 16 times in 676 plate appearances. Torgeson, the rookie, contributed greatly with his .281 batting average, 16 home runs and 78 runs batted in.

Spahn and Sain each won 21 games. Barrett, who had gone to the Cardinals in the Mort Cooper deal and then was sold back to the Braves, won 11. On June 13, the Braves traded 34-year-old Cooper to the New York Giants for Bill Voiselle, who became the Braves fourth starter and won eight games for them in the half-season he played for them. Southworth liked what he saw in Voiselle and thought he had a lot of potential as he looked to the 1948 season.

For Cooper, it was the beginning of the end of a great career, most of it spent with Southworth in St. Louis and Boston. He was 2–5 with the Braves when he was traded and 1–5 with the Giants. New York released him in 1948. He signed with the Cubs in 1949 but was released after one outing in which he pitched to three batters, gave up a walk and a hit, threw a wild pitch and surrendered a three-run homer.

With Voiselle, Barrett, Sain and Spahn as his starting pitching corps and Elliott, Holmes and Torgeson bolstering the middle of the lineup, Billy the Kid looked forward to 1948. Publicly, Southworth was the toast of the town, eschewing optimism, signing autographs, granting interview after interview.

Sportswriter Considine was right. Billy was wrapping himself up in his work, not only because that was his baseball credo, but it also helped stave off the grief that engulfed him in the quiet moments when his mind drifted to how much he missed his beloved son.

Baseball helped alleviate that. So did more than an occasional beer.

◆ 15 ◆

Spahn and Sain and...

While Bob Elliott, *Tommy Holmes* and Earl Torgeson contributed to the punch and dependability in the heart of the Boston Braves batting order, Johnny Sain and Warren Spahn offered the same durability and consistency on the mound.

Sain had come up with the Braves in 1942 and had a 4–7 record before going into the armed services. He didn't get back into baseball until 1946, Southworth's first year with the Braves, and he immediately became one of the National League's best pitchers, posting a 20–14 record. In 1947, he was even better, winning 21 and losing 12. It stood to reason that as the Braves improved as a team, Sain's numbers would improve correspondingly.

Sain didn't have a blazing fastball to challenge hitters. His strikeouts came from knowing hitters' strengths and weaknesses, keeping them off balance and fooling them with finesse. Sain said he was totally different than Warren Spahn, the Braves' lefthander who was emerging as a star: "Spahn was smooth, orthodox. I was all motion, change of speed, unorthodox. There are just as many ways to pitch as there are pitchers."[1]

Sain had the distinction of having been the last man to pitch to Babe Ruth and the first man to pitch to Jackie Robinson in the big leagues.[2]

Because Sain wasn't overpowering, he became a student of the art of pitching, learning not only hitters' habits, but umpires' habits behind the plate, situational pitching, working in concert with the catcher and all the other little things that could help him on the mound. He was also a good hitter and helped his own cause on many occasions and was often used as a pinch-hitter.[3]

Spahn was a tall lefthander who raised his right leg high before every delivery. Like Sain, he broke in with the Braves at the end of the 1942 season, went off to war and did not return until 1946. He was 8–5 under Southworth that year but turned in a 21–12 performance in 1947. Whereas Sain by his own admission was unorthodox, Spahn was consistent with the high leg kick, good fastball and good control. Also like Sain, he was a good hitter.

Three changes in the Braves lineup from 1947 to 1948 were the additions of Alvin Dark at shortstop, Eddie Stanky at second base and Jeff Heath in the outfield. Stanky was not blessed with great baseball skills but he was a hustler and he kept his head in the game, two traits that always set well with Southworth. When the Dodgers and Branch Rickey decided to make a second baseman out of Jackie Robinson, Stanky became expendable and the Braves picked him up. Dark was a rookie who gave every indication he was ready for the big leagues. He would win the Rookie of the Year award in 1948. Heath was a hard-hitting outfielder who spent most of his career with the Cleveland Indians but was with the St. Louis Browns when the Braves purchased his contract at the end of the 1947 season.

As the Braves headed into the 1948 season, they looked like a typical Southworth team — good pitching, good team speed, strong up the middle, a good mix of veterans and youngsters, a group of players with the will to win. They included Red Barrett, Danny Litwhiler, Ernie White and Johnny Beazley, who had experienced Southworth's winning ways with the Cardinals.

Billy the Kid sung the praises of his troops in spring training. He told sportswriters Sain and Spahn would be great but he told them to watch the development of another pitcher, Bill Voiselle, who he said could make the difference in a tight pennant race. Spahn, he said, was the only pitcher in baseball who had the potential of winning 30 games some day.

Billy said the Braves had improved considerably at what had been their weakest link in 1947, their double play combination up the middle. "What a difference Stanky can make for our shortstop. Alvin Dark can be a sensation," he said. He was also excited about the development of his first baseman. "I want you to watch Torgeson this year — just watch him."[4]

Southworth wasn't ready to predict a pennant in Boston but he was proud of the progress being made. "We had quite a climb to face," he said. "It was a jump one couldn't make in one or two years. But we have been moving up. I can promise you you'll have a much better ball club in 1948 than we had in 1947. I know we'll be better. And maybe a lot better with just a little luck."[5]

Despite all the hype, the Braves started the season sluggishly. Sain didn't win his first game until April 30, Spahn won only one and Boston finished the month at 5–7, languishing in seventh place. Part of the problem was injuries to key players. Torgeson missed some games because of a sore left wrist and Stanky strained a knee ligament sliding into second base, trying to break up a double play. When Sain lost a 3–2 decision to Pittsburgh on May 5, the Braves sunk to 6–9 and a season-low three games below .500.

The *Boston Post* reported on May 7 that Southworth was "disgusted" with his team's recent play and was going to shake up the batting order, moving Torgeson up to second, replacing center fielder Jimmy Russell who would bat third. Holmes, who earlier in the year batted second and was replaced in that spot by Russell, would now hit sixth. The lineup changed but the ballclub continued to sputter. It was typical of Southworth teams. Even his great Cardinal teams in the early 1940s had trouble getting out of the gate.

One bright spot was Voiselle, who won his first four decisions and, as Southworth had predicted, was coming into his own. At the end of May, Sain, Spahn and Voiselle had each won four games, accounting for 12 of the team's 17 wins. The Braves had climbed to .500 at 17–17 but, entering June, were in fifth place, albeit just three games behind the first-place Giants.[6]

Russell responded well to being moved to third in the batting order. On May 15, he supplied the only run of the game as his homer delivered a 1–0 win for Spahn, who threw the third consecutive shutout for the Braves pitching staff. Sain and Voiselle had the other two.

Another characteristic of a Southworth team took hold in June. Suddenly, everything came together. The ballclub jelled. There was no real reason for it, nothing anyone could put their finger on, but the Braves started playing with the fervor everyone expected of them at the start of the season. Sain won six out of his seven starts, Spahn and Voiselle each won four and rookie Vern Bickford won his only two starts of the month. Elliott, Torgeson and Holmes were all hitting well and Dark and Stanky were living up to their potential as a potent double play combination.

The suddenly resurgent Braves won 20 out of 30 in June. On June 7, Russell tied a National League record with four extra-base hits in one game as the Braves beat the Cubs, 9–5. A switch-hitter, Russell homered and doubled twice and did it from both sides of the plate. On June 13, Spahn got rocked in Cincinnati, allowing six runs in five innings of work. The Braves scored four in the seventh but went into the ninth inning trailing, 7–4. They rallied for four runs in the ninth. In the bottom of the ninth, Southworth went with his best and brought in Johnny Sain to pitch. Sain set the Reds down to preserve the win and propel the Braves into first place in the National League. They remained there the rest of the month.

The great play continued in July. The Braves won 19 of 30 games and got some help from some unlikely people. The big three among the starters were just 10–10 for the month with Sain at 5–4, Spahn at 2–2 and Voiselle 3–3. But Nels Potter and Murray Dickson didn't lose a game all month and Bobby Hogue, who was the winning pitcher in the 8–7 win that put the

Braves in first place on June 13, was 4–1 in July. Boston had won 39 and lost just 21 in June and July and went into August with a 5½ game lead over second-place New York. On July 8, Russell hit a grand slam home run in the eighth inning in a game at Ebbets Field in Brooklyn to break a 2–2 tie and was pelted with debris from fans when he took his position in center field. Typical of the Braves' play was the July 31 contest against the Cardinals when the Braves scrapped for four runs in the bottom of the ninth inning, without the benefit of an extra-base hit, to beat the Cardinals, 7–6. Holmes, Dark and outfielder Clint Conatser each had three hits for the Braves.

August proved to be their toughest month. They opened it by losing four in a row and never seemed to get on track. It was like April all over again. Toward the end of the month they put together a four-game winning streak but lost 19 of 33 games. Heading into the September stretch drive, Boston's lead in the National League race had shrunk to next to nothing and four teams were within two games of each other in the race. The standings were:

	W-L	GB
Boston	70–55	...
Brooklyn	68–54	0.5
Pittsburgh	66–54	1.5
St. Louis	68–57	2
New York	60–60	7.5
Philadelphia	55–68	14
Cincinnati	52–71	17
Chicago	52–72	17.5

On September 6, the Braves played a doubleheader with the Dodgers and beat them twice. Spahn pitched all 14 innings of a 2–1 victory in the opener. Sain tossed a shutout in the nightcap, winning 4–0. Boston went on a streak in which they won six straight, then after a loss, reeled off seven more wins. Spahn and Sain were a big part of it. They followed up on their doubleheader win of September 6 by winning both ends of a doubleheader against Philadelphia on September 11. This time it was Sain winning the opener, 3–1, and Spahn cruising to a 13–2 victory in the second game.

Gerald Hern, sports editor of the *Boston Post*, watched what was happening and was inspired to report on it poetically in his poem "Spahn and Spain and Pray for Rain."

As Sain and Spahn continued their dominance, Hern's poem became more well known and was eventually shortened conversationally into "Spahn and Sain and pray for rain," a phrase that became part of baseball folklore for generations to come.

On September 14, Sain beat Chicago 10–3 for his 20th victory and the following day Spahn won his 14th in a 5–2 decision over the Cubs. On September 17, Sain was the starter and winner in a 6–2 win over Pittsburgh. On September 18, Spahn beat the Pirates, 2–1. In the space of 12 days in the heat of the pennant race, Spahn and Sain had gone 8–0. On September 29, Boston beat Brooklyn, 4–3, behind Sain, clinching the National League pennant. It was the Braves' first championship in 34 years and Southworth's fourth in the last seven years.

Sain won 24 and lost 16 but was 8–2 from September 1 on. Spahn was 15–12 for the year but was 6–3 during that same span. The team as a whole was 21–7 from September 1 on so the two top pitchers got some help from the rest of the staff, though the others didn't get near the publicity. Vern Bickford, the rookie, was 11–5 and Voiselle won 13 and lost 13. Bobby Hogue, the main relief pitcher, was 8–2.

Years later, Voiselle was asked if he was resentful of being ignored in the "Spahn and Sain and pray for rain" jingle, considering he won 13 games and had a better earned run average than Spahn. "I reckon I was, in a way," he said. "We had some pretty good pitchers on that team — Spahn, Sain, Vern Bickford. Nelson Potter did real good that year and so did Red Barrett."[7]

The new faces in the lineup at the start of the year all came through. Heath hit .319 and had 20 home runs and 76 runs batted in. Dark, the rookie, hit .322 and Stanky hit .320. The starting lineup boasted two other .300 hitters, Holmes at .325 and outfielder Mike McCormick who hit .303. Elliott once again provided the big bat in the middle of the lineup with his 23 home runs and 100 runs batted in. Heath had 20 home runs and 76 RBIs. Torgeson was next productive with 10 homers and 67 runs batted in.

The turnaround of the Braves in three seasons was similar to what Southworth had done when he took over the Cardinals in 1940. One difference was the Braves had been in the National League doldrums far longer than the Cardinals had. Also, the Braves did not have the carefully crafted farm system that provided St. Louis with one good young ballplayer after another, year after year.

Frank Graham of the *New York Journal-American* pointed out the Braves finished sixth in 1945, finished fourth under Southworth in 1946 and third in 1947. "You wouldn't say, looking at it on paper, or even on the field some days, that this was a championship ball club. But it played championship ball for Southworth. How? Why?" Graham cited two reasons. First was his attention to detail. "At training camp and during the season, he goes over and over and over plays with limitless patience, never raising his voice, never berating a player but hammering, hammering, hammering away, striving for perfection." The second reason, said Graham, is the confidence he instills in his players. "He props them up and they lean on him in the beginning. But when he sees they can stand alone, he steps back because he doesn't want to take from them any of the confidence he has given them."[8]

The city of Boston was baseball crazy in September as the Red Sox in the American League were also battling for a championship and there was the possibility of having an all-Boston World Series. But the Red Sox and Cleveland Indians tied for first place, each with 96–58 records, forcing a one-game playoff at Fenway Park in Boston. On October 4, the Indians downed the Red Sox 8–3, claiming the championship and assuring the Braves would travel beyond Boston in the upcoming World Series.

The Indians and Braves were similar in several ways. Both had innovative, motivating managers in Lou Boudreau and Southworth. Both had strong starting pitching. Boudreau felt he could match Spahn and Sain with his duo of Bob Feller and Bob Lemon and their supporting casts had helped get them where they landed. Just as Boston touted its rookie pitcher, Vern Bickford, Cleveland had Gene Bearden, who, with his 20 wins, had a first season reminiscent of what Johnny Beazley did for the Cardinals in '42 when he won 21. Lemon won 20 and Feller 19. The Indians also had a rookie in the bullpen, 41-year-old Satchel Paige. Cleveland had three .300 hitters in their starting lineup: Boudreau, the shortstop, .355, and outfielders Dale Mitchell, .336, and Larry Doby, .301. Doby had the distinction of being the first black player in the American League, laying the groundwork for Paige and others to follow.

The first game of the 1948 World Series, at Braves Field, was a classic pitching duel between Sain and Feller. It was a scoreless tie going into the bottom of the eighth inning when Boston catcher Bill Salkeld coaxed a walk out of Feller. Phil Masi ran for Salkeld and went to second on Mike McCormick's sacrifice bunt. A typical Southworth "rally" was brewing. Stanky was walked intentionally to get to Sain. Sibbi Sisti, a reserve infielder, came in to run for Stanky. Sain, a good hitter, flied out and the runners held. With Tommy Holmes at bat, Feller went into his stretch, then whirled and threw to second where it appeared he had Masi picked off. But umpire Bill Stewart called Masi safe, prompting a heated protest by Boudreau, who had taken the throw. Holmes then singled, driving in Masi with what turned out to be the only run of the game. It was one of two hits allowed by Feller. Sain went the distance, allowing just four hits.

"Lou tagged Masi out by two feet," said Feller in recalling the play years later. "It wasn't even close. Everyone in the ballpark saw he was out, except one — the umpire. We hadn't just picked off Masi. We picked off Stewart too."9

In Game One of the Series, the Braves scored a run in the bottom of the first but were held in check the rest of the way by Lemon. Boudreau and Doby got key hits for the Indians who evened the Series at a game apiece with a 4–1 over Spahn and Boston.

Game Three, played before 70,306 fans at Municipal Stadium in Cleveland, proved to be another pitching gem, this one between Bearden and Bickford. Both pitchers allowed five hits, but Bickford was touched for a couple of runs while Bearden threw a shutout, Cleveland winning, 2–0, to take a two games to one lead in the Series.

The fourth game of the Series drew an even bigger crowd, 81,897, who witnessed another battle with great pitching and not much hitting. Sain took the mound for the Braves and he was as sharp as he had been in Game One, giving up just one run once again. But the Indians plated a run in the first and Doby homered in the third. That was all the run support Steve Gromek needed in holding on for a 2–1 Cleveland victory.

Bob Feller pitched a two-hitter in the opening game of the World Series but lost 1–0. Johnny Sain was the winner. It was the closest Feller ever came to winning a World Series game (National Baseball Hall of Fame Library, Cooperstown, New York).

The Braves' run came on a homer by Marv Rickert, an outfielder who was playing in place of Jeff Heath who broke his ankle in the last week of the season. Rickert played in only three games in the regular season but started five World Series games. Not much more could have been asked of Sain. He had pitched two complete games, given up two runs, and had a 1–1 record to show for it.

With Game Five possibly being the World Series clincher for the Indians, 86,288 filled the ballpark to see the only game of the Series that was a blowout. Boston, needing a win to stay alive, got two home runs from Elliott and one from Salkeld as the Braves pounded Feller and four other Cleveland pitchers in an 11–5 victory. Spahn was the winning pitcher. Fans got one treat they had been waiting for. Satchel Paige made an appearance in the seventh inning.

The Series moved back to Boston where Southworth handed the ball to Voiselle to keep the Braves' hopes alive. Billy always had confidence in Voiselle and always believed in showing confidence. With everything on the line, every other pitcher was available if needed. If Boston could get this one, Southworth would have Sain ready for Game Seven with everyone else once again available in the bullpen.

Boudreau sent Lemon to the hill for the Indians. Yet another pitchers' duel ensued. The score was tied, 1–1, in the sixth when Joe Gordon, the former Yankee, hit a two-run homer. Cleveland added another run in the eighth. The Braves rallied for two runs in the bottom of the eighth to chase Lemon. But Bearden came in, put out the fire, and set down the Braves in the ninth inning for a 4–3 Cleveland victory.

The Indians had captured the Series, four games to two. Three of the games were decided by one run, another was decided by two and still another by three. Symbolic of the Braves season was that Spahn and Sain were the two winning pitchers for Boston. Torgeson was the leading hitter with seven hits in 18 at-bats for a .389 average.

The Braves missed the power hitting of Heath, sidelined with the broken ankle. His injury occurred in the last week of the season, after the Braves had clinched the pennant, on a slide into home plate. Some questioned whether Heath should have even been playing or whether Southworth should have been resting his regulars for the World Series. Southworth said he preferred to play them and keep them sharp for the World Series.

The old adage of baseball being "a game of inches" was never more true than in the Series clincher for the Indians. In the eighth inning, with Cleveland leading, 4–1, Conatser, playing in place of the injured Heath, came to bat with the bases loaded. He hit a long drive to center field that Indians outfielder Thurman Tucker caught at the wall. A few inches higher and it would been a grand slam, putting the Braves up, 5–4. A few inches to the left or right of Tucker, it would have cleared the bases and tied the score.

While Southworth and Boston were disappointed in losing the World Series, there was good reason to believe the Braves had turned the corner and were about to be a powerhouse in the National League at the end of the decade, just as the Cardinals had been at the start of it.

16

From Better to Bitter

Just as there is often no clear-cut moment that can be pointed to when a team clicks, the same is true when a disconnect occurs. It is more likely a number of things, rather than a single event or incident, that catapults some to greatness and throws others overboard.

The Braves under Billy Southworth experienced both from 1948, the championship year with all the glory that came with it, to 1949, a year of near constant turmoil. In all his years in baseball, Southworth had never experienced anything like it, and the burden it brought took an exceedingly heavy toll.

The 1949 Braves unraveled quickly. Was it because the players felt Southworth was getting too much credit for their 1948 success? Was it because the Boston press was on a witch hunt? Was it jealousy or anger over the signing of an untried youngster for big bucks? Was it a couple of malcontents stirring things up? Was it Southworth's lingering grief over his lost son that brought back demons from the past in the disguise of beer after beer after beer?

The answer depends on who was asked, but the consensus was "all of the above." The first signs of possible trouble emerged in the middle of the pennant race in 1948 as the Braves tried to bolster their pitching staff and win their first National League championship in 34 years.

In June, they signed Johnny Antonelli, a brilliant 18-year-old lefthanded pitcher fresh out of high school for a bonus reported to be in excess of $50,000. In those days, ballclubs could entice talented youngsters to sign by offering them a bonus — in essence, upfront money. Players who received deals like this were referred to as "bonus babies." Antonelli's father was his son's top promoter. In modern baseball, he would have been considered an agent. He contacted major league teams by letter and by phone and in some cases succeeded in getting tryouts for his son.

His efforts paid off. When Antonelli signed with the Braves, he became one of the richest "bonus babies." One of the conditions for a team signing a "bonus baby" was that the player had to be added to the major league roster. So a kid fresh out of high school was thrown into the major league mix.

Antonelli fit well into the Southworth formula — a young player he could nurture on a team full of veteran pitchers from whom he could learn. Except for the money, it was not unlike taking an untried Johnny Beazley and turning him to a 20-game winner with the Cardinals in 1942. Antonelli represented a big investment but one that might have an immediate payoff in the pennant race and certainly would pay off in the future. Unlike Beazley, Antonelli's career was not likely to be interrupted by a world war.

But the signing did not sit well with many of the Braves. Here was a high school kid who had never thrown one pitch in professional baseball got more money just for signing than any of the other Braves players got for an entire season, including Elliott, the league's Most Valuable Player in 1947, and Sain, who perhaps was the best pitcher in the National League.

Sain, who at the time was on his way to his second straight 20-plus win season, was livid. Though Braves owner Lou Perini negotiated the signing, Sain was certain it couldn't have been done without Southworth's approval. Teammate Clint Conatser recalled, "It probably wasn't so but Johnny was disgusted that an unproven kid's salary was approximately four times his own." Sain complained so vehemently to management that he got a new contract with a pay raise. But he hardly spoke to Southworth after that.

The extent of Sain's bitterness is hard to measure. He said reports that he refused to speak with Southworth were exaggerated because he never fraternized with the manager. The manager was the boss, he was the employee and that was the nature of their relationship, he said.

But teammate Conatser told a different story. Sain was so incensed, he told Conatser he hoped the Braves didn't win the World Series. Conatser was shocked and asked him why. Sain said, "If we do, that little SOB will take all the credit for it." In telling the story years later, Conatser pointed out Sain shut out the Indians in the first game of the World Series and lost a 2–1 heartbreaker in his next start, so he did all he could to try to win it.[1]

Billy always had a great relationship with the press over the years and most members of the media treated him kindly. And the press unabashedly gave Southworth credit for the Braves' turnaround, often using disparaging words about his players.

In May 1949, *Look* magazine, one of the most popular periodicals in the country, read by millions of people, published a five-page feature story under the headline "Billy Southworth, Pennant Man." Writer Arthur Sampson wrote: "Southworth has shown he can win with any kind of material. With the Cardinals, he had the Swifties, the fast, powerful, never-let-up young fellows like Stan Musial, Country Slaughter, Whitey Kurowski. With the Braves, he has mainly discards. In St. Louis, he won with a hand-picked crew. He wanted to prove to the world — and to himself — he could win with a makeshift array."[2]

Though these were the opinions of one writer, they associated Southworth with words such as "discards" and "makeshift" in reference to his ballplayers.

And there was more.

Tommy Holmes, in his *Brooklyn Eagle* column: "Certainly that was not a great team of Braves in '48 and it took the old Southworth technique to hold it together. The verdict of most of us this spring: That the Braves were strictly a one-year proposition and couldn't repeat."[3]

Bob Considine in the *New York Journal-American*: "The '48 club was one of those dark horses which slip into a title now and then." In the same column, Considine wrote of the "run-of-the-mill Brave, if that isn't too redundant." The column ran under the headline "Billy's First Class Guy; Could Be Braves Ain't."[4]

Bill Corum, also in the *New York Journal-American*: "My feeling is that Billy exceeded what might have been normal expectations by winning the National League pennant last year. In other words, I don't think the Braves were a championship team and I don't think they are now."[5]

Time, the nation's most popular weekly news magazine: "Billy Southworth was quiet and thoughtful. The Boston press and Braves management were calling him the smartest manager in baseball; he had done wonders with a team of youngsters and temperamental cast-offs from other clubs."[6]

To the Braves players who actually performed on the field and won the championship, all of the hype afterwards must have seemed like "Southworth, Southworth, Southworth," and it grated on them.

Considine speculated that Billy drove his players more than they wanted to be driven. This wasn't like the old Cardinal "all for one, one for all" teams and those were the only kinds of teams Billy wanted or could even relate to.

Post-war baseball drew a different breed of ballplayer. Baseball historian and analyst Bill James wrote, "This change occurred because supervising the players became logistically complicated after the war. The cities became larger and the transportation around the cities became more convenient. Night baseball rendered the 11:30 curfew obsolete."[7]

James said another important factor was that the culture changed. The post-war ballplayers didn't want to be supervised 24 hours a day. Women still threw themselves at ballplayers like they did in the old days. Now, however, more players were taking them up on their offers. The change in attitude was profound. "The older generation of managers — McCarthy, Mack, Shotton, Southworth, Frisch — were pushed aside, in part, by this change."[8]

Two other factors were at work in the dismantling of a baseball team almost overnight, relatively speaking. One was that Southworth was drinking again. The other was a Boston sportswriter who began writing about dissention on the ball club, saying there was near mutiny against Southworth.

Some of the Braves thought all of the trades with the Cardinals were done in part so that Billy could surround himself with his old pals, as he called them, who would cover for him when things got tough. But there was a more tragic reason, in the view of some, for the recurrence of his drinking problem. Billy the Kid still grieved over the loss of his son. He tried to drown out his sorrow with baseball or just drown it, period, in beer. Four years after the fatal accident, when the Braves went to New York, Billy would sometimes return to the crash scene to be alone with his thoughts and his beer.

Billy's drinking, and the effect it had on his team, is substantiated by several of his players. Conatser roomed with Torgeson and told of the time in spring training 1949 when Torgeson left his hotel room one night to go night-clubbing. Southworth called their room and asked where Torgy was. Conatser said he didn't know. Billy slammed the phone down and began calling other rooms in the hotel in search of Torgeson. Conatser knew which nightclub Torgeson was frequenting. He called him and told him he better get back because Billy had been drinking and was on the warpath.[9]

Sain said players have a tendency to second-guess whoever the manager is. He said he resented Southworth bringing over Beazley, White and Mort Cooper from St. Louis. "They had pitched for him in St. Louis on those pennant-winning teams," he said. "They were his friends and he wanted them to hang around when he was doing too much drinking. Billy's drinking began when his son crashed his plane.... Billy would go out to that airport and just sit for hours. It was sad."[10]

While Billy tried to weather many storms, another nemesis emerged in the form of Dave Egan, a *Boston Record* sportswriter, who had a well-earned reputation for his blistering criticism of people or circumstances he didn't like, notably Ted Williams of the Red Sox. But there were others. In 1943, when then-Braves manager Casey Stengel was hit by a taxi cab and hospitalized just before opening day, Egan wrote, "The man who did the most for baseball in Boston in 1943 was the motorist who ran Casey Stengel down two days before the opening game and kept him away from the Braves for two months."[11]

In the heart of the 1948 pennant races, when both Boston teams were contenders, Egan wrote that Warren Spahn was the only Brave who would be a first-stringer with the Red Sox.[12]

On April 8, 1949, Egan wrote about dissention in the Braves spring training camp. Among the things he claimed: Southworth and Sain were not speaking to each other; Spahn wanted to be traded; outfielder Jimmy Russell was fined for breaking curfew; clubhouse attendant Doc Young was fired; there was a near fist fight between Southworth and a local radio announcer; and that Southworth was taking too much credit for the Braves winning the 1948 pennant.

The column was a bombshell whose shrapnel flew all over the baseball world. Egan's writings were widely read in New England and this particular column was quoted or referred to on sports pages throughout the country.[13]

Perini, Southworth and even some Braves players either refuted Egan's allegations or did their best to downplay them. Egan had mentioned the players held a private meeting to discuss their problems. Southworth said it was a team meeting and he was there. Conatser said he never attended a private meeting among the players and, if there was one, he would have known about it because he roomed with Tommy Holmes, the team captain. Doc Young, the equipment manager, wasn't fired.

The story seemed to follow the Braves as they traveled from one city to another, with writers on the lookout for anything that even looked like trouble among the troops. An unwritten rule in baseball is that what happens in the clubhouse stays in the clubhouse — and that made it difficult for players to contradict allegations, because in doing so they'd be referring to things that happened in the clubhouse. It was a difficult time for Southworth who knew he certainly wasn't in St. Louis anymore.[14]

When the season started, the Braves started slowly — nothing new for a Southworth-managed team. Though they were just 7–5 at the end of April, that was good for a share of first place in a bunched up National League that saw last-place Philadelphia just 2½ games out of the lead. Boston won 16 out of 28 games in May which allowed them to stay tied for first place. Boston fans were wondering: Despite all the controversy, could Southworth put together another miracle?

On July 23, the Braves lost a tough one to the Pirates who won the game in the ninth inning. Spahn had gone the distance for Boston. Twice during the game, after Spahn had singled, Stanky, who was coaching third base for Southworth, signaled a hit-and-run. Both times, the batter fouled off a pitch and both times Spahn ran, slid into second and had to retreat back to first.

After the game, there was talk that all the running had tired Spahn out. Southworth said Stanky was on his own calling for the hit-and-runs and Stanky didn't deny it. Reports in the press had two sharp edges. One was the notion that Southworth put the blame on Stanky instead sticking up for him; the other was that Stanky accepted the responsibility because he didn't like Southworth and this was a way of showing him up.

Both Stanky and Alvin Dark, Billy's double play combination at second and short, had become disenchanted with Billy. Both were in their second year with the Braves, Stanky coming over when the Dodgers decided to move Jackie Robinson to second base, and Dark coming up from the minors to win the Rookie of the Year award.

In his autobiography, Dark recalled what it was like playing for Billy. "Southworth was a mild little man who won pennants with the wartime Cardinals by exercising a lot of patience and just letting the Cardinals play. He wanted everybody to like him. His idea of strategy was to avoid getting the other team angry. He'd say things like, 'C'mon boys, just relax.'"[15]

Sometimes, the growing disrespect took the form of mockery and insubordination. One day, Stanky struck out and came back to the dugout and kicked an ice bucket in disgust. The next day, prior to the game, Southworth talked to his players and told them not to get mad when they made an out but to just have the attitude of "I'll get 'em next time." That day, after Stanky hit a pop fly that was easily caught, he returned to the dugout and, in front of everybody, began shouting, "I made an out. I made an out. Oh, goodie, I made an out. Whoopie. Hooray."[16]

On August 7 in Chicago, Jim Russell and Earl Torgeson got into a fight that resulted in Russell having two black eyes and Torgeson having a broken thumb. There were various accounts as to how it happened and Southworth did his best to downplay it. But it was another incident of unrest on the ballclub and a manager that was apparently having trouble controlling it.

Perini and other Braves executives had defended Billy all year and were of course aware that they had signed him to a multi-year contract that had over a year remaining. But something had to be done. On August 16, Southworth was given a "leave of absence" for the rest of the season due to illness. Most observers believed he was on the verge of a nervous breakdown. Coach Johnny Cooney took over the club. Billy went home to Ohio to rest. Many believed he would not be back.

Tommy Holmes — the sportswriter, not the ballplayer — summed up Billy's situation this way: "Countless rumors never confirmed or denied; a report the skipper had lapsed into his old habits; stories of cliques battling each other; 16 versions of the fight between Russell and Torgeson; roaring recriminations and yowls leveled at the manager. Lou Perini said Billy the Kid needed a rest. I shouldn't wonder."[17]

Not surprisingly, the Braves began a nosedive in the National League standings, spurred by a stretch in September when they lost 13 out of 14 games. When the long 1949 season finally ended in the first week of October, their fall from grace in the space of a year was official. The Braves were 75–79, in fourth place, 22 games behind the first-place Dodgers.

At home in Sunbury, Ohio, Southworth did his best to try to relax and get well. He had his family, his fishing pole and his hunting gear to keep him content. But events he could not control continued to intervene. On November 29, Billy got a phone call that stunned him. His lifelong friend, Bob Hooey, sports editor of the *Ohio State Journal* in Columbus, had been seriously hurt in an auto accident in Columbus. Billy and Hooey's wife Gladys were at his bedside when Hooey died the next day from his injuries.

Billy went to the cemetery and made arrangements for Hooey's burial. "It was the only thing I could do for my best friend," he told a reporter. In truth, he had now lost his two best friends, his son in a plane crash, his buddy in a car crash, in the space of four years. And once again there was profound grief.[18]

In the baseball world, his personal tragedies aside, the press and the public wondered if the Braves brass would bring Southworth back from his leave of absence to once again manage the team. That question was partially answered on December 14 when Dark and Stanky, who were thought to be the instigators of a lot of the trouble, were traded to the New York Giants. That provided an answer to the rest of the Braves team, who had voted earlier not to include Southworth in the team's share of World Series money for finishing fourth. In those days, the first four teams in the league got a piece of the World Series pie. In the case of the Braves, eliminating their manager from their share of the take gained each player about $5 each. They didn't get it, though. Baseball commissioner A.B. "Happy" Chandler overruled them and Billy got his share.

The animosity that some players had toward Southworth resulted in some exaggerated, and, in some cases, false accusations about him that lingered for years. Antonelli, the bonus baby for whom Southworth had high hopes, stated publicly after his career was over that Billy had treated him unfairly.

Antonelli said when he was 19 years old, he pitched a shutout against the Cubs. He said Dutch Leonard, who was more than twice Antonelli's age, was the losing pitcher. Antonelli said, "The next time Billy Southworth let me touch the ball, even in relief, was six weeks later. What kind of judgment was that on the part of a seasoned manager? Southworth was protecting his job."[19]

What actually happened is Antonelli beat Leonard, 2–0, on June 12, 1949. But contrary to Antonelli's account of not touching the ball for six weeks, his next start was June 19 when the Braves beat Cincinnati, 3–2. Five days later, he was the losing pitcher in an 8–4 loss to St. Louis. He didn't start again until July 17 and, including that start, lost four consecutive decisions. It was at that point he was removed from the starting rotation.[20]

Southworth declared himself fit and returned to manage the Braves in 1950 and got great pitching from Sain, Spahn and Bickford. They combined for 59 wins. But the rest of the staff won only 24 and the Braves finished at 83–71, in fourth place, eight games behind Philadelphia's surprising Whiz Kids.

It was during that season that yet another tragedy occurred, not directly to the Southworth family but one in which Billy felt compelled to get involved in. Old ballplayers were able to keep track of other former players over the years through word-of-mouth, newsletters and other communiqués. Billy was aware that an old teammate of his on the Cardinals, Wattie Holm, had fallen on hard times.

Wattie, whose real name was Roscoe, lived in Iowa with his wife and two children and had experienced a series of business failures. He and Southworth were not close. They had not stayed in touch over the years; nonetheless, Billy had heard about his old teammate's troubles.

On the morning of Friday, May 19, 1950, Holm shot and killed his wife, Ella, seriously wounded his 14-year-old daughter, Margaret, and then turned the gun on himself with a fatal blast to the head. The Holms' other child, Robert, 20, was away at school. Southworth learned of the situation and felt he needed to do something. With the permission of Holm's relatives, including son Robert, Billy made arrangements for Margaret to come live with the Southworths as soon as she recovered from her wounds.

Carole Southworth Watson does not know what motivated her father to get so personally involved. Perhaps, being no stranger to tragedy in his own life, he saw it as an opportunity where he could do something to salvage a young life. Margaret Holm lived with the Southworths for a year and half until Robert was out of school and secure enough to bring his sister home to Iowa.[21]

Meanwhile, on the ballfield, Billy fielded a team and tried to improve on the record of 1950. But in June 1951, with the Braves floundering and the fire gone from the belly of their manager, Billy resigned, saying it was time for someone else to take the reins. That someone turned out to be Billy's star outfielder Tommy Holmes, who was in his first year as a minor league manager.

Once again, Billy went home to Sunbury, but this time never again to manage.

Bill Corum, the wise and witty sports columnist for the *New York Journal-American*, summed up the ups and downs of a baseball manager after Billy took his leave of absence in 1949: "Southworth took the bows in '48, some say too personally and too emphatically. So now I suppose it is only fair that he should take the bow-wows."[22]

◆ 17 ◆

The Transition Years

Billy Southworth would have preferred to go out on top, where he spent most of his managerial career. Instead, he went home to Sunbury, Ohio, where he was a celebrity in the quiet community of 800.

But he was also "Billy" or "Mr. Southworth," the nice man with the big house on the hill. He would jump at the chance to get back into baseball, because that had been his life for 40 years, but in the meantime he was content to go hunting and spend time with his family. When an occasional writer stopped by to try to chat with him, if he didn't want to talk to him, Billy would grab his hunting gear and head out the back door.[1]

His life in baseball was a matter of record now—11 seasons as a minor league manager with six of his teams finishing first, three finishing second; 13 seasons as a major league manager with his teams winning four National League championships, two World Series championships, winning more than 100 games three years in a row, never finishing below fourth place, and having the fifth best winning percentage (.597) in baseball history.

With the exception of Stan Musial, his teams did not produce players with great individual statistics because of Billy's iron-clad resolve to play percentages and therefore platoon players, resulting in them having fewer game appearances. It didn't matter to the Cardinals. It mattered to the Braves.

Statistics show the kind of baseball Southworth's teams played. He bunted more than any other manager in his era or any manager since then. His teams led the league in bunts six times, including all three years when they won more than 100 games. Southworth's teams led the league in hits six times; complete games six times; shutouts five times; batting average five times; doubles five times; slugging percentage four times; pitchers leading the league in strikeouts four times; and in earned run average four times. His teams were fundamentally sound. In 11 years, no Southworth team ever led the league in errors or walks allowed.[2]

Leading the league in doubles five times is a significant statistic because it is an indication of hustle, of players taking the wide turn at first after a base hit and seizing the opportunity to take the extra base. It is a symbol of Southworth baseball dating back to the days when he was a young minor league manager teaching Enos Slaughter to run on his toes, not on his heels. (Slaughter hit 413 doubles in his career.)

All that was behind him now. In Sunbury, he still lived in the home he began building in 1941, on the banks of Walnut Creek, made from stones he

Billy's first love was baseball but, when he wasn't on the ballfield, he loved to go hunting. Here he is posed with rifle in hand (courtesy Southworth family).

hauled from the creek. Billy bought a horse-drawn dump wagon and hauled 104 loads of stone from the creek to the home site. The home was framed with 2 × 6, 2 × 10 and 2 × 12 pieces of lumber — not a single 2 × 4.

"An architect drew up plans, a carpenter from Johnston helped, and in the off season my father did as much building as anyone else, and the place just got bigger and bigger," said his daughter, Carole.[3]

Billy still had the same demons that plagued him during his managerial career. He still liked his beer and deep inside, he still mourned the loss of Billy Jr. Not surprisingly, every once in a while, whether he was around the house, watching Ohio State football, or on one of his hunting expeditions, he would come across something that would remind him of his son and it would just be crushing.

"It was so difficult. My father was so stoic. He carried on but you could tell when Billy Jr. died, dad just died inside," said Carole.[4]

Youngsters who grew up in Sunbury remember the fun they had in the wintertime when they took their sleds and toboggans, trudged to the top of "Mr. Southworth's Hill," and slid all the way down the snow-packed slope. Billy and Mabel often invited the children into their kitchen for cookies and hot chocolate or just to get warm. Sometimes Billy would give them a ride in his horse-drawn sleigh. When prodded, he would tell them a baseball story or two, like the one about the time long ago when he hit a home run through a knothole in a fence in Columbus.

In 1948, when Cleveland won the American League championship, most of Ohio was rooting for the Indians in the World Series — but not the people of Sunbury. They were ecstatic about Mr. Southworth and his champion Braves. Schools were dismissed early so the kids and their parents could go to the Sunbury High School gym and listen to radio broadcasts of the games.[5]

Sunbury provided a good life for Billy. It had a grocery store, a gas station, a barber shop, places to hunt. He liked the people and the people liked him. But he still had the desire to get back into baseball so when the Braves asked him to be a scout for them in the Midwest, he gladly accepted. He would be on the road watching young ballplayers in small towns but he wouldn't have the grinding schedule he once had.

It wasn't long before Billy found a youngster he thought would some day make a name for himself in the big leagues. He was a shortstop at Eau Claire, Wisconsin, in the Class C Northern League — a long way from the bigs — and he was only 18 years old. But Billy saw a bright future for this kid whose name was Henry Aaron:

Aaron has all the qualifications of a major league shortstop. He runs better than average so I would have to call him fast but not very fast.

On the latest official Northern League batting averages, Aaron is hitting .345. He is a line drive hitter although he has hit a couple of balls out of the park for home runs. He has good hands, also quick hands, gets the ball away fast and accurately. He gets a good jump on the ball and can range far to right or left. I saw him go deep in the hole to his right and field a slow-hit ball. He came up throwing and virtually shot his man out at first base. This was a big league play in my book because I did not think he had a chance to retire the man at first. He has a strong arm. Aaron started two double plays and completed one from the pivot position. Aaron throws a lot like Maranville, not over handed but side-arm. His arm is strong and he does not have to straighten up to throw.

Aaron told me he turned 18 years of age last February. Consequently, I like his chances of becoming a major league player far more than I do either Gene Baker, shortstop of Los Angeles or James Pendleton of Montreal, first because of the difference in ages; then, too, I think he has better hands than either Baker or Pendleton. He has proven his ability in the short time he has been here.

Baker and Pendleton are faster men but this boy will outplay them in all departments of the game when he has more experience. Second game — On Aaron's first trip to the plate, he hit a long home run over the left-center fence. He collected three hits for the evening and had three RBIs. He had four chances with one error. Oh, yes, he also had one stolen base.

For a baby-faced kid of 18, his playing ability is outstanding. I will see the remaining game tonight but will send in this report now because regardless of what happens tonight, it will not change my mind in the least about this boy's ability. Please don't get the impression from what I have said above that Aaron isn't a good runner, because he is fast and his running will continue to improve for the next couple of years.[6]

This was high praise from a seasoned old manager for a teenage kid but, two years later, that kid was in the major leagues as an outfielder, leading the Braves to the National League championship in 1957 and 1958 and a World Series championship in 1957. He went on to be the all-time home run king with 755 until the record was broken by Barry Bonds.

On November 6, 1956, Quinn announced that the Braves, who had been playing in Milwaukee for the past three years, were revamping their scouting setup and that Southworth would no longer be needed. He would be used in an advisory capacity the following spring at the Braves minor league training camp in Waycross, Georgia.

Tommie Ferguson, once a bat boy and now, as an adult, one of the Braves' attendants, ran into Billy in the spring of 1957 at the Waycross camp and was shocked by the accommodations the Braves had provided for him. He was holed up in a little motel room next to a prison where sirens went off periodically and a rotating search light flashed a beam through his window every so often.

Ferguson was appalled. He told Billy he had been the best major league manager of his day — four pennants, two World Series championships — and brought a championship to the Braves for the first time in 34 years. Looking around the tiny room Ferguson said, "Is this the best they could do for you?" Southworth replied, "Tommie, remember one thing. If you are a big leaguer, you are a big leaguer under any conditions."[7]

When Billy's work at Waycross was done, he returned to his beloved Sunbury. He hadn't smoked in years but in his days managing the Cardinals he was a pack-a-day man and was even featured in magazine ads promoting Camel cigarettes. And while the death of his son had triggered the demon that drove him to drink, it was the birth of a granddaughter that got him to quit. One morning in Sunbury, Billy had been upstairs. Daughter Carole and baby Cheryl were downstairs. He came downstairs, looked lovingly at his granddaughter and said, "this is ridiculous" and he never drank again.[8]

But the years of heavy smoking had taken its toll and Southworth suffered from emphysema, a condition that would get steadily worse.

In August 1969, the Cardinals had the chance to do what Billy the Kid's Redbirds had done nearly 30 years earlier — win three consecutive National League championships. They would have to fight off the Cubs and the Mets, two surprisingly good teams considering their recent past. But with future Hall of Famers Bob Gibson, Lou Brock and Steve Carlton and a team with the experience of two successful stretch drives, anything was possible. Aside from having three future Hall of Famers, something Billy never had, the '69 Cardinals were much like Southworth's teams in the 1940s — fast, fundamentally sound and strong up the middle with Tim McCarver behind the plate, Gibson and Carlton leading a strong pitching staff, Dal Maxvill and Julian Javier at short and second and speedy Curt Flood in center field.

Neal Russo, longtime sportswriter for the *St. Louis Post-Dispatch*, decided to pay a visit to Billy to get his take on the pennant race. To his surprise, the old manager said winning two championships in a row could actually be a hindrance to winning a third one. "It's always harder to win the second time than it is the first and it's even harder to win the third time than it is the second," Billy said. "A club that has won two straight pennants sometimes forgets how it won. It's not a matter of complacency. A club that has won two championships has to remember to still work hard."

As he talked, it was easy for the listener to imagine him on the field 25 years earlier, motivating his players, encouraging them and warning them not to fall into bad habits. He said players need to be constantly observing and thinking — watching the opposing pitcher to see which pitch he's getting over the plate and which he isn't; they should be alert in the field, know the tendencies of the player at bat and position themselves accordingly; and, as base runners, know which pitchers are slow to get to the plate and which catchers have the good arms and the ones who don't.

Those are the kinds of things that good teams pay attention to when they're hungry for a pennant and the kinds of things that can drift away from the mental attitude if a team is not careful, he said.

Another factor that makes it difficult for a team to win three championships in a row is what happens in the offseason that can affect players mentally and physically. When you've won a pennant, you are the toast of the town, he said. You are invited to a lot of dinners and you are told so often how good you are that a feeling of invincibility can set in.

He recalled warning his 1944 ballclub in spring training about how hard they were going to have to work if they were to win a third straight championship. "I tried to impress upon them they were farther out of condition, both physically and mentally, especially mentally, because they had all been invited here and there to speak. They had been put on a pedestal. They had been wined and dined," he said.

Southworth said yet another difficulty in winning three straight championships is that everyone else in the league is gunning for you. The other contending teams want to dethrone you, he said, and the lesser teams take great pride in being "spoilers"— knocking you out of the pennant race if they can by beating you in key games down the stretch.

Southworth had always been as concerned with the mental part of the game as the physical part and he talked about one year when his ballclub eased up too much — and it was his fault. "I remember one year (1943) when we built up a huge lead and I asked the players if they wanted to try for a record — winning the pennant by the biggest margin or the earliest clincher — or be rested," he said. "They left it up to me and I decided to rest them. I'd never do that again." He said the ballclub involuntarily let down and lost its momentum and he thinks it was a factor in losing the World Series to the New York Yankees.[9]

As it turned out, the 1969 Cardinals did not win a third straight championship, finishing fourth behind New York, Chicago and Pittsburgh.

Southworth was relaxed during the interview but he admitted his health was failing and that his baseball watching was pretty much confined to sitting in front of the color television set in his living room.

Three months later, his emphysema took a turn for the worse. On Friday, November 14, 1969, he was admitted to Riverside Hospital in Columbus where he died the next day with his family at his side. In the closing moments of his life, he squeezed the hand of his daughter Carole and whispered words that Billy had used all of his life to convey his love and respect. "We're pals, aren't we," he said.[10]

◆ 18 ◆

A Final Tribute

Like all of mankind, Billy Southworth was the human equation of the whole being equal to the sum of its parts. He was the son of a blacksmith who quoted Longfellow; a man who met his first wife when they sang duets together in a church choir; someone whose skills brought him great success as a baseball player and manager.

But he was also a man who had a fondness for drinking that intruded not once but twice on the great skills he possessed as a manager; and a man who suffered the loss of three of his four children and whose love of the game of baseball was perhaps topped only by the devotion he had for his only son, Billy Jr., taken away from him tragically and abruptly in a plane crash. It awakened a demon inside him that he had successfully pushed aside many years before.

With all of the accomplishments of a lifetime in baseball, a batting average of .297, playing in two World Series, managing teams that won more than 100 games three years in a row, managing teams that won four league championships and two World Series championships and having the fifth best winning percentage all-time for a manager at .597 — like any parent, he would have traded in all of that to have his son back. Billy's second marriage provided him with a stable home life he cherished and produced a daughter who was the apple of her father's eye and gained his ultimate distinction that he reminded her of on his death bed — that they were "pals."

Elayne Savage, a psychotherapist and motivational speaker from Berkeley, California, had an experience 10 years after Billy Jr.'s death that was similar in personal impact and she was able to identify the personal trauma and give it a name. In Savage's case, her mother and grandmother were killed in a plane crash in 1955 when she was a little girl and she spent many years trying to get over it but just couldn't shake it.

In her case, she did not continually return to the scene of the crash as Billy reportedly did. Instead, she spent many years of her adult life searching for the exact type of small plane that her mother and grandmother had been on. When she found it at a small airport, there were no passengers aboard yet so she was allowed to get inside. She knew her mother's row and seat number from 50 years earlier. She sat in it and meditated for a few minutes and then left quietly. It was closure, something she waited almost all her adult life to experience. Billy Southworth had no such experience and it left a void.

As a professional therapist, Savage wrote about her own quest for closure and called it "My Mother's Plane Keeps Crashing." In Billy Southworth's world, it is likely his son's plane kept crashing and, like Savage, it haunted him.[1]

Southworth got one vote for the Baseball Hall of Fame in 1945 and again in 1946, probably from his friend Bob Hooey of the *Ohio State Journal* in Columbus. He didn't get any votes in 1947 or 1948 and received seven in 1949, the year after his Braves played in the World Series.

In 1950, he got one vote — and it wasn't from Hooey, who died in a car accident the year before. He got four votes in 1951, shortly after he retired, one in 1952 and two in 1953. He didn't get a single vote again until 1958 when, inexplicably, he got 18. But with a requirement of 75 percent approval for induction, he was never a serious contender.

As time went by, the only possibility for the man with the fifth highest winning percentage in baseball history to get into the Hall of Fame was through the grace of the Veterans Committee, a task made more difficult because of the ever-changing makeup of the group and rules to which it was to abide by.

The Veterans Committee had its roots in 1939 when Commissioner Landis established an Old-Timers Committee to consider induction of players who played prior to 1900. In 1955, in the first of many shifts the committee would take over the years, a new format evolved in which the committee of 11 members would meet every two years — the odd-numbered years — and elect two players each time. In 1962, they made yet another change, deciding to meet every year with the requirement of electing at least two players.

In the 1970s, the Veterans Committee was accused of cronyism because among its 11 members was the outspoken old ballplayer and manager Frankie Frisch as well as J. Roy Stockton and Fred Lieb, two friends of Frisch who had covered him as a player and manager for many years. During that time period, five of Frisch's teammates were voted in by the committee.

In 1978, the makeup of the committee was changed. Instead of 11 members, it would have 15 — five Hall of Famers, five owners or executives and five sportswriters. They would meet every year to make their selections.

The next change came in 1995 when there was an effort made to give deserved recognition to players in the old Negro Leagues who never had a chance to make it to the major leagues. The new rules allowed the committee to elect at least one Negro League player, at least one player from the 19th century and two 20th century old-timers.

The most sweeping change of all occurred in 2001 when the 15-member committee was eliminated and replaced by a system in which all living Hall of Fame members as well as writers and broadcasters who had been elected to their respective wings, would do the voting. The election would be every two years. Because of the size of the "committee," the voting would be done by mail rather than having a meeting. One other change was that non-players — managers, coaches, umpires and executives — could only be considered every four years.

The outcome was predictable. With more than 200 people voting, and by mail with no discussion, none of those eligible got the required 75 percent of the vote in three straight elections — in 2003, 2005 and 2007.

In 2003, Southworth's name was not included on the ballot listing managers who, by virtue of being on the ballot, had Hall of Fame credentials. The omission incensed Raymond Mileur, an Illinois author and creator of "The Birdhouse," a fan-based St. Louis Cardinal website. He urged his legions of readers to email the Hall of Fame to register their protest that Southworth wasn't on the ballot.

"I was shocked, perhaps even outraged," said Mileur. "It was bad enough Billy had not been elected to the Hall of Fame, but to not even have his name on the ballot was more than I was willing to tolerate."[2]

Mileur said his one-man campaign included phone calls to the Hall of Fame, articles written, com-

Ray Mileur, a fan who had a website devoted to the Cardinals, spearheaded an effort to get Southworth elected to the Hall of Fame and was invited by the Southworth family to represent them at the ceremonies (courtesy Ray Mileur).

ments made on radio shows, lobbying of sportswriters and appeals on his "Birdhouse" website for fans to express their displeasure.

The outpouring from fans was so great the Hall of Fame felt compelled to respond through a letter to "The Birdhouse": "Certainly there are many worthy candidates among the 60 managers, umpires and executives that were considered for the final players' ballot by the Baseball Writers of America Screening Committee, a group completely independent of the National Baseball Hall of Fame and Museum. This screening committee of 60, consisting of two writers from each city with one team and two writers from each region with two teams, pared down the list to the 15 candidates that each individual felt to be most deserving. Though Billy Southworth is not eligible for consideration by the Hall of Fame Committee on Baseball Veterans in 2003, he will be again in 2007 when the process is repeated and every four years thereafter."[3]

In 2007, yet another set of changes took effect on the Veterans Committee. A 16-member panel would do the voting — in person rather than by mail — after receiving input from all living Hall of Fame members. It was also decided that managers, owners and umpires would be eligible every two years, instead of every four, beginning in 2008. The voting took place on December 3, 2007, for induction in 2008. And Billy Southworth's name was on the ballot.

As always, potential inductees needed 75 percent approval. Billy the Kid got 13 of 16 votes for 81.3 percent. He was in.

So was Dick Williams, manager of the great Oakland A's teams, who also got 81.3 percent. Among executives, former Pirate owner Barney Dreyfuss, former Dodger owner Walter O'Malley and former commissioner Bowie Kuhn were selected. Rich "Goose" Gossage, a fireballing relief pitcher for two decades, was elected in the regular balloting for eligible players.

Mileur doesn't want to take any credit for Southworth getting in but he thinks it might be the first time anyone was elected to the Hall of Fame after being taken off the ballot "or left off by administrative error or just gross incompetence."[4]

On the afternoon of December 3, 2007, Carole Southworth Watson received a phone call at her Sunbury, Ohio, home informing her that her father had been elected to the Hall of Fame. "My gracious, I was thrilled," she said. "The whole town of Sunbury went wild. They wanted to put up signs saying this was Billy Southworth's town but I asked them not to because I thought the next thing would be people coming and hanging around the house."

She had no doubt that the efforts of Mileur, a man whom she didn't know and had never met, were the reason Billy finally got in. "Ray just kept beating the drum, beating the drum, beating the drum," she said.[5]

The induction ceremony was in Cooperstown, New York, on July 27, 2008, but that presented a problem for Carole. She had organized a reunion of family and friends on that day in Asheville, North Carolina, where she was born when her father was managing there. It was a commitment she felt she could not break. Since Mileur had been instrumental in getting her father inducted, she asked him to go to the ceremonies and accept the honor on behalf of the Southworth family.

Mileur, who was not a Southworth and was not connected with major league baseball except for being a rabid fan, was honored and humbled to be asked — but he was afraid of trampling on Hall of Fame protocol. Hall officials wanted Cardinals president Bill DeWitt, Jr., to accept the award.

"As time drew close to the ceremony, Carole and the family insisted they wanted me to accept the award," said Mileur. "My position was somewhat difficult. I didn't want anything, like a debate about who was going to accept the award, to take away or distract from Billy Southworth's day at Cooperstown. It was not about Ray Mileur's very minor role in getting him elected, it was about Billy Southworth belonging there."[6]

As it worked out, DeWitt accepted the award with Mileur there representing the family. It was fitting that 60 years after winning his last National League championship and 38 years after his death, his family and friends did a little "platooning" at Billy's induction ceremony.

As DeWitt took the podium to accept Southworth's plaque, among the 56 Hall of Famers seated behind him were Red Schoendienst and Stan Musial, who played for him; and Lou Brock, Bob Gibson, Ozzie Smith and Dennis Eckersley, all Hall of Famers from a more recent era.

The memories flowed. "We had some great clubs with him as our manager," said Musial. "And he was a very good manager. We were all young but he treated everybody fairly."

Schoendienst's first year in the majors, 1945, was Southworth's last year with the Cardinals. Schoendienst recalled that Billy also made good use of players in the waning years of their careers. "I liked Billy. He was a good man. But if you missed a sign, he'd grab you right now," he said. Schoendienst said by 1945 Terry Moore was one of the "older guys" and was Southworth's team captain.

Whitey Herzog, another successful Cardinal manager and a future Hall of Famer, said he remembered Southworth from his high school days — and in that era, the 1940s, most managers had a dual role because they also coached third base.

Inductee Dick Williams won pennants with three different ball clubs — the Boston Red Sox, the San Diego Padres and, most famously, the Oakland A's of the early 1970s. Williams grew up in the St. Louis era and recalled how he had used one of Billy's trick plays in the 1972 World Series.

With Johnny Bench, the Cincinnati Reds great catcher, at bat, Gene Tenace, the Oakland catcher, held out his glove well beyond the strike zone as if to indicate an intentional walk. Bench relaxed momentarily and the pitcher fired a strike. It was one way of getting ahead on a tough hitter.

During his acceptance speech, Williams, a hard-nosed player and manager, said he was afraid he would get choked up and not be able to speak. He told the crowd that Hall of Famer Tony Gwynn, who played for Williams at San Diego, told him to avoid looking at his family and instead pick out a tree and talk to the tree. Williams said he would take that advice but "I just hope it's not a weeping willow."[7]

Gossage, the only modern-era player inducted, acknowledged the friendships he had with players now deceased, including Catfish Hunter and Thurmon Munson, and said he was proud to wear a New York Yankees cap on induction day. He concluded by saying, "My career was like a kid getting on his favorite ride at Disney World and not getting off for 22 years. Thanks for sharing the ride with me, you guys. It's been amazing."[8]

DeWitt was brief but succinct in accepting Southworth's plaque on behalf of the Cardinals and Billy's family. "We're all proud of Billy Southworth and his election to the Hall of Fame," he said. "He was a humble and private man who taught his children that humbleness is greatness. He was a winner in every sense."[9]

Had Billy been there to accept his plaque in person, he might have smiled and reminded the crowd that in 1944, when his Cardinals won their third straight pennant, in the World Series that year they beat the St. Louis Browns — owned by DeWitt's father, Bill DeWitt, Sr. And he might have told stories about his own father who taught him his work ethic and his brothers who taught him how to play ball and his days as a bellhop, a railroad shop worker and a hash slinger in a greasy-spoon restaurant, but always chasing a dream.

And he might have told them stories about his dealings with young ballplayers such as the time when Don Padgett asked him why he was riding the bench when he was hitting .400. "Because you're fielding .399," Southworth told him. Or he might have let them in on his speech to his players before the third game of the 1944 World Series. "Gentlemen, swinging the bat is a great exercise," he told them. "It strengthens the diaphram and loosens up pent-up emotions in your chest. And — you might hit the ball."[10]

He might have even worked in a story or two about Casey Stengel, whose playing career was entwined so closely with Billy's and whose success as a manager in the 1950s with the Yankees was much like Southworth's success with the Cardinals a decade earlier.

Billy's induction into the Baseball Hall of Fame, though a long time in coming in the view of his supporters, was carried out with the grace, dignity and forthrightness that were hallmarks of his managerial career, once described as "making sure everyone knows who's running the team without getting obnoxious about it."[11]

Appendices

A: Career Statistics

William Harold Southworth

Born: March 9, 1893, Harvard, Nebraska; Died: November 15, 1969, Columbus, Oho. 5 feet, 9 inches, 170 pounds; bats left, throws right. Inducted into the Baseball Hall of Fame, 2008

Playing Career

Year	Team	AB	R	H	D	T	HR	RBI	AVE
1913	Cleveland	1	0	0	0	0	0	0	.000
1915	Cleveland	177	25	39	2	5	0	8	.220
1918	Pittsburgh	246	37	84	5	7	2	43	.341
1919	Pittsburgh	453	56	127	14	14	4	61	.280
1920	Pittsburgh	546	64	155	17	13	2	53	.284
1921	Boston	569	86	175	25	15	7	79	.308
1922	Boston	158	27	51	4	4	4	18	.323
1923	Boston	611	95	195	29	16	6	78	.319
1924	New York	281	40	72	13	0	3	36	.256
1925	New York	473	79	138	19	5	6	44	.292
1926	NY-StL	507	99	162	28	7	16	99	.320
1927	St. Louis	306	52	92	15	5	2	39	.301
1929	St. Louis	32	1	6	2	0	0	3	.188
Lifetime Totals		4359	661	1296	173	91	52	561	.297

Transactions

February 23, 1921: Traded with Fred Nicholson, Walter Barbare and $15,000 from Pittsburgh to Boston for Rabbit Maranville.

November 12, 1923: Traded with Joe Oeschger from Boston to New York for Casey Stengel, Dave Bancroft and Bill Cunningham.

June 14, 1926: Traded from New York to St. Louis for Heinie Mueller.

World Series

Year	Team	AB	R	H	D	T	HR	RBI	AVE
1924	New York	1	1	0	0	0	0	0	.000
1926	St. Louis	29	6	10	1	1	1	4	.345
Lifetime Totals		30	7	10	1	1	1	4	.333

Minor League Managing

Year	Team	Record	Finish
1928	Rochester	90–74	First
1929	Rochester	43–23	First (Partial)
1930	Rochester	105–62	First
1931	Rochester	101–67	First
1932	Rochester	43–45	(Partial)
	Columbus	42–25	Second (Partial)
1935	Asheville	75–62	First
1936	Asheville	29–59	(Partial)
	Memphis	21–35	Eighth (Partial)
1937	Memphis	88–64	Second
1938	Memphis	77–75	Fourth
1939	Rochester	84–67	Second
1940	Rochester	31–13	First (Partial)

Major League Managing

Year	Team	Record	Finish
1929	St. Louis	43–45	(Partial)
1940	St. Louis	69–40	Third (Partial)
1941	St. Louis	97–56	Second
1942	St. Louis	106–48	First
1943	St. Louis	105–49	First
1944	St. Louis	105–49	First
1945	St. Louis	95–59	Second
1946	Boston	81–72	Fourth
1947	Boston	86–68	Third
1948	Boston	91–62	First
1949	Boston	55–54	(Partial)
1950	Boston	83–71	Fourth
1951	Boston	28–31	(Partial)
Totals		1044–704	.597 winning percentage

World Series

Year	Team	Record
1942	St. Louis	4–1
1943	St. Louis	1–4
1944	St. Louis	4–2
1948	Boston	2–4
Lifetime Record		11–11

Honors

National League Manager of the Year, 1941, 1942
International League Hall of Fame, 1947
Alabama Sports Hall of Fame, 1988
National Baseball Hall of Fame, 2008

B: War Years Managers

All major league managers faced the same challenges during the war years — having to compete with teams depleted by ballplayers going off to war and being replaced with players much younger or much older with less talent than the men they replaced. Here is a summary of the managers with the best records during the war years, 1942–1945. Several of the managerial records are worth special note. Though the St. Louis Cardinals were a powerhouse and the St. Louis Browns have a reputation of being perennial losers, the mangers of the two St. Louis teams are first and fourth in most wins. While Connie Mack ranks 13th in total wins, he is last in total losses and his teams had the worst won-loss percentage during that period. Mack survived as manager because he was also the owner. Conversely, Steve O'Neil of the Detroit Tigers is 11th in total wins, but his winning percentage is higher than many of the managers above him.

Manager	*Team*	*Wins-Losses*
Billy Southworth	St. Louis (N)	411–205
Joe McCarthy	New York (A)	365–249
Leo Durocher	Brooklyn	335–280
Luke Sewell	St. Louis (A)	324–284
Frankie Frisch	Pittsburgh	318–290
Bill McKechnie	Cincinnati	313–301
Joe Cronin	Boston (A)	309–303
Lou Boudreau	Cleveland	302–304
Jimmy Dykes	Chicago (A)	290–315
Mel Ott	New York (N)	285–326
Steve O'Neill	Detroit	254–207
Ossie Bluege	Washington	235–226
Connie Mack	Philadelphia	228–384
Charlie Grimm	Chicago (N)	172–125
Jimmie Wilson	Chicago (N)	143–174
Bob Coleman	Boston (N)	128–165
Casey Stengel	Boston (N)	106–149
Fred Fitzsimmons	Philadelphia (N)	104–180
Bucky Harris	Phil (N), Wash	101–122
Ben Chapman	Philadelphia (N)	28–57

Manager	Team	Wins-Losses
Del Baker	Detroit	73–81
Hans Lobert	Philadelphia (N)	42–109
Del Bissonnette	Boston (N)	25–34
Roy Johnson	Chicago (N)	0–1

C: The 1942 St. Louis Cardinals

Manager: Billy Southworth
Season record: 106–48, first place in National League
Defeated New York Yankees 4 games to 1 in World Series

	G	AB	R	H	D	T	HR	RBI	AVE
Walker Cooper	125	438	58	123	32	7	7	65	.281
Johnny Hopp	95	314	41	81	16	7	3	37	.258
Creepy Crespi	93	292	33	71	4	2	0	35	.243
Marty Marion	147	485	66	134	38	5	0	54	.276
Whitey Kurowski	115	366	51	93	17	3	9	42	.254
Stan Musial	140	467	87	147	32	10	10	72	.315
Enos Slaughter	152	591	100	188	31	17	13	98	.318
Terry Moore	130	489	80	141	26	3	6	48	.288
Jimmy Brown	145	606	75	155	28	4	1	71	.256
Ray Sanders	95	282	37	71	17	2	5	39	.252
Ken O'Dea	58	192	22	45	7	1	5	32	.234
Harry Walker	74	191	38	60	12	2	0	16	.314
Coaker Triplett	64	154	18	42	7	4	1	23	.273
Erv Dusek	12	27	4	5	3	0	0	3	.185
Buddy Blattner	19	23	3	1	0	0	0	1	.043
Gus Mancuso	5	13	0	1	0	0	0	1	.077
Sam Narron	10	10	0	4	0	0	0	1	.400
Estel Crabtree	10	9	1	3	2	0	0	2	.333
Jeff Cross	1	4	0	1	0	0	0	1	.250

	W-L	G	IP	H	R	BB	SO	ERA
Mort Cooper	22–7	37	278.2	207	55	68	152	1.78
Johnny Beazley	21–6	43	215.1	181	51	73	91	2.13
Max Lanier	13–8	34	161	137	53	60	93	2.96
Ernie White	7–5	26	128.1	113	36	61	67	2.52
Lon Warneke	6–4	12	82	76	30	15	31	3.29
Harry Gumbert	9–5	38	163	156	59	59	52	3.26
Murry Dickson	6–3	36	120.2	91	41	61	66	2.91
Howie Krist	13–3	34	118.1	103	34	43	47	2.51
Howie Pollet	7–5	27	109.1	102	43	39	42	2.88
Whitey Moore	0–1	9	12.1	10	6	11	1	4.38
Bill Lohrman	1–1	5	12.2	11	2	2	6	1.42
Bill Beckmann	1–0	2	7	4	0	0	0	0.00
Clyde Shoun	0–0	2	1.2	1	0	0	0	0.00

D: The 1943 St. Louis Cardinals

Manager: Billy Southworth
Season record: 105–49, first place in National League
Lost to New York Yankees 4 games to 1 in World Series

	G	AB	R	H	D	T	HR	RBI	AVE
Walker Cooper	122	449	52	143	30	4	9	81	.318
Ray Sanders	144	478	69	134	21	5	11	73	.280
Lou Klein	154	627	91	180	28	14	7	62	.287
Marty Marion	129	418	38	117	15	3	1	52	.280
Whitey Kurowski	139	522	69	150	24	8	13	70	.287
Stan Musial	157	617	108	220	48	20	13	81	.357
Harry Walker	148	564	76	166	28	6	2	53	.294
Danny Litwhiler	80	258	40	72	14	3	7	31	.279
Johnny Hopp	91	241	33	54	10	2	2	25	.224
Debs Garms	90	249	26	64	10	2	0	22	.257
Ken O'Dea	71	203	15	57	11	2	3	25	.281
Jimmy Brown	34	110	6	20	4	2	0	8	.182
Frank Demaree	39	86	5	25	2	0	0	9	.291
George Fallon	36	78	6	18	1	0	0	5	.231
Coaker Triplett	9	25	1	2	0	0	1	4	.080
Buster Adams	8	11	1	1	1	0	0	1	.091
Sam Narron	10	11	0	1	0	0	0	0	.091

	W-L	G	IP	H	R	BB	SO	ERA
Mort Cooper	21–8	37	274	228	70	79	141	2.30
Max Lanier	15–7	32	213.1	195	45	75	123	1.90
Harry Gumbert	10–5	21	133	115	42	32	40	2.84
Howie Pollet	8–4	16	118.1	83	23	32	61	1.75
Ernie White	5–5	14	78.2	78	33	33	28	3.78
Howie Krist	11–5	34	164.1	141	53	62	57	2.90
Harry Brecheen	9–6	29	135.1	98	34	39	68	2.26
Murry Dickson	8–2	31	115.2	119	46	49	44	3.58
Red Munger	9–5	32	93.1	101	41	42	45	3.95
Al Brazle	8–2	13	88	74	15	29	26	1.53
Bud Byerly	1–0	2	13	14	5	5	6	3.46

E: The 1944 St. Louis Cardinals

Manager: Billy Southworth
Season record: 105–49, first place in National League
Defeated St. Louis Browns 4 games to 2 in World Series

	G	AB	R	H	D	T	HR	RBI	AVE
Walker Cooper	112	397	56	126	25	5	13	72	.317

	G	AB	R	H	D	T	HR	RBI	AVE
Ray Sanders	154	601	87	177	34	9	12	102	.295
Emil Verban	146	498	51	128	14	2	0	43	.257
Marty Marion	144	506	50	135	26	2	6	63	.267
Whitey Kurowski	149	555	95	150	25	7	20	87	.270
Stan Musial	146	568	112	197	51	14	12	94	.347
Johnny Hopp	139	527	106	177	35	9	11	72	.336
Danny Litwhiler	140	492	53	130	25	5	15	82	.264
Ken O'Dea	85	265	35	66	11	2	6	37	.249
Augie Bergamo	80	192	35	55	6	3	2	19	.286
George Fallon	69	141	16	28	6	0	1	9	.199
Debs Garms	73	149	17	30	3	0	0	5	.201
Pepper Martin	40	81	15	24	4	0	2	4	.279
John Antonelli	8	26	0	4	1	0	0	1	.190
Bob Keely	1	0	0	0	0	0	0	0	.000

	W-L	G	IP	H	R	BB	SO	ERA
Mort Cooper	22-7	34	252.1	227	69	60	97	2.46
Max Lanier	17-12	33	224.1	192	66	71	141	2.65
Ted Wilks	17-4	36	207.2	173	61	49	70	2.64
Harry Brecheen	16-5	30	189.1	174	60	46	88	2.85
Red Munger	11-3	21	121	92	18	41	55	1.34
Freddy Schmidt	7-3	37	114.1	94	40	58	58	3.15
Al Jursich	7-9	30	130	102	49	65	53	3.39
Blix Donnelly	2-1	27	76.1	61	18	34	45	2.12
Bud Byerly	2-2	9	42.1	37	16	20	13	3.40
Harry Gumbert	4-2	10	61.1	60	17	19	16	2.49
Bill Trotter	0-1	2	6	14	9	4	0	13.50
Mike Naymick	0-0	1	2	2	1	1	1	4.50

F: The 1948 Boston Braves

Manager: Billy Southworth
Season record: 91–62, first place in National League
Lost to Cleveland Indians 4 games to 2 in World Series

	G	AB	R	H	D	T	HR	RBI	AVE
Phil Masi	113	376	43	95	19	0	5	44	.253
Earl Torgeson	134	438	70	111	23	5	10	67	.253
Eddie Stanky	67	247	49	79	14	2	2	29	.320
Alvin Dark	137	543	85	175	39	6	3	38	.322
Bob Elliott	151	677	99	153	24	5	23	100	.283
Mike McCormick	115	343	45	104	22	7	1	39	.303
Tommy Holmes	139	585	85	190	35	7	6	61	.325
Jeff Heath	115	364	64	116	26	5	20	76	.319
Jim Russell	89	322	44	85	18	1	9	54	.264
Sibby Sisti	83	221	30	54	6	2	0	21	.244

	G	AB	R	H	D	T	HR	RBI	AVE
Clint Conatser	90	224	30	62	9	3	3	23	.277
Bill Salkeld	78	198	26	48	8	1	8	28	.242
Frank McCormick	75	180	14	45	9	2	4	34	.250
Connie Ryan	51	122	14	26	3	0	0	10	.213
Bobby Sturgeon	34	78	10	17	3	1	0	4	.218
Danny Litwhiler	13	33	0	9	2	0	0	6	.273
Al Lyons	16	12	2	2	0	0	0	0	.167
Marv Rickert	3	13	1	3	0	1	0	2	.231
Ray Sanders	5	4	0	1	0	0	0	2	.250

	W-L	G	IP	H	R	BB	SO	ERA
Johnny Sain	24-15	42	314.2	297	91	83	137	2.60
Warren Spahn	15-12	36	257	237	106	77	114	3.71
Bill Voiselle	13-13	37	215.2	226	87	90	89	3.63
Vern Bickford	11-5	33	146	125	53	63	60	3.27
Red Barrett	7-8	34	128.1	132	52	26	40	3.65
Bobby Hogue	8-2	40	86.1	88	31	19	43	3.23
Nels Potter	5-2	18	85	77	22	8	47	2.33
Clyde Shoun	5-1	36	74	77	33	20	25	4.01
Ernie White	0-2	15	23	13	5	17	8	1.96
Jim Prendergast	1-1	10	16.2	30	19	5	3	10.26
Johnny Beazley	0-1	3	16	19	8	7	4	4.50
Al Lyons	1-0	7	12.2	17	11	8	5	7.82
Ed Wright	0-0	3	4.2	9	1	2	2	1.93
Johnny Antonelli	0-0	4	4	2	1	3	0	2.25
Glenn Elliott	1-0	1	3	5	1	1	2	3.00
Ray Martin	0-0	2	2.1	0	0	1	0	0.00

G: Winning Managers

Best Winning Percentage

Manager	W-L	Pct.
1. Joe McCarthy	2,125-1,333	.615
2. Jim Mutrie	658-419	.611
3. Charles Comiskey	840-541	.608
4. Frank Selee	1,284-862	.598
5. Billy Southworth	1,044-704	.597
6. Frank Chance	946-648	.593
7. John McGraw	2,763-1,948	.586
8. Al Lopez	1,410-1,004	.584
9. Earl Weaver	1,480-1,060	.583
10. Mickey Cochrane	348-250	.582
11. Harry Wright	1,225-885	.581
12. Eddie Dyer	446-325	.578
13. Cap Anson	1,295-947	.578
14. Fred Clarke	1,601-1,181	.576

Manager	W-L	Pct.
15. Joe Girardi	550–412	.572*
16. Davey Johnson	1,280–991	.564*
17. Monte Ward	412–320	.563
18. Pat Moran	748–586	.561
19. Steve O'Neill	1,879–1,040	.559
20. Walter Alston	2,040–1,613	.558

*Still active; includes portion of 2012 season

Three Consecutive 100-Win Seasons

Manager	Years	Team
Connie Mack	1929–1931	Philadelphia A's
Billy Southworth	1942–1944	St. Louis Cardinals
Earl Weaver	1969–1971	Baltimore Orioles
Bobby Cox	1997–1999	Atlanta Braves
Joe Torre	2002–2004	New York Yankees

Chapter Notes

Chapter 1

1. Carole Southworth Watson, Billy's daughter, made the Father Confessor reference in an interview with the author on February 6, 2012.
2. Bob Broeg, *Stan Musial: The Man's Own Story* (New York: Doubleday, 1964), p. 260.
3. John Daly, *"Billy Southworth,"* Society for American Baseball Research Baseball Biography Project, 2009, p. 1.
4. In 1915, when the Federal League was competing for sites in Major League cities, Charles Somers, owner of both the Cleveland and Toledo franchises, moved the Toledo ball club to Cleveland where they played their home games in the Cleveland ballpark when the major league team was on the road. This was to prevent the Federal League from operating a team in Cleveland — because there was no available ballpark for them.
5. Carole Southworth Watson, interview with author, February 6, 2012.
6. Many comparisons between Billy Southworth and Casey Stengel have been made over the years. They were products of the same era — Stengel born in 1890, Southworth in 1893 — they both were outfielders who made the Major Leagues as teenagers, and they were teammates on the Pittsburgh Pirates (Southworth was brought up to the Pirates from the minor leagues when Stengel was injured). In 1923, they were part of a multi-player trade in which they were, in effect, traded for each other. Southworth was the most successful manager of the 1940s, his teams winning four pennants and two World Series, Stengel was the most successful manager of the 1950s, his teams winning five consecutive World Series championships beginning in 1949 and winning two more American League championships in 1957 and 1958 and a World Series championship in 1958.
7. Joe Williams, "Southworth's Boy Once Shot, Flag Incentive," *New York World Telegram*, August 28, 1949.
8. Carole Southworth Watson, recalling how her mother described Billy, interview with author, February 6, 2012.
9. *Ibid.*
10. *Ibid.*
11. Daly, *Billy Southworth*, p 2.
12. Arthur Daley, "Sports of the Times: A Strange Career," *New York Times*, November 26, 1969.
13. Bob Hooey, "Major Billy Southworth, Unscathed in Combat Flights, Dies in B-29 Crash," *The Sporting News*, February 28, 1945.
14. Carole Southworth Watson, interview with author, February 17, 2012.
15. *Ibid.*
16. Bill Corum, "A Harvard Man Wins in the Hub," *New York Journal American*, September 28, 1948.
17. Tommy Holmes, "Up-to-Date Saga of Billy the Kid," *New York Herald Tribune*, August 17, 1949.

Chapter 2

1. Harry T. Brundidge, "Billy Southworth, Son of Village Smithy, Forges Flag Winners," *The Sporting News*, October 30, 1930.
2. *Ibid.*
3. Lenny Lepola, "Remembering Billy Southworth, My Dad," *Sunbury News*, July 24, 2008.
4. Bob Hooey, "Billy the Kid: Born to Game," *The Sporting News*, October 26, 1944.
5. Family legend has it that a teacher wrongfully accused Billy of throwing a spitball in class and that Billy walked out and never returned to school. In interviews over the years, Billy never mentioned it when he talked about his school days.
6. Hooey, "Billy the Kid."
7. *Ibid.*
8. Brundidge, "Billy Southworth."
9. Hooey, "Billy the Kid."
10. *Ibid.*
11. Portsmouth's baseball heritage includes many major league players who were born there.

They include Pinky Swander and Harry Blake, who played in the late 1800s; Larry Hisle, a slugging outfielder for several teams; Al Oliver, the first major league player to have 200 hits and 100 RBIs in a season for two teams, one in the American League, one in the National League; Del Rice, major league catcher and manager; Rocky Nelson, journeyman who played on Pittsburgh's 1960 World Series champion; and Johnny LeMaster, the only player in baseball history to hit an inside-the-park home run in his first major league at-bat.

12. Ted Williams, the great Boston Red Sox player, contended that Jackson should have been elected to the Hall of Fame after his death because his punishment had been a "lifetime ban."

13. The pitch thrown by Carl Mays struck Ray Chapman with such force that the ball bounded back toward the mound. Mays picked it up and threw to first before he realized it wasn't a batted ball.

14. John Drohan, *Boston Braves Media Guide*, 1948.

15. "Billy Southworth: Miracle Man of '42," *The Sporting News*, October 1, 1942.

16. *Ibid.*

17. *Ibid.*

18. The scouting report, unsigned, is included in the Billy Southworth files in the research library at the National Baseball Hall of Fame in Cooperstown, New York.

Chapter 3

1. Bezdek managed the Pirates through 1919, then accepted an offer to be athletic director, football coach and baseball coach at Penn State. He was remarkably successful in both sports. His football teams were 65–30–11 with two undefeated seasons and one trip to the Rose Bowl. His baseball teams compiled a record of 129–76–1. In 1937, he was hired as football coach for the Cleveland Rams in the National Football League. Bezdek is the only man to have managed a major league baseball team and coached a professional football team.

2. baseball-reference.com.

3. Tommy Holmes, "Yanks May Strike Terror But Not in Mr. Southworth," *Brooklyn Eagle*, August 29, 1940. Harry Greb started his professional boxing career in Pittsburgh in 1913 and met Southworth four years later. Greb was known as a powerful puncher whose career hit its peak on May 23, 1922, when he defeated Gene Tunney for the world middleweight boxing championship. Greb suffered many injuries during his career. In 1926, he underwent surgery and never came out of the anesthesia, dying at the age of 32.

4. "Hail Southworth as a Phenom: Pirates's New Outfielder Gets Away to a Brilliant Start," *The Sporting News*, July 6, 1918.

5. Hendrix and Hollocher's careers with the Cubs took strange turns. Hendrix, a three-time 20-game winner, was suspected of trying to fix a game in 1920 between the Cubs and the Philadelphia Phillies. Cub management had received several reports that Hendrix had bet against the Cubs in a game he was scheduled to pitch. Chicago started Grover Cleveland Alexander instead and still lost. Nothing was ever proven against Hendrix but the Cubs released him at the end of the season. Hollocher's career was interrupted many times by a stomach ailment that sidelined him sometimes for weeks. The cause of the problem was never medically determined and some observers thought it was an imaginary illness. Whatever it was, it forced an early retirement for the promising young shortstop. In 1940, after he was out of baseball, Hillocher committed suicide with a shotgun to his head. He was 44.

6. "On His Way to Lead Again," *The Sporting News*, July 3, 1919.

7. Cooney was one of Southworth's coaches in Boston and took over as interim manager in 1949 when Billy took a leave of absence because of health issues.

8. Whitman is quoted in a *Saturday Evening Post* article, "The Red Birds Fly Again," by J. Roy Stockton, published August 9, 1941.

9. Hooey, "Billy the Kid."

10. *Ibid.*

Chapter 4

1. Charles C. Alexander, *John McGraw* (New York: Viking, 1988), p 34.

2. *Ibid.*

3. *Ibid.*, frontispiece.

4. Since the inception of the World Series, it has been played during two World Wars, the Great Depression and other times of national strife. Only twice has it been cancelled—in 1994 because of the players' strike and 1904 because of McGraw.

5. Southworth's daughter, Carole Southworth Watson, said she believed her father began drinking more heavily when he joined the Giants. She steadfastly maintains he was not an alcoholic but said he was susceptible to "one beer leading to two." Interview with author, February 17, 2012.

6. Frank Graham, "Graham's Corner: Billy Southworth and Mr. McGraw," *New York Journal-American*, February 1, 1946.

7. Alexander, *John McGraw*, p. 253.

8. *The Sporting News*, October 9, 1924, p. 2.

9. *New York Times*, October 7, 1924, p. 13.

10. baseball-almanac.com/ws/yr1924ws.shtml.
11. J. Roy Stockton, "The Redbirds Fly Again," *Saturday Evening Post*, August 9, 1941, p. 62.
12. Graham, "Graham's Corner."
13. Hooey, "Billy the Kid."

Chapter 5

1. www.baseballlibrary.com/ballplayers.
2. The stories of Rhem's drinking escapades are well documented. One account is his biography in www.baseballlibrary.com/ballplayers.
3. John P. Carmichael, *My Greatest Day in Baseball* (New York: A.S. Barnes, 1945), pp. 180–181.
4. Jack Kavanaugh, *Ol' Pete: The Grover Cleveland Alexander Story* (South Bend: Diamond Communications, 1996), p 95.
5. Carmichael, *My Greatest Day in Baseball*, p. 181.
6. *Ibid.*, p. 182.
7. *Ibid.*, p. 181–183.

Chapter 6

1. Hooey, "Billy the Kid."
2. Carmichael, *My Greatest Day in Baseball*, p. 183.
3. Kavanaugh, *Ol' Pete*, pp. 104–106.
4. Alexander won nine games for the Cardinals in 1929. His ninth win gave him 373, one more than Christy Mathewson, making him the winningest pitcher in National League history. But his alcohol problems had become so disruptive that manager Bill McKechnie, with Sam Breadon's blessing, sent him home, causing him to miss the last six weeks of the season. The Cardinals released him and he was picked up by the Philadelphia Phillies, the team he broke in with and had achieved great success. But he lost his first three decisions in 1930 and retired. Years later, researchers discovered that Mathewson had not been credited with a victory he should have received. The victory was added to his total, giving him 373 and tying him with Alexander. If Alex had not missed the last six weeks of the 1929 season, it is reasonable to believe he would have won at leas one more game. Because he didn't, he is still tied with Mathewson as the all-time National League leader in wins.
5. As great a player as Hornsby was, he had a stretch where he played for four teams in four years. After being traded from the Cardinals after the 1926 season, he played for the New York Giants in 1927, the Boston Braves in 1928 and the Chicago Cubs in 1929.
6. Frederick G. Lieb, *The St. Louis Cardinals: The Story of a Great Baseball Club* (New York, G.P. Putnam's Sons, 1947), p. 126.
7. *Ibid.*
8. Lieb, *The St. Louis Cardinals*, pp. 127–128.
9. *Ibid.*

Chapter 7

1. Joe Williams, "Southworth's Boy, Once Shot, Flag Incentive," *The Sporting News*, August 28, 1941.
2. Hooey's three-part series on Southworth's career, published in three consecutive issues of *The Sporting News* in October and November 1944, was a detailed biography of his friend, offering vivid details to the high points in his life and glossing over or ignoring important events or circumstances that were not complimentary.
3. Lieb, *The St. Louis Cardinals*, p. 133.
4. The story of the clubhouse dispute has been recounted many times over the years in many reliable resources, including Fred Lieb's history of the St. Louis Cardinals and Bob Hooey's lengthy account of Southworth's career in his series in *The Sporting News*. None of the accounts mention who the two players were who were feuding with one another, keeping intact the old axiom "What happens in the clubhouse stays in the clubhouse."
5. Hooey recounts the locker room scene in the November 9, 1944, installment of his biography of Southworth in *The Sporting News*, 17 years after it occurred. While the substance of what happened is accurate, based on others' accounts, Hooey was not in the locker room when it occurred and is most probably telling the story as Southworth told it to him, including what he quotes Southworth as saying.
6. "Slump Ends When Southworth Returns," *The Sporting News*, June 14, 1928.
7. *Ibid.*
8. Jim Mandelaro and Scott Pitoniak, *Silver Seasons and a New Frontier: The Story of the Rochester Red Wings* (Syracuse: Syracuse University Press, 2010), p. 27.
9. Williams, "Southworth's Boy Once Shot, Flag Incentive."
10. *Ibid.*
11. *Ibid.*
12. Mandelaro and Pitoniak, *Silver Seasons and a New Frontier*, p. 28.
13. E.J. Lanigan, "Fanning with Lanigan," *The Sporting News*, November 29, 1928.
14. *Ibid.*
15. "Scribbled By Scribes," *The Sporting News*, November 29, 1928.
16. *Ibid.*
17. Hooey, "Billy the Kid." *The Sporting News*, November 9, 1944.

Chapter 8

1. Cullen Cain, "Breadon Is Confident Billy Southworth Will Make Good Manager," *The Sporting News*, March 2, 1929.
2. Ibid.
3. Ibid.
4. Lieb, *The St. Louis Cardinals*, p. 139. The clubhouse dispute over the trip to Miami is well documented in several publications. Lieb's account, written in the style of the day, includes direct quotes even though Lieb was not present at the meeting. He reported what happened based on what those who were there told him.
5. Jerome Mileur, *High-Flying Redbirds: The 1942 St. Louis Cardinals* (Columbia: University of Missouri Press, 2009), p. 18.
6. Lieb, *The St. Louis Cardinals*, pp. 138–139.
7. Hooey, "Billy the Kid."
8. Mandelaro and Pitoniak, *Silver Seasons and a New Frontier*, p. 38.
9. Ibid., pp. 39–40.
10. Ibid., p. 40.
11. Ibid., p. 36.
12. Starr continued to have a career where he struggled for success and acceptance. The Cardinals brought him up in 1932 and he was 1–1 in limited action. In 1933, he pitched sparingly for both the New York Giants and Boston Braves, compiling 0–1 records for both clubs. He then languished in the minor leagues for eight years before resurfacing with Cincinnati in 1941. Then he pitched for Pittsburgh where, at the age of 36, he had his best year, winning 15 and losing 13. He closed out his career with the Cubs in 1945, pitching in relief for Chicago's pennant winner.
13. Sisler's all-time, single season hit record remained for 84 years until Ichiro Suzuki of the Seattle Mariners topped him with 262 in 2004.

Chapter 9

1. Author interview with Carole Southworth Watson, May 17, 2012.
2. Arthur Daley, "Billy Southworth Twice Rose to Top of Game," *New York Times*, November 30, 1969.
3. Hooey, "Billy the Kid."
4. Daly, "Billy Southworth." SABR Baseball Biography Project, 2009, p 4.
5. Author interview with Carole Southworth Watson, May 17, 2012.
6. Tom Meany didn't refer to a bar room fight as the cause, but did report Terry's black eye in *The New York Times*. Jon Daly, Southworth's biographer for SABR, said Terry and Southworth did not get along and "Southworth's drinking may not have helped matters" (p. 5). Hooey, Southworth's friend and biographer for *The Sporting News*, did not mention alcohol or the black eye or the alleged fight. He wrote, "Bluntly speaking, Billy the Kid, after five years of managing, did not come up to Terry's expectations as a manager." "Billy the Kid, Life Story of Southworth," *The Sporting News*, November 9, 1944. Southworth's daughter Carole said Terry teased Southworth about his middle name, Harold, which he hated, and Billy decked him. Alcohol surely played a part in it, she said.
7. J. Roy Stockton, "The Redbirds Fly Again," *The Saturday Evening Post*, August 9, 1941.
8. Author interview with Carole Southworth Watson, May 17, 2012.
9. Ibid.
10. The Southworth family history is sketchy during this time period. There are no family records available to verify dates and events. Previous published accounts say Lida Brooks Southworth died of a cerebral hemorrhage in 1934 and that Billy married Mabel Steman two years after that. But court records and newspaper accounts confirm Billy and Lida Southworth were divorced after Lida filed the papers in September 1934, that Billy and Mabel Steman were married shortly after that and their daughter, Carole Southworth Watson, was born in August of 1935. Public records also confirm the death of Lida Brooks Southworth in 1936.
11. Arthur Daley, "Sports of the Times," *New York Times*, November 26, 1969.
12. Many sources, including asheville.com/area_info/baseball.
13. Daniel Okrent and Harris Lewine, *The Ultimate Baseball Book* (Boston: Houghton Mifflin, 1991), pp. 231–232.
14. Mandelaro and Pitoniak, *Silver Seasons and a New Frontier*, p. 64.
15. Ibid., p. 66.

Chapter 10

1. Jesse Abramson, "Blades Fired as Cardinals Manager," *St. Louis Post Dispatch*, June 8, 1940.
2. Ibid.
3. Arthur E. Patterson, "St. Louis Wins Fifth Straight," *New York Herald Tribune*, June 18, 1940.
4. "Cardinal Fans Tip Lid to Billy the Kid," *The Sporting News*, August 8, 1940.
5. Everett Morris, "Southworth Lays Cards Rise to Team's Spirit and Will to Win," *New York Daily News*, April 30, 1941.
6. Ibid.
7. Stockton, "The Redbirds Fly Again."
8. Excerpt from diary of Billy Southworth, Jr., as published in *New York Times*, June 19, 2005.
9. "Meet the Missus," *The Sporting News*, August 21, 1941.
10. Public document available in many re-

sources, including David Pietrusza, *Judge and Jury: The Life and Times of Judge Kenesaw Mountain Landis* (South Bend: Diamond Communications, 1998), p. 433.

Chapter 11

1. Jerome Mileur, *High-Flying Birds: The 1942 St. Louis Cardinals* (Columbia: University of Missouri Press, 2010), pp. 12–14.
2. Stockton, "The Redbirds Fly Again."
3. *Ibid.*
4. *Ibid.*
5. Joe King, "Southworth Hopes to Make Braves Terror on Bases," *New York World-Telegram*, February 20, 1946.
6. Mileur, *High-Flying Birds*, p. 54.
7. *Ibid.*, pp. 70–71.
8. Herb Goren, "Southworth Thinks Series Not Crucial," *New York Sun*, June 19, 1942.
9. Frank Angelo Joseph "Creepy" Crespi had 334 plate appearances in 1942 and had six extra base hits — four doubles and two triples. He played parts of four years with the Cardinals. After the 1942 season, he went into the Army and broke his leg playing baseball. He broke it again in a wheelchair game he was participating in. That ended his baseball career at the age of 24.
10. John Kiernan, "Dodgers Take Care of Cardinals," *New York Times*, June 23, 1942.
11. *Ibid.*
12. Dick Young, "Still in the Race, Card Boss Says," *New York Daily News*, July 31, 1942.
13. Frank Graham, "Setting the Pace," *New York Sun*, September 8, 1942.
14. J. Roy Stockton, "Cardinals Morale Stays High," *St. Louis Post Dispatch*, September 2, 1942.
15. Mileur, *High-Flying Birds*, p. 180.
16. *Ibid.*, p. 181.
17. Tommy Holmes, "Cards Top Yankees Again," *Brooklyn Eagle*, October 1, 1942.
18. Mileur, *High Flying Birds*, p. 220.
19. Hooey, "Billy the Kid."
20. Hy Turkin, "Biog of Billy," *New York Daily News*, October 4, 1942.

Chapter 12

1. "Columbus Enjoys Big Chunk of Series Glory," *Columbus Dispatch*, October 15, 1942.
2. Billy Southworth, "The Greatest Ball Club on Earth," *Saturday Evening Post*, June 5, 1943.
3. *Ibid.*
4. www.baseball-almanac.com/ws/yr1943ws.shtml.
5. Lieb, *The St. Louis Cardinals*, p. 209.
6. *Ibid.*, p. 211.
7. *Ibid.*

8. *Ibid.*, p. 212.
9. The Seattle Mariners, managed by Lou Piniella, won 116 games in 2001, tying the record of the 1906 Cubs.
10. Since the 1942–44 Cardinals, three other teams have won 100-plus games three years in a row — the 1969–71 Baltimore Orioles, managed by Earl Weaver; the 1997–99 Atlanta Braves, managed by Bobby Cox; and the 2002–2004 New York Yankees, managed by Joe Torre.

Chapter 13

1. Tommy Holmes, "Billy Southworth Has a Youngster," *Brooklyn Eagle*, October 5, 1944.
2. "New War Chapter in Game's History," *The Sporting News*, January 21, 1943.
3. "Billy the Buckeye Buckaroo," *Ohio State Journal*, January 21, 1943.
4. "Manage Like Dad," *The Sporting News*, February 22, 1945
5. "DFC for Capt. Billy," *Columbus Dispatch*, August 12, 1943.
6. Stroberg had a long, successful career as a movie producer. Among his credits when young Southworth met him were *The Thin Man* and *Pride and Prejudice*.
7. Michael Shapiro, "Father-Son Bond Remains Alive in Wartime Diary," *New York Times*, June 19, 2005.
8. Holmes, "Billy Southworth Has a Youngster."
9. Frank Graham, "Story of a Boy Who Went to War," *New York Sun*, May 18, 1943.
10. "Maj. Southworth Killed in Bomber," *New York Times*, February 17, 1945.
11. "Southworth Search Continues," *Dunkirk Daily Observer*, February 23, 1945.
12. www.baseballinwartime.com/in_memoriam/southworth_billy_jr.htm.
13. Lieb, *The St. Louis Cardinals*, p. 218.
14. Interview with author, February 6, 2012.
15. Arthur Daley, "Father and Son," *New York Times*, September 1, 1945.
16. *Ibid.*

Chapter 14

1. Burt Whitman, "Southworth Signs to Manage Braves," *Boston Herald*, November 7, 1946.
2. *Ibid.*
3. Tommy Holmes, "Stars May Follow Billy to Boston," *Brooklyn Eagle*, November 10, 19456.
4. Lawton Carver, "Southworth Given Richest Job Among Baseball's Managers," *The Sporting News*, November 16, 1945.
5. Bob Considine, "On the Line," *New York Journal-American*, June 17, 1947.

6. Leonard Cohen, "The Sports Parade," *New York Post*, June 18, 1947.
7. *Ibid.*
8. *Ibid.*

Chapter 15

1. Richard Goldstein, "Johnny Sain, 89, Who Inspired Baseball Rhyme, Dies," *New York Times*, November 9, 2006.
2. On July 28, 1943, when Sain was in the military, he participated in an exhibition game at Yankee Stadium, in which Babe Ruth, age 48 and long retired, made a guest appearance at the plate. Sain walked him. On April 15, 1947, Jackie Robinson made baseball history by becoming the first black ballplayer in the major leagues. Robinson grounded out.
3. When Sain's career was over as a pitcher, he became a pitching coach with several teams and is credited with developing many young hurlers into stars. In stints with the Yankees, Twins, Tigers, White Sox and Atlanta Braves, pitchers such as Whitey Ford, Jim Bouton, Jim "Mudcat" Grant, Earl Wilson, Denny McLain, Wilbur Wood, Stan Bahnsen and Jim Kaat all won 20 games for the first time in their careers, in some cases, the only time. In 1968, he was the pitching coach for McLain, who won 31 games and is the last 30-game winner in the major leagues.
4. Grantland Rice, "Look Out for Billy Southworth." *New York Herald-Tribune*, March 9, 1948.
5. *Ibid.*
6. Howell Stevens, "Tribe in Another Shakeup," *Boston Post*, May 7, 1948.
7. Interview with author in 1994 and quoted in *Inside Pitch: A Closer Look at Classic Baseball Moments* (Jefferson, N.C.: McFarland, 1996), pp. 46–47.
8. Frank Graham, "Graham's Corner," *New York World Telegram*, October 4, 1948.
9. Bob Feller, *Now Pitching: Bob Feller* (New York: Birch Lane Press, 1990), p 165.

Chapter 16

1. Mort Bloomberg, "Number 30, Billy Southworth, Manager," *Boston Braves Historical Newsletter*, Spring 2008.
2. Arthur Sampson, "Billy Southworth, The Pennant Man," *Look*, May 24, 1949.
3. Tommy Holmes, "Up to Date Saga of Billy the Kid," *Brooklyn Eagle*, August 17, 1949.
4. Bob Considine, "On the Line — Billy's First Class Guy; Could Be Braves Ain't," *New York Journal-American*, August 21, 1949.
5. Bill Corum, "In My Book, He Was Great," *New York Journal-American*, August 17, 1949.
6. *Time*, "Sport Headaches," August 29, 1949.
7. Bill James, *The Bill James Guide to Baseball Managers from 1870 to Today* (New York: Scribner, 1997), p. 119.
8. *Ibid.*
9. Bloomberg, "Number 30, Billy Southworth, Manager."
10. Danny Peary, *We Played the Game* (New York: Hyperion, 1994), p. 18.
11. *Boston Braves Historical Association Newsletter*, Spring 2011.
12. Bayard Hooper, "Egg in Your Beer," *Harvard Crimson*, October 5, 1948.
13. Bob Considine even referred to it in his *New York Journal-American* column four months later, on August 21, 1949.
14. Carole Southworth Watson said Egan made life miserable for Billy, Both she and her mother would rather have had Billy come home to Sunbury than to put up with the abuse of Egan who she described as "a mean man." Her disdain was still evident 63 years later, in an interview with the author on February 17, 2012.
15. Though Southworth might have lost the respect of some of his players, the facts do not support some of their criticisms. While Dark says "his idea of strategy was to not anger the opponent," the facts are that Southworth was well known for strategy: playing percentages, platooning and his teams consistently led the league in bunting to accommodate his strategy of moving runners into scoring position and playing for the early lead. Dark's comments about Southworth are in his book that, ironically is titled, *When in Doubt, Fire the Manager*.
16. Alvin Dark and John Underwood, *When in Doubt, Fire the Manager: My Life and Times in Baseball* (New York: E.P. Dutton, 1980), pp. 44–45.
17. Holmes, "Up-to-Date Saga of Billy the Kid."
18. *Columbus Messenger*, August 2, 2008.
19. Peary, *We Played the Game*, p. 87.
20. Game logs for the 1949 season can be found at www.retrosheet.org/boxesetc/1949/VBSN01948.htm.
21. Carole Southworth Watson, interview with author, July 31, 2012.
22. Bill Corum, "But Coming or Going, He's a Good Manager," *New York Journal-American*, August 17, 1949.

Chapter 17

1. Carole Southworth Watson recalls her father heading out the back door, saying, "I'm

going squirrel hunting" in 1949 when a reporter came to the house after Billy came home on sick leave.

2. James, *The Bill James Guide to Baseball Managers from 1870 to Today*, pp. 280, 283–284.

3. Lepola, "Remembering Billy Southworth, My Dad."

4. *Ibid.*

5. "Billy Southworth Always Batted 1,000 with the Smallfry of Sunbury," *Utica Observer-Dispatch*, November 18, 1969.

6. Letter from Billy Southworth to John Quinn, written in 1952, date unknown, and published in *The Sporting News*, July 6, 1968.

7. Bloomberg, *Boston Braves Historical Society Newsletter*, Spring 2008.

8. Interview with Carole Southworth Watson, February 6, 2012.

9. Neal Russo, "Don't Count Cardinals Out, Says Ex-Pilot Southworth," *The Sporting News*, August 9, 1969.

10. Interview with Carole Southworth Watson, February 6, 2012.

Chapter 18

1. Author interview with Elayne Savage, February 6, 2009. Her comments were in connection with a story on the impact of plane crashes on surviving family members published in the *Mason City* (IA) *Globe Gazette*, February 9, 2009.

2. Author email correspondence with Ray Mileur, June 28, 2012.

3. Mileur wrote about the campaign for Billy in a blog for BaseballGuru.com. The blog contains the letter from the Hall of Fame. It can be found at baseballguru.com/articles/analysis/raymondmileur01.html.

4. Correspondence with Mileur, June 28, 2012.

5. Author interview with Carole Southworth Watson, June 28, 2012.

6. Correspondence with Mileur, June 28, 2012.

7. Rick Hummel, "An Unsung Skipper: Southworth Among Game's Most Proven Winners," Baseball Hall of Fame newsletter, July 20, 2008.

8. Barry M. Bloom, "Emotions run high on hall induction day," mlb.com, July 7, 2008.

9. Carole Southworth Watson said her father taught her two lessons: "Humbleness is greatness" and "Save your money" (interview with author February 6, 2011).

10. Paul Dickson, *Baseball's Greatest Quotations* (New York: HarperCollins, 1991), p. 404.

11. Rob Neyer and Eddie Epstein, *Baseball Dynasties: The Greatest Teams of All Time* (New York: W.W. Norton, 1993), p. 173.

Bibliography

Books

Alexander, Charles. *John McGraw*. New Yrk: Viking, 1988.
Anderson, Dave. *Pennant Races: Baseball at Its Best*. New York: Doubleday, 1994.
Armour, Mark, and Daniel Levitt. *Paths to Glory: How Great Baseball Teams Got That Way*. Dulles, VA: Brassey's, 2003.
Broeg, Bob. *Stan Musial: The Man's Own Story*. New York: Doubleday, 1964.
Carmichael, John P. *My Greatest Day in Baseball*. New York: A.S. Barnes, 1945.
Corcoran, Dennis. *Induction Day at Cooperstown: A History of the Baseball Hall of Fame*. Jefferson, N.C.: McFarland, 2011.
Creamer, Robert. *Stengel: His Life and Times*. New York: Dell, 1984.
Dark, Alvin, and John Underwood. *When in Doubt, Fire the Manager*. New York: E.P. Dutton, 1980.
Dickson, Paul. *Baseball's Greatest Quotations*. New York: HarperCollins, 1991.
Durocher, Leo, and Ed Linn. *Nice Guys Finish Last*. Chicago: University of Chicago Press, 1975.
Durso, Joseph. *Casey: The Life and Legend of Casey Stengel*. Englewood Cliffs, N.J.: Prentice-Hall, 1967.
Feller, Bob, and Bill Gilbert. *Now Pitching: Bob Feller*. New York: Birch Lane Press, 1990.
Gaus, Ed. *Beerball: A History of St. Louis Baseball*. Lincoln: iUniverse.com, 2001.
Goldstein, Richard. *Spartan Seasons: How Baseball Survived the Second World War*. New York: Macmillan, 1980.
James, Bill. *The Bill James Guide to Baseball Managers from 1870 to Today*. New York: Scribner, 1997.
_____. *The Politics of Glory: How Baseball's Hall of Fame Really Works*. New York: Macmillan, 1994.
Kavanaugh, Jack. *Ol' Pete: The Grover Cleveland Alexander Story*. South Bend: Diamond Communications, 1996.
Lieb, Frederick. *The St Louis Cardinals*. New York: G.P. Putnam's Sons, 1947.
Litwhiler, Danny. *Living the Baseball Dream*. Philadelphia: Temple University Press, 2006.
Mandelaro, Jim, and Scott Pitoniak. *Silver Seasons and a New Frontier: The Story of the Rochester Red Wings*. Syracuse: Syracuse University Press, 2010.
Mileur, Jerome, *High-Flying Birds: The 1942 St. Louis Cardinals*. Columbia: University of Missouri Press, 2009.
Musial, Stan, and Bob Broeg. *Stan Musial: The Man's Own Story*. Garden City, N.Y.: Doubleday, 1964.
Neyer, Rob, and Eddie Epstein. *Baseball Dynasties: The Greatest Teams of All Time*. New York: W.W. Norton, 2000.
Nowlin, Bill. *Spahn, Sain and Teddy Ballgame*. Burlington, MA: Rounder Books, 2008.
Okrant, Daniel, and Harris Lewine. *The Ultimate Baseball Book*. Boston: Houghton Mifflin, 1988.
Peary, Danny. *We Played the Game*. New York: Hyperion, 1994.
Peterson, Richard. *The St. Louis Baseball Reader*. Columbia: University of Missouri Press, 2006.
Pietrusza, David. *Judge and Jury: The Life and Times of Kenesaw Mountain Landis*.

South Bend: Diamond Communications, 1998.
Pitoniak, Scott. *Baseball in Rochester.* Charleston, S.C.: Arcadia, 2003.
Szalontai, James. *Teenager on First, Geezer at Bat, 4-F on Deck: Major League Baseball in 1945.* Jefferson, N.C.: McFarland, 2009.

Newspapers, Magazines and Other Print Sources

Abramson, Jess. "Blades Fired and Southworth In." *The Sporting News*, June 8, 1940.
Arace, Michael. "Southworth Deserves to Have His Story Told." *Columbus Dispatch*, July 28, 2008.
"Billy Southworth Always Batted 1,000 with the Smallfry of Sunbury." *Utica Observer-Dispatch*, November 18, 1969.
"Billy Southworth: An American Success Story." *Boston Braves 1948 Player Roster.*
"Billy Southworth. Miracle Man of '42." *The Sporting News*, October 1, 1942.
Bloomberg, Mort. "#30, Billy Southworth, Manager." *Boston Braves Historical Society Newsletter*, Spring 2008.
"Boston Fans Ready." *Columbus Dispatch*, October 6, 1948.
Brundidge, Harry T. "Billy Southworth, Son of Village Smithy, Forges Flag Winners." *The Sporting News*, October 30, 1930.
Cain, Cullen. "Breadon Is Confident Billy Southworth Will Make Good as Manager." *Brooklyn Eagle*, September 1, 1928.
Cannon, Jimmy. "This is Billy Southworth." *Baseball Digest*, May 1949.
"Cardinal Fans Tip Lid to Billy the Kid." *The Sporting News*, August 8, 1940.
"Cards Hit .662 Pace Under Southworth." *The Sporting News*, August 29, 1940.
"Cards to Hustle, Fight, Billy the Kid Promises." *The Sporting News*, October 7, 1943.
Christine, Bill. "The No-Place-But-Home Series." *Los Angeles Times*, October 11, 1989.
"Citizens of Sunbury Wild; Have a Reason." *Sunbury News*, October 6, 1948. "Cleveland Lineup Is Shifted for Second Game." *Columbus Dispatch*, October 7, 1948.
"Columbus Enjoys Big Chunk of Series Glory." *Columbus Dispatch*, October 15, 1942.
Considine, Bob. "Billy Southworth, Jr., Bombed Foe Wearing Dad's Baseball Cap." *The Sporting News*, August 5, 1942.
_____. "Billy's First Class Guy; Could Be Braves Ain't." *New York Daily Mirror*, August 21, 1949.
_____. "On the Line: Southworth Not Conceding Pennant." *New York Daily Mirror*, May 23, 1942.
_____. "On the Line: What Interests You?" *New York Daily Mirror*, June 10, 1947.
Corum, Bill. "A Harvard Man Wins in the Hub." *New York Journal American*, September 28, 1948.
_____. "He's an Ideal Pilot for Young Players." *New York Journal American*, July 1, 1943.
_____. "In My Book, He Was Great." *New York Journal American*, August 17, 1949.
Daley, Arthur. "Billy Southworth Twice Rose to Top of Game." *New York Times*, November 30, 1969.
_____. "Sports of the Times: Father and Son. *New York Times*, August 7, 1948.
_____. "Sports of the Times: A Strange Career." *New York Times*, November 26, 1969.
Daly, Jon. "Billy Southworth." Society for American Baseball Research Biography Project, 2009.
_____. "Billy Southworth in a Box." *The Hardtimes Baseball Annual*, 2008. New York: ACTA, 2007.
Daniel, Dan. "Brooklyn's Own Boston Manager," *New York World Telegram*, June 20, 1951.
_____. "Southworth Sees Braves Stronger." *New York World Telegram*, April 11, 1951.
_____. "Theodore Still Rasping Scribes," *New York World Telegram*, April 28, 1951.
Drohan, John. "Billy Southworth." *Boston Braves Media Guide*, 1948.
"Feller, Sain Pitching Amazes Southworth." *Ohio State Journal*, October 7, 1948.
Graham, Frank. "Billy Southworth and Mr. McGraw." *New York Journal-American*, February 1, 1946.
_____. "A Challenge Met." *New York Journal-American*, August 7, 1948.
_____. "Even Without Mize and Newsom."

New York Herald Tribune, September 8, 1942.

"Hail Southworth as Phenom: Pirates' Outfielder Gets Away to a Brilliant Start." *The Sporting News*, July 6, 1918.

Hillman, J.B. "Billy Southworth: Sparkplug player, troubled manager." *Sport Collectors Digest*, February 9, 1996.

Holmes, Tommy. "Billy Southworth Has a Youngster." *Brooklyn Eagle*, October 4, 1944.

_____. "Up-to-Date Saga With Billy the Kid." *New York Herald Tribune*, August 17, 1949.

_____. "Yanks May Strike Fear But Not in Mr. Southworth." *Brooklyn Eagle*, August 29, 1940.

Hooey, Bob. "Billy the Kid: Born to Game." *The Sporting News*, October 26, 1944.

_____. "Billy the Kid: Life Story of Southworth." *The Sporting News*, November 9, 1944.

_____. "Major Billy Southworth, Unscathed in Combat Flights, Dies in B-29 Crash." *The Sporting News*, February 28, 1945.

Hooper, Bayard. "Egg in Your Beer." *Harvard Crimson*, October 5, 1948.

"Johnny Sain, Who Inspired Baseball Rhyme, Dies." *New York Times*, November 9, 2006.

King, Joe. "Southworth Hopes to Make Braves Terrors on Bases." *New York World-Telegram*, February 20, 1946.

Lanigan, E.J. "Fanning With Lanigan." *The Sporting News*, November 29, 1928.

Latimer, Sandi. "Hard Times Couldn't Keep Him Down." *Columbus Messenger*, August 2, 2008. Lepola, Lenny. "Remembering Billy Southworth, My Dad." *Sunbury News*, July 24, 2008.

Lieb, Frederick. "Flashbacks: Billy Southworth." *The Sporting News*, September 28, 1944.

"Maj. Southworth Killed in Bomber." *New York Times*, February 17, 1945.

"Meet the Missus." *The Sporting News*, August 21, 1941. Mileur, Raymond. "Billy the Kid Ignored by Baseball's Hall of Fame Veterans Committee." Baseball Guru.com, May 2003.

Minshew, Wayne. "Southworth Never More Right Than in '52 Report on Aaron." *The Sporting News*, July 6, 1968.

Needham, Russ. "Cleveland's Last World Series Loaded with Records Still in the Book." *Columbus Dispatch*, October 6, 1948.

Patterson, Arthur. "Southworth Won't Be Coaxed into Claiming Flag for Cards." *New York Herald-Tribune*, August 14, 1943.

Pitarresi, John. "Good for the Goose." *Utica Observer-Dispatch*, July 28, 2008.

Rice, Grantland. "Look Out for Billy Southworth." *New York Herald-Tribune*, March 22, 1948.

_____. "Setting the Pace." *New York Herald-Tribune*, September 18, 1950. "Robert Hooey Dies." *Columbus Dispatch*, December 1, 1949.

Russo, Neal. "Don't Count Cardinals Out, Says Ex-Pilot Southworth." *The Sporting News*, August 9, 1969.

Sampson, Arthur. "Billy Southworth, the Pennant Man," *Look*, May 24, 1949. Shapiro, Michael. "Father-Son Bond Remains Alive in Wartime Diary." *New York Times*, June 19, 2005.

Smith, Red. "Views of Sport: Billy Southworth." *New York Herald Tribune*, June 21, 1951.

Southworth, Billy. "The Greatest Ball Club on Earth." *Saturday Evening Post*, June 5, 1943. "Southworth Caps Checkered Career." *The Sporting News*, September 27, 1942.

"Southworth Given Richest Job Among Baseball Managers." *Boston Herald*, November 9, 1945.

"Southworth Lays Cards' Rise to Team's Spirit and Will to Win." *The Sporting News*, April 30, 1941.

"Southworth Pitching Bombs Over Europe." *Chicago Tribune*, February 4, 1943.

"Southworth Rates Braves' Enemies in Series Highly." *Ohio State Journal*, October 6, 1948.

"Southworths at Sunbury Lions Club." *Sunbury News*, February 3, 1944.

"Southworths Divorce." *Steubenville Herald-Star*, September 12, 1932.

"Sport: Headaches." *Time*, August 29, 1949.

Stevens, Howell. "Tribe in Another Shakeup." *Boston Post*, May 7, 1948.

Stockton, J. Roy. "The Redbirds Fly Again." *Saturday Evening Post*, August 9, 1941.

"That's Hooey." *Ohio State Journal*, October 7, 1948.

Whitman, Burt. "Billy Not Always Model Manager." *Boston Herald*, November 13, 1945.

Williams, Joe. "Bonus Babies Stir Resentment in Spring Camps." *New York World Telegram*, March 11, 1953.

_____. "Boston Braves Are All Set — For World War." *New York World Telegram*, March 16, 1951.

_____. "One Inning May Have Won Flag for Cards." *New York World Telegram*, September 16, 1942.

_____. "Southworth's Boy Once Shot, Flag Incentive." *New York World Telegram*, August 28, 1942.

_____. "Well, Anyway, Giants Got Best of the Big Deal." *New York World Telegram*, October 11, 1950.

Young, Dick. "Still in Race, Card Boss Says." *The Sporting News*, July 31, 1942.

Index

Aaron, Henry 175, 176
Adams, Babe 32
Alexander, Grover Cleveland 10, 28, 30, 50, 51, 52, 54, 55, 57, 60, 61, 64, 65, 66, 70, 72, 87, 106
Andrews, Nate 149
Anken, A.L. 142
Antonelli 164, 165, 170, 171
Asbell, Jim 95
Asheville Moonshiners 91
Asheville Tourists 13, 91, 100, 137

"Bad Check" 131, 138
Bailey, Gene 84
Baker Bowl 70
Baltimore Orioles 35, 36
Bancroft, Dave 34
Barbare, Walter 31
Barnes, Virgil 40, 41, 42
Barnhart, Clyde 44
Barnum, P.T. 117
Barrett Red 150, 152, 154, 155, 157, 160
Bearden, Gene 161, 162, 163
Beazley, Johnny 9, 105, 110, 114, 116, 117, 119, 121, 122, 123, 126, 127, 131, 148, 152, 157, 161, 165, 167
Bell, Hi 47, 63, 73, 74, 75, 82, 85
Bell, Les 48, 51, 52, 57, 62, 64
Bentley, Jack 40, 41, 42, 43
Benton, Larry 54
Berly, Jack 83, 84, 85
Bezdek, Hugo 26, 27, 30, 70
Bickford, Vern 158, 160, 161, 162, 171
Bigbee, Carson 27, 32
Birdhouse 3, 182, 183
Birmingham, Joe 21, 78, 80
Bissonnette, Del 149
Black Sox scandal 39, 70, 104
Blades, Ray 13, 48, 57, 94, 97, 98, 102
Blum, Fred 13, 138
Bonds, Barry 176
Bonham, Tiny 121, 129, 130
"Bonus Babies" 164
Book-of-the-Month Club 46
Borowy, Hank 95, 122, 129, 130
Boston Braves Historical Society 3

Boston Post 158, 159
Boston Record 167
Bottomley, Jim 47, 51, 57, 60, 61, 64, 66, 72, 79
Boudreau, Lou 161, 162
Bowman, Bob 98, 101
Brady, Bob 3
Branch, Norman 95
Braves Field 55
Brazle, Al 2, 126, 130, 131
Breadon, Sam 5, 6, 11, 12, 13, 60, 66, 67, 68, 72, 73, 76, 77, 78, 79, 80, 81, 93, 96, 97, 98, 101, 114, 123, 130, 131, 143, 145, 147, 148, 149, 150
Brecheen, Harry 126, 128, 131, 135, 143, 148
Bricker, James 133
Brock, Lou 177
Brockhart, Smith W. 46
Brooklyn Eagle 117, 122, 136, 148, 166,
Brown, Jimmy 101, 107, 118, 120, 121, 131
Brown, Joe 83, 85

Cain, Cullen 78, 79
Callahan, Jim 25, 26, 27
Camelli, Hank 152
Capital Cities League 18
Capital City Products 12, 90
Caray, Harry 1
Carey, Max 27, 30, 32, 44
Carlton, Steve 177
Carleton, Tex 82, 83
Carrigan, Bill 66
Carver, Lawton 148
Casey, Hugh 114, 115
Caton, Buster 28
Chandler, Happy 170
Chandler, Spud 120, 121, 129, 130
Chapman, Ray 21
Clark, Cap 92
Clarke, Fred 25, 26
Cleveland Bearcats 22, 23
Cobb, Ty 46, 66, 69
Cody, William F. 17
Cohen, Leonard 153
Coleman, Bob 149
Collins, Eddie 66

207

Collins, Rip 74, 75, 81, 83, 84, 86
Columbus Redbirds 12, 88
Combs, Earl 60, 64
Conatser, Cliff 159, 163, 165, 167, 168
Considine, Bob 3, 152, 155, 166
Cooke, Dusty 94
Cooney, Jimmy 51
Cooney, Johnny 32, 168
Cooper, Mort 98, 99, 101, 102, 110, 112, 114, 116, 117, 118, 119, 120, 122, 125, 127, 128, 129, 130, 131, 132, 133, 135, 143, 149, 150, 152, 154, 167
Cooper, Robert 129
Cooper, Walker 99, 102, 107, 110, 111, 119, 120, 121, 122, 123, 125, 126, 129, 130, 131, 132, 143, 148, 149, 150, 151
Cooper, Wilbur 28, 30, 32
Corum, Bill 3, 5, 14, 166, 172
Crabtree, Estel 94, 95, 102
Crespi, Creepy 99, 112, 120, 122, 126
Crosley Field 12
Cubs Win the Pennant 2
Cullenbine, Roy 121
Cunningham, Bill 34
Curlee, Bill 92
Cutshaw, George 28, 30, 32
Cuyler, KiKi 32

Daly, Arthur 87, 143, 144
Daly, Jon 88
Daniel, Dan 3
Dark, Alvin 157, 158, 159, 160, 169, 170
Davis, Curt 112
Davis, Harry 95
Dean, Dizzy 84, 85
Decatur, Art 74
Derringer, Paul 82, 83, 85, 127
Detroit Lions 20
Dickey, Bill 130
Dickson, Murray 105, 107, 125, 126, 127, 128, 131, 158
DiMaggio, Joe 119, 121, 123, 129
Doby, Larry 161, 162
Dolan, Cozy 39
Donnelly, Blix 135
Douthit, Taylor 48, 51, 57, 60
Dreyfuss, Barney 25, 30
Dugan, Joe 61, 63
Durocher, Leo 9, 101, 108, 112, 117, 123, 127

Ebbets Field 54, 98, 110, 111, 112, 115, 159
Egan, Dave 167, 168
Elliott, Bob 152, 154, 155, 156, 158, 160, 163, 165
Etten, Nick 129

Federal League 22
Feller, Bob 161, 162, 163
Ferguson, Tommie 176, 177
Flood, Curt 177
Frisch, Frank 13, 36, 39, 40, 48, 67, 68, 70, 97, 167, 181

Galehouse, Denny 133, 135
Gas House Gang 51, 81, 84, 99, 108
Gehrig, Lou 53, 57, 60, 62, 63, 64, 108
Gelbert, Charlie 74
Gibson, Bob 47, 177
Gibson, George 30
Giles, Warren 83
Gillenwater, Carden 149
Godoy, Arturo 100
Goetz, John 82
Gonzalez, Mike 97, 113
Gordon, Joe 121, 123, 129, 163
Goslin, Goose 41
Gould, Jim 68
Gowdy, Hank 32, 42, 43, 73
Graham, Frank 116, 160, 161
Greb, Harry 27
"Green Light" letter 104
Griffith Stadium 41
Grimm, Charlie 32
Groh, Heinie 40, 44
Gromek, Steve 162
Gumbert, Harry 127, 128

Hafey, Chick 47, 51, 60, 62, 63, 64, 79
Haines, Jesse 47, 51, 52, 54, 56, 62, 64, 71, 72, 79, 80
Hall of Fame 3, 21, 39, 47, 57, 92, 94, 181, 183
Hallahan, Bill 51
Hamilton, Earl 28, 30
Hanlon, Ned 35
Harris, Bucky 41, 42
Hartnett, Gabby 48
Hassett, Buddy 120
Hawley, Dan 66
Head, Ed 114
Heath, Jeff 157, 160, 162, 163
Hendrix, Claude 30
Herman, Billy 152
Hern, Gerald 159
Heydler, John 39, 70
Higbee, Kirby 114
Hill, Carmen 85
Hocking Valley Railroad 18, 19
Hogue, Bob 158, 160
Hollocher, Charlie 30
Holm, Ella 171
Holm, Margaret 171
Holm, Robert 171
Holm, Wattie 63, 171
Holmes, Tommy (ballplayer) 149, 150, 154, 155, 156, 158, 159, 160, 161, 168, 172
Holmes, Tommy (sports writer) 3, 14, 122, 136, 139, 148, 166, 169
Hooey, Bob 19, 70, 77, 81, 87, 138, 170, 181
Hooey, Gladys 170
Hooper, Harry 33
Hopp, Johnny 99, 102, 111, 114, 120 121, 122, 123, 132, 150
Hornsby, Rogers 11, 46, 48, 49, 50, 51, 55, 57, 58, 59, 60, 62, 64, 65, 66, 67, 68, 69, 70, 72, 76, 77, 78, 80, 81, 96, 108, 129

Hotel Chase 136, 139, 141, 148
Hoyt, Waite 57, 64
Huggins, Miller 57, 108

Inside Pitch 3
International News Service 149

Jablonski, Ray 1, 2
Jackson, Joe 21, 69, 70
Jackson, Travis 36, 40, 42
James, Bill 166
Javier, Julian 177
Jennings, Hugh 35, 37, 39, 40
Johnson, Si 94
Johnson, Walter 41, 42, 43, 48, 69
Jolson, Al 21
Jones, Sam 22, 57
Joost, Eddie 150
Joss, Addie 21

Keeler, Willie 35
Keen, Vic 47, 56, 73, 74
Keller, Charlie 121, 122, 129
Kelly, George 36, 39, 40, 41
Kenton Reds 19
Kiernan, John 112, 113
Killefer, Bill 51
Kiner, Ralph 154
Klein, Lou 129, 131
KMOX 1
Koenig, Mark 62, 64
Kramer, Jack 135
Krist, Howard 102, 112, 114, 127, 128, 131
Kurowski, Whitey 9, 95, 102, 105, 110, 111, 114, 118, 120, 121, 122, 123, 126, 129, 131, 132, 136, 148, 166

Lajoie, Napoleon 21, 69
Landis, Kenesaw Mountain 21, 39, 40, 104, 123
Lanier, Max 99, 102, 110, 111, 116, 118, 120, 125, 127, 128, 129, 130, 131, 135
Lanigan, E.J. 76
Lazzeri, Tony 10, 57, 60, 62, 64, 65
Lee, Bill 151
Lemon, Bob 161, 162, 163
Leonard, Dutch 170, 171
Lieb, Fred 67, 80
Liebold, Harry 88
Lindell Towers 9
Lindstrom, Freddie 36, 42
Little World Series 74, 75, 76, 82, 84, 86, 95
Litwhiler, Dan 126, 129, 130, 131, 135, 150, 157
Logan, Bob 149
Lohrman, Bill 105
Lolly Willows 46
Long, James J. 77
Longfellow, Henry Wadsworth 16, 21, 90, 180
Look 165
Louis, Joe 100

Mack, Connie 19, 135, 167
Macon, Max 118

Mancuso, Gus 107
Maranville, Rabbit 28, 31
Marberry, Firpo 41
Marion, Marty 94, 99, 108, 110, 111, 114, 116, 120, 122, 123, 126, 129, 130, 131, 133, 148
Martin, Pepper 83, 84, 85, 92, 99, 132, 153
Masi, Phil 150, 161, 162
Mason City Globe Gazette 3
Mathewson, Christy 50
Maxvill, Dal 177
Mayer, Erskine 28, 30
Mays, Carl 21
McAllister, Jack 66
McCarthy, Bill 83
McCarthy, Joe 51, 120, 130, 167
McCarthy, John 105
McCarver, Tim 177
McCormick, Frank 154
McCormick, Mike 160, 161
McGee, Bill 99, 102
McGeehan, W.O. 91
McGraw, John 6, 9, 10, 27, 29, 32, 34, 35–45, 47, 49, 53, 56, 59, 60, 69, 71, 78, 80, 83, 85, 87, 89, 99, 100, 108
McInnis, George 66
McKechnie, Bill 5, 6, 11, 13, 27, 28, 72, 77, 80, 81, 96, 131
McNeely, Earl 42, 43
McPhail, Larry 111
McPhail, Lee 88
McQuillan, Hugh 40, 41
McQuinn, George 133
Meany, Tom 89
Medwick, Joe 101, 111
Memphis Chicks 13, 92
Meusel, Bob 60, 64, 66
Meusel, Emil 40, 44
Mileur, Jerome 80
Mileur, Ray 4, 182
Miller, Heinie 49
"Miracle Braves" 26, 145
Mitchel Field 14, 142
Mitchell, Dale 161
Mitchell, Fred 32, 34, 78
Mize, Johnny 99, 102, 105, 108, 125
Mollwitz, Fritz 28
Moore, Gene 133
Moore, Herb 92
Moore, Terry 99, 102, 108, 110, 111, 119, 120, 122, 125, 126, 131, 148
Moore's restaurant 37
Morarity, George 66
Morrow, Bob 74
Mother Shields Restaurant 19
Mueller, Heinie 48
Mugbridge, George 42
Munger, George 126, 128, 131, 132
Municipal Stadium 162
Murphy, James 117
Murtaugh, Danny 94
Musial, Stan 1, 9, 102, 105, 107, 108, 109, 110, 111, 112, 114, 116, 118, 119, 120, 121, 122, 123,

127, 128, 129, 131, 132, 135, 143, 144, 148, 166, 173
"My Mother's Plane Keeps Crashing" 181

National Exhibition Company 38
Naylor, Earl 126
Neal, Greasy 22
Nehf, Art 40, 41, 42
New York Herald Tribune 98
New York Journal-American 160, 166, 172
New York Post 153,
New York Sun 116
New York Times 87, 91, 112, 113
Newark Bears 97
Newsom, Bobo 117, 126
Nicholson, Fred 31

O'Connell, Jimmie 39, 40
O'Dea, Ken 105, 120, 135
O'Farrell, Bob 11, 48, 51, 55, 57, 62, 64, 66, 68, 70, 72, 76, 81, 96, 97
Ogden, Curly 42
Ohio State Journal 19, 70, 137, 170, 181
Ohio State League 32
Ohio State University 69, 101, 103, 137, 142, 175
"Ole Pete" 106
O'Neill, Steve 84
Orengo, Joe 99, 101

Paige, Satchel 161, 163
Parks Air College 101
Parrott, Jacob 19
Paschal, Ben 63
Patterson, Arthur 98
Pearl Harbor 7, 104
Pendleton, Jim 176
Penn State University 30
Pennock, Herb 57, 60, 63, 64
Pepper, Ray 83, 85
Perini, Lou 145, 148, 149, 165, 168, 169, 170
Petty, Jess 48
Piedmont League 91, 137
Pittsburgh Sun Telegraph 77
Pollet, Howard 102, 107, 108, 110, 117, 122, 126, 127, 128, 131
Polo Grounds 42, 48, 56, 108
Portland Beavers 10, 22, 23, 136
Portsmouth Spartans 20
Potter, Nelson 135, 158, 160
Priddy, Gerry 123
Psalm of Life 16

Raffensberger, Ken 95
Reinhart, Art 47, 56, 62
Reiser, Pete 112, 114, 115
Rhem, Flint 47, 51, 53, 54, 55, 56, 70, 72, 79
Rice, Grantland 3
Rice, Sam 41
Rickert, Marv 162
Rickey, Branch 6, 12, 13, 20, 25, 46, 48, 71, 72,
81, 82, 83, 85, 86, 88, 91, 92, 93, 95, 99, 102, 105, 106, 123, 124, 126, 131, 157
Ring, Jimmy 67
Rizzo, Johnny 112
Rizzuto, Phil 120, 121, 122
Robinson, Jackie 156, 157, 169
Robinson, Wilbert 35
Rochester Red Wings 5, 11, 13, 72, 73, 78, 81, 82, 93, 96, 102
Roe, Preacher 94, 95
Rome Colonels 100, 137
Rommel, Ed 48
Roosevelt, Franklin D. 104
Rose Bowl 26
Ruel, Muddy 42, 43
Ruether, Dutch 62
Ruffing, Red 120, 123, 129
Russell, Jimmy 158, 168, 169, 170
Russo, Mario 130
Russo, Neal 177
Ruth, Babe 53, 57, 60, 62, 64, 66, 73, 77, 87, 91, 94, 108, 156
Ryan, Connie 150
Ryan, Jerry 20
Ryan, Rosy 41

Sain, Johnny 3, 150, 154, 155, 157, 158, 160, 162, 163, 165, 167, 168, 171
St. Louis Post-Dispatch 77, 116, 177
St. Louis Star 68
Salkeld, Bill 161, 163
Sampson, Arthur 165
Sand, Heinie 39
Sanders, Ray 120, 125, 126, 130 131, 132, 136, 150
Saturday Evening Post 125
Sauer, Hank 2
Savage, Elayne 3, 180
Schalk, Ray 66
Scheckard, Jimmy 22, 23
Schmidt, Walter 28
Schoendienst, Alfred "Red" 2, 143
Schuessler, Arian 3
Sewell, Luke 132, 136, 139
Shawkey, Bob 64
Sherdel, Bill 47, 51, 52, 54, 55, 60, 63, 70
Shocker, Urban 57, 60
Shotton, Burt 72, 167
Shoun, Clyde 99
Singleton, Elmer 152
Sisler, George 66, 86
Sisti, Sibby 161
Slaughter, Enos 9, 93, 94, 99, 102, 107, 110, 111, 114, 115, 116, 118, 119, 120, 121, 123, 125, 126, 131, 148, 166, 174
Smith, Ira 73, 83
Smith, Red 3
Snyder, Frank 40
Somers, Charles 22
Sothoron, Alan 54
Southern Hotel 18, 19
Southworth, Arley 9, 16, 17, 90

Southworth, Billy, Jr. 2, 5, 7, 10, 11, 14, 23, 67, 68, 69, 71, 74, 75, 76, 90, 91, 92, 100, 101, 104, 125, 136–144, 175, 180
Southworth, Calvin 9, 16, 17
Southworth, George Irvin 9, 16, 17
Southworth, Gracie 16
Southworth, Lida Brooks 5, 6, 10, 11, 12, 23, 67, 68, 71 74, 75, 87, 89, 90, 91, 137
Southworth, Mabel Stemen 5, 12, 13, 14, 90, 91, 102, 103, 134, 135, 142, 175
Southworth, Marriah 9, 16
Southworth, Opal 16, 31
Southworth, Orlando 9, 16, 20
Southworth, Pressley 9
Spahn, Warren 3, 150, 151, 154, 155, 157, 158, 159, 160, 162, 163, 168, 169, 171
"Spahn and Sain and Pray for Rain" 159
Speaker, Tris 66
Sporting News 19, 29, 31, 33, 70, 74, 76, 77, 78, 81, 87, 98, 102, 103, 137
Sportsman's Park 52, 54, 62, 63, 114, 116, 127, 130, 132
Stagg, Amos Alonzo 26
Stallings, George 80
Stanky, Eddie 2, 157, 158, 160, 161, 168, 169, 170
Starr, Ray 85, 86
Stengel, Casey 10, 24, 27, 28, 34, 40, 110, 112, 113, 167
Stewart, Bill 161, 162
Stockton, J.Roy 106, 116, 181
Stoneham, Charles 38
Street, Gabby 13, 96
Stromberg, Hunt 139, 143
Syracuse Red Wings 72

Terry, Bill 12, 36, 41, 51, 89
Thevenow, Tommy 48, 62, 63, 64, 66
Time 166
Tobin, Jim 149
Toledo and Ohio Railroad 18
Toledo Mud Hens 21, 22
Toporcer, George 48, 73, 75, 82, 83, 85, 86, 88
Torgeson, Earl 152, 154, 155, 156, 157, 158, 160, 163, 167, 169, 170
Toronto Maple Leafs 101, 137
Tost, Lou 108, 109
Traynor, Pie 32
Triplett, Coaker 111, 125, 126
Tucker, Thurman 163
Tyler, Lefty 30

United Airlines 46
University of Arkansas 26
University of Chicago 26
University of Oregon 26

Vander Meer, Johnny 108, 127
Vaughn, Hippo 30

Verban, Emil 132
Veterans Committee 181, 183
Village Blacksmith 17, 90
Voiselle, Bill 3, 154, 155, 157, 158, 160, 163

Wagner, Honus 25, 26, 27, 28, 32, 70
Walker, Dixie 111, 126
Walker, Harry 125, 126, 129, 131
Walter Varney Airlines 46
Waner, Lloyd 32, 76
Waner, Paul 32, 7
Warneke, Lon 99, 101, 107, 110, 112, 114
Warner, Sylvia Townsend 46
Watkins, George 82
Watkins, Tom 92
Watson, Carole Southworth 3, 5, 10, 12, 13, 89, 90, 91, 103, 134, 135, 140, 141, 143, 171, 175, 177, 179
Watson, Cheryl 177
Watson, Mule 40
WBBM 1
WCFL 1
Weiss, George 67, 68
Wentzel, Stan 152
West Side High School 18
Wetherell, Dick 93
WGN 1
Wheat, Zach 24
White, Ernie 99, 102, 110, 112, 121, 122, 125, 127, 131, 150, 157, 167
Whitman, Burt 33
"Whiz Kids" 7, 171
Wietelman, Whitey 152
Wilks, Ted 132, 135
Williams, Dick 183
Williams, Joe 3
Wilson, Hack 36, 39, 40
Wilson, Jimmy 79
WIND 1
"Winning Run" 131, 138
WLS 1
Workman, Chuck 149
World Series 5, 8, 10, 11, 12, 13, 21, 36, 40–43, 46, 47, 48, 56, 57, 58, 59, 62, 64, 66, 68, 69, 70, 73, 76, 77, 78, 79, 96, 117, 122, 123, 126, 129, 141, 145, 161, 163, 180
World War I 30
Worthington, Red 83, 84
Wray, John 77
Wright, Ed 149, 151
Wrigley Field 1, 39
Wyatt, Whitlow 112, 118

Yankee Stadium 59, 60, 64, 69, 121, 129
Young, Cy 32
Young, Doc 168
Youngs, Ross 36, 39, 40

Zachary, Tom 41, 42

JOHN C. SKIPPER HAS ALSO PUBLISHED THE
FOLLOWING BOOKS FROM MCFARLAND

*Showdown at the 1964 Democratic Convention:
Lyndon Johnson, Mississippi and Civil Rights* (2012)

*A Biographical Dictionary of Major League
Baseball Managers* (2003; paperback 2011)

*The Iowa Caucuses: First Tests of Presidential
Aspiration, 1972–2008* (2010)

*A Biographical Dictionary of the Baseball
Hall of Fame*, 2d ed. (2008)

*Charlie Gehringer: A Biography of the Hall of
Fame Tigers Second Baseman* (2008)

*Dazzy Vance: A Biography of the Brooklyn
Dodger Hall of Famer* (2007)

*Wicked Curve: The Life and Troubled Times of
Grover Cleveland Alexander* (2006)

*The Cubs Win the Pennant! Charlie Grimm, the
Billy Goat Curse, and the 1945 World Series Run* (2004)

*Take Me Out to the Cubs Game: 35 Former
Ballplayers Speak of Losing at Wrigley* (2000)

*Umpires: Classic Baseball Stories from the
Men Who Made the Calls* (1997)

Inside Pitch: A Closer Look at Classic Baseball Moments (1996)

www.ingramcontent.com/pod-product-compliance
Lightning Source LLC
Chambersburg PA
CBHW021914180426
43198CB00035B/537